SPY HUNTER

Robert W. Hunter, with Lynn Dean Hunter

SPY HUNTER

Inside the FBI Investigation
of the Walker Espionage Case

Naval Institute Press   Annapolis, Maryland

Library of Congress Cataloging-in-Publication Data
Hunter, Robert W., 1936–
   Spy hunter : inside the FBI investigation of the Walker espionage
   case / Robert W. Hunter with Lynn Dean Hunter.
         p.   cm.
     ISBN 1-55750-349-4 (alk. paper)
     1. Walker, John Anthony, 1937– . 2. Walker family.
   3. Whitworth, Jerry, 1939– . 4. Espionage, Soviet—United States—
   History—20th century. 5. Hunter, Robert W., 1936– .
   I. Hunter, Lynn Dean, 1948– . II. Title.
   UB271.R92W34375   1999
   327.1247073—dc21   98–45372

Printed in the United States of America on acid-free paper ∞

06 05 04 03 02 01 00 99   9 8 7 6 5 4 3 2

First printing

To the American service men and women
who died in Vietnam because of the
treachery of John Walker

Contents

	Acknowledgments	ix
1	On a Collision Course	1
2	The Case Is Born	3
3	The Game Begins	9
4	The Bomb Is Ticking	12
5	A Painful Reunion	14
6	The Voice of Evil	17
7	The Spy Catchers	20
8	The Keys to the Kingdom	25
9	A Visit from Barbara	28
10	Listen and Wait	35
11	Cat and Mouse	48
12	All Those People—My God, I Had No Idea	61
13	The Wheels of Justice Begin to Turn	66
14	K.I.S.S.	70
15	Overwhelming Evidence	76
16	The Motherlode	81
17	Like Father, Like Son	94
18	Am I My Brother's Keeper?	103
19	Arthur's Trial	111
20	The Mystery of Art Walker	117
21	Recollections in Tranquillity	127
22	"D" Is for Jerry	134

23	Were Others Involved?	145
24	N.I.S.	154
25	A Proffer, Preparations, and the Vienna Procedure	160
26	A Deal Is Struck	170
27	Debriefing a Spy	177
28	Presentence Happenings	190
29	The Sentencing	193
30	Damage Done	202
31	Afterlife	208
	Postscript: A Chat with the Adversary	215
	Appendix A. Advice-of-Rights Form Signed by John Walker	219
	Appendix B. No-Parole Recommendation Filed by Judge Alexander Harvey	220
	Appendix C. Affidavit Submitted by Adm. William O. Studeman	222
	Index	243

Acknowledgments

I want to thank my wife and co-author, Lynn Dean Hunter, for her wonderful support and literary expertise. This book would not have been written were it not for her.

I would like to thank the following people for their support, encouragement, and guidance during the investigation of John Walker and his associates:

Susan J. Miltenberger, Deborah (Debbie) L. Williams, and Theresa (Terry) M. Swindell, intelligence information analysts and computer specialists in the Norfolk FBI office.

The investigative and support staff of the Norfolk FBI office, all of whom played important roles in the case.

John (Jack) C. Wagner, special agent in charge, Norfolk FBI office (now retired).

Joseph R. Wolfinger, Foreign Counterintelligence Squad supervisor, Norfolk FBI office.

Many thanks also to Pete Earley, author of *Family of Spies,* who encouraged me to write this book. Pete graciously lent me his copy of the transcript of the Jerry Whitworth trial, which was an invaluable aid.

Tony Germanotta, public-life editor for the *Virginian Pilot,* supported this project and helped write the earliest draft. My thanks go to him.

Mary Yates, my copy editor, was a wonderful help in preparing the manuscript for publication.

I also wish to thank my father-in-law, William (Bill) Charles FitzGibbon, retired editor for the *New York Times,* for his support, advice, and professional guidance in the preparation of this book.

Special thanks go to retired FBI agents Barry D. Colvert, James L. Kolouch, Gerald B. Richards, and Richard L. Ault Jr., Ph.D., for their expertise and assistance during the investigation as well as their help and comments during my writing of this book.

My love and gratitude go to my mother, Goldie E. Hunter, for her unwavering support, regardless of how moody I might have been during the nine years it took to give birth to this book.

Finally, I want to thank my late father, Robert Taylor Hunter, and my "uncle" Bobby Walsh. In my boyhood, when they took me hunting and fishing in the fields and streams of Pennsylvania, they taught me patience, integrity, persistence, faith, and self-discipline. Those lessons were crucial to the capture of John Walker.

SPY HUNTER

1

On a Collision Course

I remember sitting around with the guys in the FBI office in Norfolk, Virginia, after my transfer from New Orleans in June 1967, and talking about how there must be at least one master spy working for the Soviets in our community. After all, this was home to the largest military complex in the free world. We were at ground zero.

Little did I know that U.S. Navy radioman John Anthony Walker Jr. had transferred to Norfolk a couple of months before I had and was to embark on a career of espionage for the Soviets later that same year. His career as a spy would span the next eighteen years of mine as an FBI agent. For those eighteen years, we each pursued our professions. We traveled the same city streets, never meeting, neither one knowing that the other existed. As I honed my skills as an investigator, Walker shaped himself as a master spy. We were on converging paths, destined to meet at gunpoint in the early-morning hours of 20 May 1985.

I spent the first half of my FBI career on the criminal side, chasing bank robbers, fugitives, deserters, and other lowlifes. After ten years of hearing the same stories about why they did what they did, I changed my investigative focus to the field of counterintelligence. I wanted to try my hand at catching that elusive master spy I knew was out there.

In the early 1980s I succeeded in identifying a young Navy enlisted man who had tried to sell Top Secret information to the Soviets. Brian Patrick Horton was assigned to the Nuclear Strike Planning Branch at CINCLANTFLT (the Commander-in-Chief, Atlantic Fleet, compound) at the Norfolk Naval Station. His job was to put the strike packages together for Navy pilots. A strike package would include location and photographs of targets, strike routes, and any other information a pilot would need to complete his mission, escape the strike area, and return to his carrier. Horton wanted to sell that information to improve his quality of life. I worked closely with the Naval Investigative Service after I identified Horton as an active-duty sailor. He was arrested and convicted in a court-martial of attempting to sell classified information to a foreign power. He got six years in the brig and a dishonorable discharge for his efforts.

I felt good about the case because we had been able to prevent someone from doing grave harm to this nation's defense interests. Not so with John Walker, I'm sorry to say. Far from it.

By February 1985 I was one of the senior members of the Foreign Counterintelligence Squad in the Norfolk office. The squad was a well-balanced group: seasoned agents and first-office agents fresh out of the FBI Academy at Quantico, Virginia. I was the primary relief supervisory for Joe Wolfinger, who ran the squad. When he needed to be doing other things, I sat in for him "on the desk."

Joe was out of town on 22 February when a letter arrived from the Boston FBI office. Special Agent Randy Waldrup had been handling the squad's mail while I was out for an hour or two. When I returned, he handed me the letter and said I should take a look at it. It was a letter that would change many lives forever.

2

The Case Is Born

The letter—an "airtel," in Bureau parlance—contained the results of an interview of Barbara Joy Crowley Walker, conducted by Special Agent Walter Price in late November 1984. Barbara had called the Boston FBI office and alleged that her former husband, John Anthony Walker Jr., had been selling secrets to the Russians for about nineteen years. She wanted to talk to an agent. Price got the assignment—unaware, of course, that he was about to conduct the first interview in what would become a worldwide investigation of the largest and most damaging espionage ring of American citizens in the history of our nation.

Price went to Barbara's apartment in West Dennis, Massachusetts. In his report he mentioned that when Barbara answered the door she appeared to have been drinking, and that she drank a water glass full of vodka as they talked.

Barbara told Price she and John had been married in June 1957 and divorced at Norfolk, Virginia, in June 1976. They had four children: Cynthia, born in 1959 and living with Barbara at the time she called the FBI; Margaret Ann, born in 1957, living in Norfolk; Laura, born in 1960 and living in Buffalo at the time of her call; and

Michael, born in 1962 and serving in the U.S. Navy on board the aircraft carrier USS *Nimitz.*

Barbara said John had enlisted in the Navy in 1955 and served as a radioman. In 1966 he was promoted to the rank of chief warrant officer. He retired from the Navy in 1976 and eventually became a private detective running his own agency, Confidential Reports, in Virginia Beach, Virginia.

I would learn later that John's enlistment in the Navy was somewhat less than heroic. He had been a small-time thief as a teenager, pulling several burglaries in his home town of Scranton, Pennsylvania. He was caught, convicted, and put on probation. John's brother, Arthur James Walker, had joined the Navy in 1953 and came home on leave after John's conviction in early 1955. Art had a heart-to-heart talk with John and persuaded him to join the Navy, but the local recruiter wouldn't take him; Navy regulations wouldn't permit someone to join who was on probation from the criminal justice system. Art hustled John over to see the judge and convinced him that it would make a better citizen out of John if the judge would release him from probation and let him join the Navy. The judge agreed and, I suspect, told John to get his ass out of town. If the judge had been in a disagreeable mood that day, he might have saved this country from the most damaging espionage case in history!

Barbara continued her story to Agent Price, reporting that in 1967 she and John had opened a beer joint called the Bamboo Snack Bar in Ladson, South Carolina, near Charleston, where John was assigned with the Navy on a ballistic-missile submarine, the USS *Simon Bolivar* (SSBN 641). They immediately began having financial problems. John had been promoted to chief warrant officer, and soon after they opened the bar he was transferred to the Norfolk Naval Station, where he was assigned as communications watch officer/message center officer on the staff of Commander, Submarine Forces Atlantic (SUBLANT), located in the CINCLANTFLT compound.

Barbara recalled that John went to Norfolk in the spring of 1967, not very long after his promotion. He was to get himself set up in

Norfolk and then eventually send for the family. She would stay and tend to the kids and run the bar in Ladson until then. John visited them on weekends.

Late in 1967 Barbara began to get suspicious of John. During his weekend visits he always had $400 or $500 extra money with him. When she asked him where he was getting the money, he told her he earned it by driving rental cars from Norfolk back to Washington, D.C., for which he was paid $500 per car.

In a few months John had enough money saved to move the family to Norfolk. They found someone to run the bar, and Barbara and the kids joined John in March 1968. She told Agent Price that John had rented an apartment in a high-rise building in an exclusive section of town. The Algonquin House was a rather upscale place for a Navy man with a wife and four children. A mayor of the city had lived there, as well as other well-heeled individuals.

Barbara told Price she and John paid cash for new furniture when they moved into their new place. John also bought a sailboat, and they bought some property for several thousand dollars cash.

Barbara became more suspicious of John's activities and new-found wealth soon after she joined him in Norfolk. She went through his desk one day while he was at work and found several photographs of bushes, trees, and unfamiliar roads. The pictures had arrows and instructions written on them. She also found papers with instructions having to do with rotors. She told Price she thought the pictures and writing were instructions to John telling him where to place and retrieve packages. She also found $1,500 in a locked tin box in his desk. She instinctively knew at that point that her husband was a spy.

Barbara confronted John a short time after finding the items in his desk and accused him of being a spy. He became enraged and struck her, giving her two black eyes. Barbara told Price she began drinking heavily during that period of her life.

Barbara admitted that she had accompanied John on a couple of trips to Washington, to exchange packages with people she believed were Soviets. Later, during cross-examination at Jerry Whitworth's trial on 12 May 1986, when asked why she went with

John on these drops, she would explain, "I wanted him to know how much I cared."

On the first trip to Washington, they flew in and then rented a car. Using instructions and photographs John had brought with him, they drove to a location near a stop sign, and John got out of the car and placed a package on the ground. They followed the instructions to another location, where John picked up a package containing a large amount of cash. They spent the night at a local motel and flew back to Norfolk the next day.

The other trip occurred after John had been transferred to San Diego in 1969. He was assigned to the USS *Niagara Falls,* a Navy supply ship. They were living in Union City, California, at the time. John asked Barbara to go to D.C. with him. She remembered that they rented another car in D.C. Again using pictures and instructions he had brought along, John placed a package in one location and picked one up at another. This time there was $35,000 in his package.

Barbara later told us she remembered that the money was tightly rolled when John got it, and he wanted her to put it in the lining of her coat to transport it back to California. She had to iron it flat in their motel room so that she could conceal it in her coat lining.

During this initial interview with Agent Price, Barbara said she thought John had recruited his brother Arthur into his espionage ring. She recalled Arthur telling her, one time in 1968, that he had been involved with the Russians too, but not to the extent that John was involved. I would learn more about that later in the investigation, a part of this story that definitely qualifies it for a place at the top of the list of sleazy tales.

Barbara also told Price that John had tried to recruit their daughter Laura into his espionage business when she was in the Army in 1978, and that she thought he had recruited his good friend "Jerry Wentworth," who had been in the Navy with him in California; she would later recall his correct name to be Jerry Whitworth.

When Price asked Barbara why she had not come forward with her story before, she was somewhat evasive. Her explanation was twofold. First, John had refused to pay her a monthly stipend when she asked for one during a visit to Norfolk in the summer of 1984.

The second reason had to do with their daughter Laura. Barbara explained that when Laura and her husband, Philip Mark Snyder, separated, the husband had taken their baby son Christopher. Snyder knew of John's attempt to recruit Laura to commit espionage, and he told Laura that if she made any attempt to get custody of their son, he would tell the authorities what he knew about John. Nothing like a little family blackmail to heat things up! Barbara told Price that Laura was desperate to get her son back. She had not seen him in two years. Laura told Barbara they had to turn John in so that she could try to get Christopher back. Barbara agreed, and made the call.

The airtel from Boston also advised that Laura had called the Boston office, after Price's interview with Barbara, and said she also wanted to talk to an agent about her dad's activities. Laura was living in Buffalo and going to cosmetology school at the time.

I now recall with interest and some amusement that the letter from Boston ended with words to this effect: "Boston is aware of the possibility that Mrs. Walker's allegations might be a result of her alcohol abuse and hostile feelings toward her ex-husband. This information is being furnished to Norfolk and Buffalo for whatever action deemed appropriate. Boston anticipates no further investigation unless requested to do so." That was a standard ending to an FBI communication when the sending office either doesn't have any further investigation in its territory or feels that the information requires no further action. Boston did not send a copy of the airtel to FBI Headquarters, as has been erroneously reported in many accounts of this case. FBI Headquarters had no knowledge of the interview of Mrs. Walker until I notified them of it after the case was assigned to me.

I read Boston's letter several times that day in mid-February 1985 and recall feeling in my gut that this one was for real. I also remember thinking, regardless of Boston's observations, that sometimes a person might have to get drunk to work up the nerve to call the FBI. Barbara was a smart lady. She knew full well what the ramifications of her phone call might be. Her story included many details that matched up perfectly with what we knew about actual Soviet espionage operations. The one detail I was skeptical of was the alleged $35,000 she and John had picked up in that "dead drop"—an espionage term for placing (or retrieving) a package at (or from) a prearranged location with no personal contact involved—in D.C., and her estimation that John made over $1 million in his nearly twenty years as a Soviet agent. Those figures were unheard of. If she was right, John Walker was indeed that master spy I had been looking for.

I wrote a brief note to Joe Wolfinger telling him to read Boston's airtel closely because I thought Barbara's story demanded our attention. I put it in Joe's "in" box and went to the Y for a workout.

3

The Game Begins

When I got to work the next day, Joe Wolfinger was there. He called me into his office, and we discussed Boston's airtel. Joe agreed with me that the details in Barbara's story about the drops and the paraphernalia she found in John's desk could not be things she had made up. He was skeptical about the amount of money Barbara said John had received, but we agreed that we should open a case and begin an investigation. Joe asked me if I wanted to handle the case, and I jumped at the chance. I'll never forget that day. It was 25 February 1985.

I recall feeling excited about the prospects of catching John, but I also recognized several very serious problems with the case:

1. John and Barbara had divorced in 1976 and had not lived together in ten years. The information she had given us was over ten years old. In fact, some of the things she had told Price had happened seventeen years earlier. How in the world was I going to prove something that happened that long ago?
2. Was John Walker still an active agent for the Soviets, or had he retired? If he was still active, where was he getting the classified

information to sell to the Soviets? He had been out of the Navy for ten years when Barbara came forward; he no longer had access to military secrets. That meant, of course, that he had to have at least one other person with access working for him. Who was it? How would I catch him?

3. If John had retired, it would be even more difficult than usual proving an espionage case against him.

Espionage is one of the most difficult crimes to prove in court, for several reasons. We never have the other side—the Soviets, in this case—as witnesses who come into court and say "Oh, yes, John gave us classified documents that would have enabled us to kick your butt if we had gone to war." Furthermore, hard evidence is very difficult to come by in an espionage case. Usually the material that is passed is either photographed or copied and the original document is put back in its designated place, making it very difficult to prove what information has been passed. Also, it's difficult dealing with classified information in a court of law; sometimes the U.S. government chooses not to do so, and a case just doesn't get prosecuted.

From the very beginning of the investigation, I took a rather simple approach as to how to work the case. I figured that if John had retired from the espionage business, I would just have to hunker down, dig into his entire military career, learn as much about him as possible in an attempt to build a case, and then probably confront him and hope to get a confession. On the other hand, if he was still active, I would try to catch him in the act. I was well aware of the fact that the FBI had never caught an American citizen suspected of espionage in the act.

The first thing I did was send a copy of Boston's airtel to FBI Headquarters and to the Washington FBI field office, along with a request to Boston and Buffalo to reinterview Barbara and interview Laura for additional details about John's activities. I also asked them to try to persuade Barbara and Laura to submit to a polygraph examination. I asked that Special Agent Barry Colvert of the Washington field office be assigned to conduct the examinations. I had worked with Barry previously on the Horton case and knew he was an outstanding polygraph man; in fact I think he was the best in the Bureau for years. I sent the requests out two or three days after the case was assigned to me. All I could do then was sit back and wait for the results of the interviews. I had to have the results before I could take any further action. I needed to know that Barbara and Laura were credible and that they were willing to cooperate with us further. I realized that the agent faced with the most difficult problem was Walter Price. He had to attempt to maintain Barbara's confidence in us and try to keep her under control. She was an admitted alcoholic, and Price had his work cut out for him.

Agent Paul Culligan of the Buffalo FBI office was the first to respond to my request. In early March he notified me that he and Agent Charlie Wagner had interviewed Laura. She confirmed that John had tried to recruit her to provide classified documents to him when she was a radio operator in the U.S. Army in 1978; she said she refused. She agreed to cooperate with us in the investigation of her father. Culligan suggested to me that we have Laura call her father and tell him she was broke, which was true, and that she was considering going back into the military. The objective of the call would be to dangle a carrot in front of John and see how he would react. He would realize, of course, that if Laura went back into the military she would have access to classified information. We had no idea whether John was still an active agent, but if he was, Laura's call could give us a hint.

I liked Culligan's idea and talked it over with Wolfinger; he agreed. I called Culligan and told him I would get permission from the Bureau (Headquarters) to have Laura make the call and record the conversation for us.

Culligan told me Laura was living with a guy in a small apartment in Buffalo in near-poverty conditions. She was attending cosmetology school and struggling with some pretty severe problems of her own. She certainly didn't give the impression of stability.

I began to worry that one of the Walker family members might tip John off to the fact that we were on to him. True to my fears, Culligan called me a couple of days later and gave me some news that both angered me and elevated my heartbeat.

4

The Bomb Is Ticking

I was sitting at my desk, working on an airtel to request copies of the military records of John and his brother Arthur, when Culligan called. Laura had just called him to say that Barbara had called John and Arthur and told them that she had turned them in to the FBI. Laura said Barbara told her that John didn't believe her.

This was the first of many moments when the case looked to be down the tubes. There I was, in the early stages of an investigation of what appeared to be a serious breach of our national security, and it might be over before it even got off the ground. I went in and told Wolfinger, and together we moaned and groaned. We made a quick call to Walter Price and asked him to go find out from Barbara exactly what she had said to John and Art.

I returned to my desk wondering what would happen next. I called a friend in the Naval Investigative Service (NIS) and found out that John's son, Michael Lance Walker, was in the Navy assigned to the nuclear-powered aircraft carrier USS *Nimitz* somewhere in the Mediterranean. I wondered if he was involved with his father, but there was no way of knowing.

At this point I was conducting what in the Bureau was called a preliminary investigation. The attorney general's guidelines for such an investigation in the counterintelligence field are quite restrictive. Basically I was limited to doing some background stuff and conducting record checks. I knew that if I was to work the case the way it needed to be worked, I was going to need a full field investigation. Only Headquarters can authorize an FFI. I requested their authorization during the second week of March 1985. I also asked for permission to have Laura make the telephone call to her dad and record it for us. Around the same time, I sent a request to our San Francisco office and asked them to begin some discreet efforts to locate and identify "Jerry Wentworth," as we were still calling him.

Headquarters granted my request for a full field investigation in a matter of three or four days. They also granted my request regarding Laura's telephone call to John. The FFI opened the door to all sorts of neat investigative tools. Now I could get authorization for wiretaps, telephone toll records, and surveillance of John, among other things.

We decided that the case needed a code name, both for security reasons and for brevity when preparing the hundreds of communications to come. I suggested the name Family Affair, but Dave Szady, the supervisor at Headquarters handling the case at that level, said it was "too tacky." He named the case Windflyer, after a horse he had won money on at the track.

When the Bureau gave us the authority to monitor Laura's call to her father, they emphasized that we could do it only if she consented. If Barbara had really told John she turned him in, Laura might not want to make this call. I wasn't sure if we would get the chance to monitor anyone's conversations but our own. I needed that call back from Walter Price!

5

A Painful Reunion

After a couple of days, Price called. He had talked to Barbara, and she had told him that she *had* told Arthur that she turned John in to the FBI, but she had *not,* after all, told John. She had been drinking when she called Arthur. Arthur's response to her was something like "Why did you do it after all these years?" I figured she was starting to crack under the pressure. I felt little relief in the news that she hadn't told John, but it gave me some hope that the investigation wasn't down the chute.

On 25 March I flew to Buffalo to meet Laura and talk to her before she called John. Culligan met me at the airport. I was impressed by his intelligence and wonderful sense of humor. He is a former Air Force pilot who also served as a pilot for the Bureau in the Buffalo area.

I have to digress to tell my favorite story about Culligan. As we got to know each other, we swapped tales about life in the Bureau. Culligan's story involved his supervisor. We street agents had to go into our supervisor's office for "file reviews" every three months or so. We would sit before him while he reviewed our cases and made astute comments about them. It was something we had to endure. Culligan was blessed with one supervisor who had absolutely no sense of humor. Cully took great exception to this, and he made it his goal to get the guy to loosen up. His major effort occurred during one of his file reviews, at which he appeared wearing his tuxedo and carrying two glasses and a nice bottle of wine on a silver tray. The supervisor looked at him, never changed his expression, and made not one comment about Cully's attire.

At any rate, as we drove to Laura's apartment Culligan and I discussed how we would handle our meeting with her. This would be my first meeting with any member of the Walker family.

Laura met us at the door. She was strikingly attractive and obviously nervous about the call she was about to make. I learned that she had not talked to her father in over two years. She had pretty much cut herself off from the family for a while and really hadn't been doing too well. I was very much aware how difficult it would be for her to call her dad at the request of the FBI, no matter how strained or miserable her relationship with him had been.

We talked with her for thirty minutes or so and told her, in general terms, what we wanted her to say. You can't give people a script under those circumstances; you have to give them room to be themselves. She understood that the objective of the call was to put the possibility of access to classified information in front of her dad and see how he would react. She was not to ask him anything about his business with "his friends in Europe," as he had called them when he tried to recruit her. When Culligan and I felt comfortable that Laura was ready to make the call, we hooked the recorder up to her telephone and told her we would be back in an hour. It was early evening on 25 March 1985.

This was another of those critical points in the investigation. Was Laura going to be able to pull it off? Would she crack under the pressure and tell her dad she and her mom had turned him in? Culligan and I went and got a cup of coffee and sat in his car sweating bullets until it was time to go back to Laura's.

Some might question the wisdom of leaving Laura on her own to make that call. I had wanted to come to Buffalo to meet her and to form my own impression of whether she was capable of making the call. I felt that she was, and that we should not be there when she actually made the call. The presence of two FBI guys in the room might have altered her natural style of conversation.

After an hour we went back to Laura's. She was visibly shaken and upset; she knew that she had just helped the FBI tighten the noose of justice around her dad's neck, if ever so slightly. We spent some time consoling her, and she was feeling a little better by the time we took the tape from the recorder and left. We hurried to the car, anxious to hear how the conversation had gone. We had no idea what we were about to hear.

6

The Voice of Evil

We played the tape as soon as we got into the car. The initial minute or two of their conversation was relatively normal, I suppose. At first John didn't recognize Laura's voice. He was obviously quite surprised to hear from her. When she asked how he was, his response was that he was doing great. He added that he was in good shape and weighed in at about 150 pounds naked and wringing wet. I thought that was a strange way for a father to describe himself to his daughter.

After the initial pleasantries, John wasted no time in cussing Laura out for not having kept in touch with the family. He used the word *fuck* in ways I had never heard before in describing how he felt about Laura's absence. He saved his best shot for a woman who had befriended Laura and comforted her during the time she cut herself off from her parents. John had learned the woman's identity and had contacted her in an effort to locate Laura, but she had apparently refused to tell him where Laura was. Now John worked himself into a rage, calling the woman every obscene name imaginable. Culligan and I were jolted when we heard him shout, "That f—ing bitch should have had her f—ing tits cut off!"

Cully and I looked at each other. We wondered aloud just what kind of man we were dealing with.

As they talked, we learned that John's current live-in girlfriend was P.K. Carroll, a rookie cop with the Norfolk Police Department. That was a particularly important piece of information to me. When I was first assigned the case, Wolfinger and I had talked about our approach to the investigation. We agreed that we had to be extremely discreet and cautious, for a couple of reasons. If John was still an active Soviet agent, he had probably been given an escape plan to use in the event that he got wind we were on to him. (It has happened. Edward Lee Howard, a disgruntled CIA employee who was fired in 1983 and contacted the Soviets, became aware of the FBI's interest in him and fled to the Soviet Union. He is still living safely outside the United States. And in 1985 Glenn Michael Souther, a suspect in an espionage case in Norfolk, fled the country and went to the Soviet Union two weeks after my associate Butch Holtz interviewed him. Souther committed suicide a couple of years later.)

We had figured we couldn't let the local police know about our interest in Walker because as a private investigator he might have contacts in the local departments, and someone might inadvertently tip him off. As it turned out, he couldn't have been much closer to the Norfolk PD, since he was sleeping with one of their recruits. Later, as the investigation progressed, Ms. Carroll and two other officers of the department were fired for furnishing Walker information from police files in connection with his detective business. I felt bad about the two officers because they were old-timers nearing retirement. I knew them both.

Culligan and I listened to Laura talk with her dad. She skillfully got around to the point of the call. She told John she was attending cosmetology school in Buffalo, but her life was in the toilet and she was broke all the time. When she told John she was considering going back into the service, his response was not hard evidence we could use in court against him, but from my point of view as an investigator, it was definitely interesting.

The pitch of his voice rose, and he began counseling her as to which branch of service would be best for her to join. He sounded somewhat excited at the prospect and definitely interested. He told her that opportunities for promotion were very tough in the Navy, and that although the Army had, as he put it, a lot of "f—ing n—gg—rs," it would probably be her best bet. I had never expected him to say anything like "Great, now you can commit espionage with me like I asked you to before." I simply wanted to get his reaction to the new possibility. I was pleased with what I was hearing.

Then Laura put a real bombshell on the table for John. She said, "I even thought about going into the CIA, but I didn't think I could pass the polygraph." John's response: "You had a legitimate problem there." Again, nothing that would convict him, but it certainly went a long way toward establishing credibility that John had indeed been and might still be a spy.

Culligan and I finished listening to the tape. We both commented on how filthy and vulgar John had been when talking to his daughter. We also detected something in his voice and manner of speaking that indicated how much control he had over her. It was as though we had been listening to a voice of evil.

I took a flight back to Norfolk the next morning, pleased with what we had accomplished but well aware that I still did not have one piece of hard evidence against John Walker. The whole case could be blown out of the water by one phone call to John by Barbara or Laura. They were both getting antsy and didn't understand why we hadn't arrested John yet. I couldn't help wondering how long we could keep them in check. I said many times that "the Man Above" would have to be on our side in this case, and as it turned out, He was.

One thing I didn't know until after we arrested John is that he went to Washington, D.C., on 31 March, just six days after Laura's call. He insisted that it was a business trip with his business partner, Laurie Robinson. But we have always thought he probably made an emergency drop for the Soviets to advise them that he had Laura on the hook as a new member of his ring.

7

The Spy Catchers

When I got in to work after my trip to Buffalo, I met with Wolfinger and other members of the Foreign Counterintelligence (FCI) Squad to brief them on the case and to play the tape of Laura and John's conversation.

The Norfolk FBI office at that time was on the eighth floor of the new Federal Building in downtown Norfolk. We had a panoramic view of the harbor and the expressway out of town. The squad area was an open bay with a couple of rows of desks. We literally worked side by side in the office as well as on the street.

To my right sat John Hodges, a proud graduate of the Citadel, a former Air Force pilot and Vietnam veteran. John had worked FCI cases in Washington, D.C., before transferring to Norfolk, and he had many years in the trenches. A devout Catholic and dedicated family man, he was known for an occasional outburst about the downfall of American morals and values. We dubbed him "Doctor Doom and Gloom." He thought the world was going to hell in a handbasket. He was probably right. Hodges would be the observer in the air surveillance of John Walker and, along with first-office agent Beverly Andress, would handle the numerous confessions and the arrest of Arthur Walker.

Bev Andress, a former teacher and employee on the staff of Senator Alan Cranston's Presidential Advisory Committee, was one of the first female agents assigned to the Norfolk office. In addition to participating in the surveillance of Walker from Norfolk to Washington and taking part in the interviews and arrest of Arthur, she testified for hours in federal court during Arthur's trial in August 1985. Andress helped pave the way for female agents to be accepted as professionals in the Norfolk office. Bev's husband, Rod, is also in the FBI, so she came to Norfolk with prior experience in training male agents.

One of those she had to train on our squad was Kevin Kenneally, a fellow first-office agent. A well-read, world-traveled Bostonian, Kenneally was a perfectionist in his work. When he first came to Norfolk, he went so carefully by the book that it was sometimes painful to watch. Bev just had to jerk his chain once in a while. One time he took some notes on a peanut-shop bag (I can only assume he had forgotten his pad of paper). When they got back to the office, Andress insisted that he file the original notes exactly as they were—on the bag. Rules were rules, she said. Kevin put the bag in the file.

To my left sat Richard L. "Butch" Holtz, a former Marine sergeant and Vietnam vet; at least that's what he told me. One thing I have never been able to live down is that when Holtz applied to the Bureau, I recommended him—the reason I was never promoted to supervisor, I'm sure. We had met when I was working bank robberies and he was a Virginia state probation and parole officer in Norfolk. I knew that he was, shall I say, different. "Bizarre" is probably a better description. Judge for yourself: Holtz was seriously injured during a training exercise at Quantico and underwent eleven hours of heart valve replacement surgery. This led to many subsequent hospital stays, during which he wrought havoc on the staff with his demented pranks. Once, before surgery, he prepared himself by drawing an anatomical map on his chest with a Magic Marker and writing instructions to the surgeon on his abdomen. Another time he tied his bedsheets together, hung them out the window, hid in the bathroom, and watched with glee as the nurses panicked, thinking he had gone out the fourth-floor window. As I've

OFFICIALLY NOTED

told Holtz many times, I've met a lot of people in my day, but he's not one of them. I don't remember what he did in the Walker case, but I'm sure it was spectacular.

If the squad had an aristocratic member, it was Dan McNally, an ex–Marine officer with the bearing of an English gentleman. We called him "Squire." One morning after I watched him make his way through the office, I told him he must be the personage for whom *Pomp and Circumstance* had been written. He grinned and agreed. McNally was to be my liaison between Norfolk FBI and the Naval Intelligence Service at the Norfolk Naval Station, an assignment no one on the squad envied. Dan was the perfect choice.

Francis "Ed" Schrader II, a former Navy Seal and naval officer, and a Vietnam vet, sat a couple of desks to my left. A silent, dependable man, Schrader had been a tough competitor on the swim team at Vanderbilt University. His contributions to the Walker investigation were to help monitor the wiretaps (all squad members got a turn at that), conduct interviews, and search Walker's residence in Norfolk after his arrest.

Ray Zicarelli, Paul Galvydis, and Kathy Williams were three more first-office agents on the squad during this case. Each made a valuable contribution in his or her own right. I put Zicarelli in charge of handling the evidence we collected—a monumental job, as it turned out. He also did interviews after we arrested John. Galvydis and Williams assisted in monitoring the telephone taps and also conducted interviews.

Ed Hale, a grizzled FBI veteran, completed the squad. Affectionately known as "Stump," he had graduated from East Carolina University and spent several years in the Newark, New Jersey, office before transferring to Norfolk. Stump handled the maintenance of the massive quantity of tapes and written logs generated by the wiretaps we were to place on John's telephones.

I have to take a minute to relate my favorite story about Stump. I was at my desk one morning when he came in with smoke erupting from both ears. He was really stoked about the traffic he had endured on his way in to work. It had apparently been especially bad on the Norfolk–Virginia Beach Expressway, near the western end, where it dumps traffic into downtown Norfolk. The road had been under repair for some time and was a bear to negotiate during rush hour. Stump had been bitching about his commute for some time, and this particular morning I guess he had had enough. Along with John Hodges, I watched with interest as Stump, his face beet red, picked up his phone and announced that he was going to call the mayor's office and complain. He dialed a number and ground his teeth as he waited for someone to answer. When they did, he lit into them and chewed ass about the insufferable traffic congestion he had been forced to endure. When he finished, he got a strange, confused look on his face and hung up. Hodges and I congratulated him for a fine performance and asked what was wrong. He looked at us and said, "That was the mayor's office in Portsmouth, not Norfolk. I dialed the wrong number." Hodges and I fell out of our seats. Stump got up from his chair and went out for coffee. It was his finest moment.

Joseph R. Wolfinger was the squad supervisor. I'm sure that you realize by now that he had his hands full. Joe graduated from Randolph Macon College, a small school in Ashland, Virginia. He got his law degree from the University of South Carolina. He spent his early years as an agent assigned to the Detroit Division. Joe is a smart guy, and he rose rapidly through the ranks. He was a supervisor at Headquarters prior to his transfer to Norfolk in the early 1980s. A big man of German descent, Joe was well liked and highly regarded by his peers. He had friends at the Headquarters level, a fact that would help this investigation considerably in getting through the bureaucratic morass.

"Wolfie" likes to play the part of a Southern gentleman and good ol' country boy. He *is* a gentleman, but certainly not a poor, slow-witted country boy. Far from it. He loves to tell stories about his experiences. My favorite is the one he tells about when he was a member of his high school wrestling team. It was his turn to take the mat and face his opponent who, as luck would have it, was blind. Joe said the worst thing about having to wrestle the blind guy was how the crowd booed him when he would sneak around behind the guy trying to gain a little advantage. I think the blind guy pinned him. It's a cruel world.

· · ·

As the investigation progressed, everyone in the Norfolk office, agents and support staff alike, became involved. The case consumed our office, the third smallest in the nation. In fact, before the case was over nearly every FBI field office in the country, including Honolulu and Hawaii, and legal attachés in London, Bonn (West Germany), and Bern (Switzerland), had people out covering leads.

The president of the United States, the director of the CIA, the secretary of defense, the secretary of the Navy, and some congressional intelligence committees were briefed at various times during the course of the investigation. And as case agent or lead investigator, I was the one who bore the ultimate responsibility for the investigation. An awesome responsibility it was. When I am asked to speak about the case, I tell the audience that I was six feet six inches tall and had dark hair when the case was assigned to me. By the time the case ended, I was down to five ten, and the hair was nothing but gray.

8

The Keys to the Kingdom

In March 1985 the military records of John and Arthur arrived. Those records told me that Art Walker joined the Navy as an enlisted man in 1953. He rose through the ranks and retired as a lieutenant commander in 1973. He served in the submarine service and eventually became an instructor in antisubmarine warfare at the Little Creek Amphibious Base, which straddles the Norfolk/Virginia Beach boundary. He had a Top Secret clearance during most of his career. That clearance gave him access to highly classified and sensitive military information.

John Walker's records showed that he joined the Navy in the fall of 1955. After completing his basic training at the Great Lakes (Illinois) Naval Training Center, he was sent to basic Radioman School. He was given the rate of radioman when he completed that training and was sent to his first command on the destroyer escort USS *Johnny Hutchins.* John earned 4.0 performance ratings, the highest rating possible, during his entire career, with very few exceptions. I noticed that his performance dropped below the 4.0 mark one rating period in 1968, which I later learned corresponded with the period of time just after he had started selling Navy secrets to the

Soviets. I guess it made him a little nervous at first, serving two masters. He quickly regained his form, though, and went back to those 4.0 ratings for the rest of his career. I've often wondered what John's former commanding officers, the authors of all those glowing 4.0 performance ratings, thought when the news broke that John had been a spy for the Soviets for nearly twenty years.

John rose through the ranks rapidly and became a first-class petty officer within six years. He made chief petty officer three years later, and senior chief petty officer three years after that. John then made warrant officer and retired in 1976, at the rank of warrant officer 3. When it comes to describing John Walker's role as a radioman in the U.S. Navy, I think Adm. William O. Studeman, director of naval intelligence, said it best in his affidavit to the U.S. District Court, District of Maryland, on 4 November 1986, prior to John's sentencing in that court on 6 November:

> The Navy occupation . . . of Radioman is one of the most important and responsible jobs in the fleet. The individuals chosen for that occupation are among the best and brightest, necessarily so because the tasks are demanding and the responsibilities are significantly greater than most young men are required to assume. The Radiomen of the U.S. Navy, and their counterparts in the other services, hold the keys to the nation's secrets. They transmit and receive the communications containing those secrets, and they care for and protect the cryptographic equipment, logic and enciphering systems that prevent the exposure of transmitted messages to hostile powers. It was into this select group that John Walker was placed. . . . It was nearly ten years after his retirement before the United States would learn that its confidence in John Walker was sadly misplaced.

(For the complete text of Admiral Studeman's affidavit, see appendix C.)

Of course, that same trust was misplaced in Jerry Alfred Whitworth, another Navy radioman, recruited into John Walker's espionage ring.

Soon after I received John's and Arthur's Navy records, Wolfie and I asked the National Security Agency—the folks responsible for making the cryptographic equipment used by our nation's military and other government agencies—to send someone to Norfolk to review the files and discuss the potential damage John and his cohorts could have caused if they had taken advantage of their access to this country's secrets.

Steve Carter arrived a few days later. After reviewing John's and Art's files, shook his head sadly and said, "If these people gave the Soviets the information they had access to, the damage will be not only grave, it will be catastrophic." Steve was visibly shaken.

They did indeed have the keys to the kingdom!

9

A Visit from Barbara

In mid-March, after the Bureau gave us authorization to conduct a full field investigation, we developed all sorts of information on John, his son Michael, and his brother Arthur. I wanted to know as much about them as I possibly could. We checked passport, telephone, real estate, financial, birth, court, arrest, and any other records I could use to build my profile of John Walker. The information started pouring into the file. It was my job to assimilate it and put it to use.

At the end of March I compiled a forty-five-page teletype to Bureau Headquarters, which contained enough information for them to prepare an affidavit for the Foreign Intelligence Surveillance Court in Washington and request permission to place a wiretap on John's and Arthur's telephones.

Also, near the end of March, Agent Barry Colvert called me on the secure phone and told me he had just finished the polygraph examination of Barbara Walker, and she had passed. I'll never forget what Barry said: "Put your helmet on, Bubba, because you are in for a hell of a ride." He knew we were dealing with an espionage case of epic proportions, and the pressure would be tremendous.

Walter Price called me to say that Barbara was coming to Norfolk to visit daughter Margaret for ten days. She was scheduled to arrive on 2 April. I asked him how her drinking problem was, and he told me she was into the bottle big time. I knew that her visit would make it much easier for her to have a few pops and call John, Arthur, or Michael's wife, Rachel, and tell any or all of them that she had turned John in to the FBI; they all lived within a few miles of each other in the Norfolk/Virginia Beach area. Since she would be staying with Margaret, I assumed she would definitely tell her. I knew this would be another of those times when "the Man Above" would have to look out for us.

Price gave Barbara my office phone number, and she called me soon after she arrived. I had been having frequent meetings about the investigation with Wolfinger and squad members since early on in the case. Everyone involved was kept advised of where we were and what was happening. Wolfie and I had agreed that when Barbara arrived, Bev Andress and I would spend as much time with her as possible.

Barbara called me from Margaret's apartment after she arrived on 2 April. She and Margaret were going to spend some time together, so I made arrangements to pick her up the next morning after Margaret went to work. I instructed her to meet us a few blocks from Margaret's place. That would give us a chance to check out the neighborhood and try to determine whether John, or any suspicious character who might work for him, was watching Margaret's place or following Barbara.

When Barbara got into the car, I got the impression that she had been drinking, but she didn't appear to be drunk. It was obvious where Laura got her beauty, although the years of worry and drinking had taken their toll on Barbara. She smoked heavily and appeared tired and nervous. No wonder; she had been going through hell for a long time, and now she was involved in an endeavor that would put the man she loved in jail for the rest of his life.

It took Barbara a few minutes to loosen up and decide that she could place her trust in us. She wanted to know why John hadn't been arrested yet. I explained how difficult it is building a case of espionage against someone. She understood but didn't necessarily like my answer. We went for coffee and talked for a couple of hours. She seemed to like Bev and was pleased that she had another woman to talk to.

Barbara said she planned to stay in Norfolk ten days, and she was sure that sometime during that period John would demand to see her. She explained that he always met with her when she was in town so that he could remind her to keep her mouth shut about the "family secret," the term the family used when referring to John's spying activities. I asked her whether she had tipped John off about turning him in, and she said she had not. She said she had called Art, though, and told him. She didn't know what Art had done with the news, but she figured he probably told John. She had not received any calls from John, so she wasn't sure. I told Barbara I wanted her to put the inevitable meeting with John off until the end of her visit, if at all possible. She agreed to try. I asked her not to discuss her dealings with the FBI with anyone, including Margaret. She agreed not to, and I felt that her response was sincere. I also knew that if that devil in the bottle got hold of her, there was no telling what she would do.

Barbara agreed to meet with Bev and me every day she could while Margaret was at work from 9:00 A.M. until 5:00 P.M. or so. Margaret did not work weekends, and Barbara planned to spend that time with her. Bev and I gave her our office and home phone numbers and asked her to call us any time, day or night, if she needed to talk. We dropped her off a few blocks from Margaret's place and went back to the office. I was convinced that Barbara's visit was going to be the longest ten days of my life.

Barbara called me and Bev at least once every day to check in. There were a few days during her visit when she had things to do and neither Bev nor I got together with her, but most days we were able to meet with her. Bev took her shopping a couple of times and kept her occupied. I met with her several times, and we usually talked about John's activities and the effect his spying had had on the family. According to Barbara, before John started spying in late 1967, he had been a good husband and father; after he became a spy, though, he began to drink, became a womanizer, and neglected her and the family. Quite frankly, based upon what I had heard in the conversation between John and Laura, I found it hard to believe that he had ever been anything but self-centered, vulgar, and amoral.

Each day we met with Barbara, it appeared that she had been drinking hard the night before. My concern that she might get drunk and call John, or tell other family and friends in the Norfolk area that she had turned him in, never abated.

I did have some very helpful meetings with her. I went over her entire story about what she knew about John's espionage activities. Her memory astounded me. She recalled many more details than the average person usually does. She told me of going on a couple of dead drops with John near Washington, D.C. One time was in 1968, not long after she had gone through his desk and found out he was a spy. The other time was when they were living in California; John returned from a cruise and asked her to go to D.C. with him. She said that on each occasion John took his instructions from the Soviets, and during the afternoon they would check out the areas where he was to drop his package and pick up the Soviet package. Then they would return to their hotel, have dinner, and return to the drop area under cover of darkness and conduct the acts of espionage according to a schedule provided by the Soviets. Barbara said she went on three or four drops with John, and he did the same routine every time. That bit of information would turn out to be very important later on in the investigation.

Barbara revealed another aspect of John's sterling character when she told me of an incident that occurred soon after they opened the Bamboo Snack Bar in Ladson, South Carolina. It seems they were having problems meeting the payments on a loan they had obtained from a local bank, and one of the loan officers came by one day to discuss the problem. John wasn't there, so he and Barbara talked. Barbara said the banker suggested that she could work some of the debt off "in trade." When she told John, he told her that if the guy wanted her to prostitute herself to help pay the bills, she should go ahead and do it. Every time I thought I had heard the worst of John's character, another story would pop up, each one more outrageous than the last.

Barbara also told me she had tried to turn John in to the FBI twice before. The first time was when they were living in California, in 1974. John was assigned to the USS *Niagara Falls,* where he was communications officer, Top Secret control officer, and communications control officer. By then he had been spying for nearly seven years. Barbara called the FBI office and asked if a person could be protected if he or she knew that someone was committing a crime and then turned that person in to the authorities. Whoever she talked to told her no. Barbara hung up the phone and didn't call back. To think that she came so close to ending John's espionage career ten years sooner just boggles my mind. If the conversation went exactly as she said, I would have to say shame on the FBI employee who mishandled that call.

Barbara's other attempt to turn John in occurred when she was in Norfolk, visiting their son Michael and his wife, Rachel, in July 1984. Michael was at work in Fighter Squadron VF-102 at the Oceana Naval Air Station in Virginia Beach, and she and Rachel were at home. Barbara had been drinking, she said, and she told Rachel that John was a spy and she was going to turn him in. She wanted Rachel to drive her down to the FBI office, but Rachel called Michael, who got on the phone and talked Barbara out of it. If she went to the FBI, he said, it would ruin his own career in the Navy. This bit of news got my attention, and I wondered if Michael was also spying with his dad. I also couldn't help but wonder just how many people knew that John Walker was a spy. I was starting to think I was the last to know.

During one meeting with Barbara, I asked what made her believe that John had recruited his brother Arthur into the espionage business. Her reply blew my mind. She told me she and Art had had an extramarital affair that lasted about ten years. It began when they were living in the Charleston, South Carolina, area in 1966 or 1967. John was at sea on the USS *Simon Bolivar,* a "boomer," or ballistic-missile submarine. Art came to visit, and the combination of his raging hormones, Barbara's booze, and John's neglect led them to the bedroom. The affair took on a life of its own and followed them from city to city.

Barbara said that one day, after she had discovered John was a spy, Art came by their apartment in the Algonquin House in Norfolk for an afternoon of frolic while John was at work at the Norfolk Naval Station. As they played, Barbara began lamenting the fact that John was a spy. According to Barbara, Art said, "If it makes you feel any better, I did the same thing while I was assigned at Groton, Connecticut, only not to the extent that John has."

This was turning out to be the darnedest case. I never knew what to expect, except that whatever it might be, the chances of it being bizarre were pretty good.

Barbara was right: John put tremendous pressure on her to meet with him from the time she arrived in Norfolk. He even showed up at Margaret's place one evening after she had been there a few days and demanded that she go with him to talk for a couple of hours. She was able to convince him that she didn't feel well. She did a great job of putting him off until the evening before she was scheduled to go back to her place in West Dennis, Massachusetts.

Bev and I met with her the day of the meeting. She wanted to wear a wire and record their conversation, but I was against the idea. I knew that John hadn't survived nearly twenty years as a master spy by being careless. I also knew that he was an electronics expert and might have the capability of detecting a wire. There was also the possibility that he might pat her down looking for a wire. After all, she had called Art and told him she had turned John in to the FBI, and Art might well have passed that information along. We argued about the wire briefly, but I simply refused to use one and told her she would just have to pay attention and remember what John said during their meeting. I also told her she had to convince him that she still loved him—which, strangely enough, she still did—and that she had not called the FBI; I told her to convince him that she didn't have the nerve to do it.

We dropped Barbara off in Margaret's neighborhood around 3:00 P.M. on 11 April 1985. John was to pick her up for dinner at 7:00, and Barbara was to call me as soon as possible after the meeting. Bev and I went back to the office and waited for her to call. I was still afraid Barbara would get loaded and spill her guts to John at dinner; I just didn't see how she could pull it off. On the verge of apoplexy, I went into Wolfie's office and told him what was going on, and he nearly went into convulsions. To say we were uptight would be putting it mildly.

Barbara called later that evening and gave me some basic details of how the meeting went; then we made arrangements to meet the next morning. When Bev and I picked her up, she was in reasonably good shape. Their meeting had gone pretty well, she said. John, being the big spender, had taken her to McDonald's. He warned her to keep her mouth shut about him and pointed out that if he went to jail, he would not be the only one to suffer. She asked him if he meant that their son Michael was involved with him, but he refused to give her a direct answer. He also didn't deny that he was still a spy. He asked her if she had turned him in. She told him she hadn't and didn't have the nerve to. He said he was glad to hear that and warned her again to keep her mouth shut. He told her he didn't want to end up being interviewed in a jail cell on *60 Minutes* someday. (Strangely enough, John requested and got an interview by Mike Wallace on the CBS show *60 Minutes* five years later at the federal correctional institution in Marion, Illinois. He requested the interview because he wanted a chance to say publicly how unfairly he thought his brother Arthur had been treated in the sentence he received after his conviction for his part in John's espionage business. John's complaint fell on deaf ears.)

I took Barbara to the Norfolk airport later that day and put her on a plane back to Massachusetts. I told her to call me any time she thought of anything she felt I needed to know, or if she simply needed to talk. I received many calls from her over the next couple of years, often late at night after she had soaked her soul in vodka. She was a tragic figure in those days.

I returned to the office to see how things were coming with the installation of the wiretaps on the telephones in John's home, business, and houseboat. My request had been approved on my birthday, 5 April, and we were to go on line that day, 12 April 1985.

10

Listen and Wait

The process of getting a wiretap approved by the Foreign Intelligence Surveillance Court (FISC) in Washington, D.C., is not necessarily simple. Contrary to what many people believe, we can't just decide one day that we want to tap someone's telephones. I first had to convince my boss, Wolfinger, that a tap was needed, and that I had enough information developed to send to Headquarters to support an affidavit, which the supervisor there would then compile, with the help of the Bureau's Legal Division, and submit to the attorney general of the United States. Once the AG approved the affidavit, the Bureau supervisor—in this case, Dave Szady—would take it to a judge at the FISC for his approval and authorization.

A fellow named John Martin was then chief of the Internal Security Division at the Department of Justice. He readily agreed to a tap on John's phones, but he disagreed with Szady, Wolfinger, and me and wouldn't sign off on a request for a tap on Arthur's telephone. He wasn't convinced Art was involved.

Then Szady went to see the judge, who read the affidavit, and asked, "Why haven't you asked for a tap on Arthur Walker's telephone? It appears to me that he is involved, too." Szady grumbled that the DOJ wouldn't go along with a tap on Art's phone.

We had the taps on John's telephones by the time Barbara got back home to Massachusetts. John had one phone line in his residence at 8524 Old Ocean View Road in Norfolk and a telephone on his houseboat, which he kept docked in the Willoughby Spit section of Norfolk. He also had three phone lines in his offices at 405 South Parliament Drive in Virginia Beach. From those offices he ran three small businesses. One was his private detective agency, Confidential Reports, which primarily handled divorce and insurance or workman's compensation fraud cases. He also had a company he called Electronic Counterspy, which was engaged in the business of "sweeping" office spaces and conference rooms for "bugs" (hidden microphones). He could also check telephones to determine if they were bugged. His third company, Associated Agents, was mainly an outlet for the sale of electronic equipment.

A telephone tap is one of the fastest ways for a case agent to burn up manpower and draw the ire of his fellow squad members. In this case I needed three agents for each of three eight-hour shifts, twenty-four hours a day, seven days a week. I could only hope that we would get a break and move on John Walker before the troops got restless. I knew from experience that sitting on a phone tap isn't all fun and romance. The novelty wears off after about ten minutes, and then it becomes a tedious, tiresome job.

I met with the squad and other agents who had volunteered to help monitor the equipment (headphones and recorders) and briefed them on what I expected to get out of the taps. I hoped to develop a list of John's friends and acquaintances, whom we could interview about him when the time came. I certainly expected to learn more about John Walker, the person. This kind of knowledge would give me an edge and an insight on how to deal with him. I wanted to learn as much as I possibly could about his personality, his life, his interests, and his weaknesses and strengths before I came face to face with him.

One thing I didn't expect to hear on the phones was John Walker talking to anyone about his espionage activities. I didn't have one solid piece of evidence that John was still an active agent for the Soviets—or had ever been, for that matter. And I figured that if he was, he wasn't going to talk about it on the phone.

Of all the things I asked the agents to listen for, the most important was any indication that John was going to go out of town. Based upon past experience and upon what we knew about Soviet intelligence operations, I doubted that the Soviets would come to Norfolk to deal with John. Because of the high concentration of U.S. military bases, the entire Norfolk area, including Williamsburg, was officially "off limits" to the Soviets; they were not allowed to travel to the area without U.S. State Department approval. I didn't think they would risk coming to Norfolk to deal with John Walker. If they filed with the State Department to come to Norfolk, they knew we would be aware of their plans and would be out to see what they were up to. If they came unannounced, they would be running a great risk of getting caught. I figured that if John was still active, he must be exceptionally valuable to them. They would pay him to come to them, probably in the D.C. area, just as Barbara said they had done in the past.

So we settled in, listening to John's telephone conversations around the clock. After several weeks it was clear that we were wasting our time on the midnight-to-eight shift. We made some scheduling adjustments, and that made life a little easier for the people in the "hole."

Every morning I read all of the telephone logs (agents' summaries of pertinent conversations). If a conversation was of particular interest to me, I listened to the actual tape. We were getting an earful of John—his vulgarity, his sense of humor, his deceptiveness. As Wolfinger remarked, "John was a man who lied even when the truth would have served him better."

As I listened, I was getting to know John Walker. I was surprised to note his work ethic. He put in long hours and seemed committed to making his detective agency a success. He was also good at "reading" people, and he used them to his own ends. I got the impression that he took advantage of the distraught women who called him to investigate their straying husbands. These women were vulnerable—and John got them into the sack any time he could.

. . .

While the wiretaps continued, other aspects of the case went forward. In early April, John Hodges and I went to see our old friend and former boss, Dick Rafferty. Dick had been our squad supervisor before he retired. He worked as a private investigator for a while after his retirement, then took a job as head of security for a local hospital. Dick had also been a cop in Boston and an agent with the Naval Investigative Service before coming into the Bureau. Obviously he had been around the block a few times. I figured that if anyone in the community knew John Walker, Rafferty would. This was to be the first and only interview of anyone, other than Barbara and Laura, conducted before the arrest of John Walker. I was determined that this was going to be an absolutely discreet investigation. No one was to be contacted about John until I felt that the time was right. Rafferty was a man of the highest integrity, and he would honor my request to hold our conversation in strict confidence.

I called him at his office at Portsmouth General Hospital, and we made arrangements to meet. When we arrived at his office, he took us to coffee. We chatted about old times. Rafferty is a husky, red-headed, blue-eyed Irishman with a fine mind and a keen wit. He knew instantly that we had something serious to discuss. I told him we were working on a major case he would be proud to be a part of—but, because it was classified, I couldn't tell him any of the details. He laughed and said he understood. I asked him if in the many years he had lived in the Norfolk area he had ever run into John Walker. He rolled his eyes and said, "Oh, yes, I know the bastard."

Rafferty went on to tell us that in his opinion John Walker was an amoral man who would do anything he had to do to achieve his goal. He said John was an expert in electronics and would not hesitate to bug the FBI office, telephones, and cars to try to confirm any suspicion he had that we were on to him. He said John would be surveillance-conscious, and we should be very circumspect in our investigation of him. He also said John was only an average investigator, at best. And the last comment he made about John stuck in the back of my mind. He warned, "Be careful, because he carries a gun."

In the FBI, when an agent develops information that a subject of a case might carry a weapon, all communications prepared in the case have to carry a cautionary statement indicating that the subject should be considered armed and dangerous. This, of course, serves as a warning to all agents working the case. From the day I talked to Rafferty, I put the "A&D" statement on every communication sent in the Walker case. I caught a lot of flack from fellow agents in other field offices, especially the large ones like the Washington field office. Having an "A&D" subject in an espionage case was unheard of. Our subjects were often strange or weird, but not dangerous. I let the statement stand, though, and laughed off the good-natured taunts.

As the days passed, I continued to build my profile of the man John Walker. The wiretaps were going pretty much as I had expected. The troops were performing well, with very little bitching and moaning over what I knew was a tough assignment.

One morning I came into the office and began my routine of reviewing the previous day's telephone logs. My attention was caught by a notation about a call to John's office concerning telephone taps. I ran the tape and to my great pleasure heard a local citizen asking John whether he could find a tap on his telephone. John told the man he would check it out for him, but he had to warn him that he couldn't find an FBI tap! I breathed a sigh of relief. I had wondered what the chances were that John, with all his training in electronics, could find our taps. Silently, I thanked him for the compliment.

It was during the wiretaps that we learned the identities of the two Norfolk police officers who were running record checks for John and giving him information from police records. At an appropriate time after John's arrest, we notified the chief, and their careers were over. I'm sure John has never given them a second thought.

You never know what you are going to hear on a wiretap. Ed Hale pointed out one conversation in which a man asked John if he needed any investigators at his detective agency. John asked him what his background was, and the guy said he was a retired FBI agent! I checked his name, and sure enough, he was. I can only imagine what

John Walker, master spy, must have thought. John played along with the guy, who called back several times, but never hired him.

We also learned a bit about John's family. His parents were divorced. John had been born in Washington, D.C., on 28 July 1937. Two years later the family moved to New York City, where they stayed until 1942 or 1943, when they moved to Richmond, Virginia. In 1948 they made their last move, to Scranton, Pennsylvania, where John's parents split up. His mother still lived there.

One evening John got a call at home from a woman at his mother's house. She was related to John—a cousin, I think. As they talked, the woman told John his mother had a new favorite word and asked him if he could guess what it was; John couldn't guess. The woman put the elderly Margaret Walker on the line, and she said "Oh, Johnny, I learned a new word!" John asked what it was, and she said, "Oh, Johnny, it's f—!" They both laughed uproariously. At that point I couldn't help but agree with John Hodges's assessment that our society is going to hell in a handbasket. One thing for sure, I wasn't dealing with a group that was going to win any All American Family awards.

After the wiretaps had been in place for two weeks or so, we put nearly every other case on our squad in an inactive status. The Walker case was all-consuming. Everyone on the squad was dedicated to it.

Not all cases on the other squads became inactive, however. My longtime friend Marty Houlihan had a case on Tom and Carol Manning, two extremists on the FBI Ten Most Wanted list for murdering a New Jersey state trooper. Marty had information that a woman with a name the same as one of Carol Manning's aliases had rented a mailbox at a business on Witch Duck Road in Virginia Beach. Marty set up surveillance on the mailbox and was waiting for something to develop. He had no idea whether it was actually Mrs. Manning who had rented the box. He was able to determine that the box had not been used for some time but was still rented.

On the afternoon of 24 April, Bev Andress and I had been out at the location where the wiretap equipment was monitored. A short time after we left the site, Marty came on the radio and said a woman had just been to the mailbox. He requested assistance in the surveillance. Bev and I joined the chase. The lady drove a rather circuitous route to a shopping center at Ward's Corner in Norfolk. She was obviously looking for surveillance as she drove. We kept our distance from her, arriving at the shopping center a short time after she parked and went into a grocery store. When she came out, Bev and I pulled our car in behind hers, blocking her exit. She bore a striking resemblance to Carol Manning. Although she denied being Carol Manning, we took her into custody. Another agent stayed with the woman's car and waited for arrangements to be made to have it impounded. As Bev and I headed back to the office, we got Marty on the line and told him we had Carol Manning in custody, although she was still denying her identity. Marty asked me if I was positive it was Carol Manning. I said I would bet my next paycheck on it. I was fortunate to have a pretty good ability to look at someone and match the person with a photograph.

I turned to the woman, who was handcuffed in the back seat, and remarked that we would definitely know who she was as soon as we got to the office and checked her fingerprints. At that point, she said, "All right, I'm f—ing Carol Manning."

Carol was nasty and foul-mouthed. She had an empty, desperate look in her eyes. When I asked her for the names of her two young children, she paused. For a few seconds, she couldn't recall what names they were using. She explained that they had been on the run for several years and had used many aliases. Life on the run apparently isn't as glorious and romantic as some would have us believe.

Marty found out where the Mannings had been living. He and a van full of agents went to the house they had rented in a quiet little neighborhood in Norfolk, not too far from the grocery store where we had arrested Carol Manning. They were able to arrest Tom Manning without any particular problems, although they did have to wrestle him to the ground. Later, at the office, when Manning filled out his fingerprint card, he wrote "Revolutionary" in the space for "Occupation."

The Mannings' children were both at home with Tom Manning at the time of the arrest. They were placed in the custody of the Social Service Bureau in Norfolk and subsequently released to the custody of a relative who had also been one of the FBI's Ten Most Wanted fugitives. He had been caught and either was acquitted or did his time for the crime of blowing up some power lines out west. I often think about those kids and wonder what ever became of them.

One evening in late April, John called Laura at her apartment in Buffalo. When she answered her phone John said "Hi, this is Jaws," a nickname he had given himself and obviously enjoyed using; in fact he referred to himself as Jaws in many conversations we overheard on the wiretaps. He had called Laura ostensibly to wish her a happy birthday. After doing so, he directed the conversation to her efforts to reenlist in the military. He encouraged her to get moving on the idea and strongly urged her to try to get into the Navy, not the Army. Laura handled herself well and said nothing to make him suspicious. John also told her about Barbara's recent visit to Norfolk and the meeting he had had with her. I can still hear him telling Laura that he thought he had persuaded Barbara to "shut her face" about the "family secret."

Laura reported the call to Paul Culligan the next day. That particular call went a long way toward convincing me that the man who called himself Jaws was still an active Soviet agent.

A day or two later Barry Colvert called me and said Laura had passed the polygraph examination regarding her knowledge of John's espionage activities and his efforts to recruit her. Laura told Barry that she had been in the U.S. Army for two years, 1978–79. She became a communications specialist, and when John learned that, he made several attempts to get her to steal classified Army documents for him to sell to "his man in Europe." He never told Laura that he was actually dealing with the Soviets, although Laura knew that he was; her mother had told her.

Talking with Colvert, Laura recalled that John often told her and the other kids that they were stupid and would never amount to anything. On one of his trips to try to recruit Laura, John told her that if she cooperated with him, she would be financially set and would make more money than she ever could otherwise. He gave her $500 in advance for her cooperation. Laura never furnished any documents to him, although she admitted being very tempted to do so.

Laura and Philip Mark Snyder met and married while she was in the Army. When she got pregnant, she decided to leave the Army and have the baby. When John learned of her pregnancy, he visited her and berated her for wanting to have the baby. He told her she should have an abortion, stay in the Army, and work for him; she could always have babies later.

Laura chose to leave the Army, however, and later gave birth to her son Christopher.

During the first week of May, Wolfinger and I hosted a conference in the Norfolk FBI office, attended by most of the major players in this investigation, including Dennis DeBrandt, FBI Headquarters unit chief; Supervisory Special Agent Dave Szady from DeBrandt's unit; Supervisory Special Agent A. Jackson Lowe of the Washington field office; Special Agent James "Dr. K" Kolouch, my counterpart in Washington Field; and Special Agent Paul Culligan from Buffalo. All of these people were intimately involved in the Walker investigation. The purpose of the conference was to discuss and plan how we were going to continue to conduct the investigation and what we were going to do in the event that we got a chance to surveil John Walker. We planned to continue on the course we had established for as long as we could, until the strain on our manpower or other circumstances required us to take a different approach. We were going to sit on the wiretaps, continue to develop intelligence on John, and wait for him to make a move.

We agreed that our objective in the investigation was to build a prosecutable case against John. We discussed and quickly dismissed any consideration of attempting to recruit or "turn" him to work for us against the Soviets. Our assessment was that if John had been or was still an active agent for the Soviets, he had done grave harm to this country, and we should make every effort to send him to prison.

We also discussed in great detail what we would do in a surveillance of John. I remarked that the way I intended to make a case against him was to catch him in the act of espionage. The guys from Headquarters and the Washington field office were a little skeptical and reminded me that what I was suggesting had never been done in the history of the FBI. That is, we had never followed an American citizen suspected of espionage and caught him in the act. I told them we would do our part, they would do theirs, and we would succeed.

We decided that if we saw John put a package down, we would allow him to leave the area, and then we would take the package; we did not want to risk another piece of classified material getting into the hands of the Soviets. We talked about what we would do if a Soviet came to the location where John had placed his package: we were going to confront him. If he turned out to be a Soviet diplomat, we would have to turn him over to his embassy. If he was not a diplomat, he would not have diplomatic immunity and would be subject to arrest.

We had a heated discussion about putting a tracking beeper on John's vehicle so that we could find him should we lose him during surveillance. The guys from Washington were very much in favor of it. I was opposed. My position was that John was an electronics expert, and he hadn't survived nearly twenty years as a master spy by being stupid. I thought he was likely to check his vehicle over before he took off on an espionage run and might find a beeper. I stood my ground, a stand I almost came to regret a couple of weeks later. Wolfinger supported me, and the Washington guys caved. There would be no beeper.

We discussed every aspect of the investigation we could think of that day. It was the single most important meeting we had during the investigation. I was very much aware that the guys from Washington had more experience in espionage cases than we had in Norfolk, and that they believed in this case only because of Wolfie's reputation at the Bureau and the fact that I had been successful in the Horton case a few years earlier.

We also discussed the possibility that John might fly out of Norfolk, either in his own plane, a single-engine Grumman Tiger—which was faster than our airplane—or by commercial airline. If he went commercial, we could put agents on the plane with him; however, if he attempted to get on an overseas flight, we would have to confront him and try to get him to agree to an interview. That was the last thing I wanted to have happen, though. I was reasonably certain that he would not talk to us, he would probably flee the country, and the case would go down the tubes. I figured my best chance of catching John was if he moved by car. If he went by plane, the case would probably be lost. Unlike many cases I had worked, this one was very much beyond my control. I felt a sense of helplessness on more than one occasion during this investigation.

We ended the meeting that day with dinner at the Lynnhaven Fish House in Virginia Beach. All of the out-of-towners went back to their respective offices the next day to get started on plans for the part they would play in a surveillance of John Walker. Dave Szady was to brief John Dion, an attorney in John Martin's National Security Section at the U.S. Department of Justice. Paul Culligan was to continue to maintain regular contact with Laura. Jim Kolouch was to develop a surveillance plan for the Washington field agents to follow in the event that we surveiled John to the D.C. area. We agreed that if we did follow John to D.C., we would turn the surveillance over to Kolouch and his associates, since they were much more familiar with their territory than we were.

I had no way of knowing where John would go to deal with his Soviet handler if he was still active. Barbara had said he always went to the D.C. area or Europe; I put my money on D.C. and prayed I was right.

A week or so after our meeting, Michael's wife, Rachel, called John at home. They discussed her graduation from Old Dominion University in Norfolk, which was scheduled to take place in a few days. Rachel was getting a degree in marine biology. John asked her several questions about the field and told her he might be able to get her a position with the Navy. He asked for her résumé and told her he would give it to a Navy buddy of his to see if any jobs were available for which she might be qualified. I would learn later that John had passed Rachel's personal information to the Soviets, and they had expressed an interest in his recruiting her.

On Friday morning, 17 May, I reviewed a series of wiretapped calls made on the previous evening. Around 8:00 P.M. John had taken a call from his mother, Margaret Walker, in Scranton. She told John, "Aunt Amelia has cashed in her chips"—a rather unusual way to announce a death in the family, I thought. As I listened to the conversation, I learned that Aunt Amelia had been one of John's favorite relatives. Apparently he had lived with her for a while when he was a boy. John's mother told him the funeral was to be on Saturday, 18 May, and asked him to come. John told his "mommy," as he always called her, that he had something to do and although he really wanted to, he just couldn't come to the funeral.

After John finished talking with his mother, he called Art and told him about Aunt Amelia's death. They agreed to send one arrangement of flowers from both of them, and they had a brief argument over who would pay for it.

John then spoke with his fiancée, P.K. Carroll. When he told her he wasn't going to the funeral, she chewed him out and told him he really should go. At that point he told her he couldn't go because he had something to do that only he could do. In the investigative business that kind of a statement is considered to be a clue. At least I thought it was; it certainly got my attention. I alerted Wolfinger that I thought we should consider putting our surveillance plan into effect for the coming weekend. Wolfie agreed. I called the people who were monitoring the wiretaps and asked them to be especially alert that day for any calls in which John might mention his plans for the weekend.

Throughout that Friday, 17 May, we overheard John telling people different stories about where he was going for the weekend. He told one person he was going to Nags Head; he told another he was going to Charlotte. He was obviously lying to someone. A few minutes before closing his office, John picked up the telephone and dialed three or four digits, then stopped to speak to some people in the office who were leaving for the weekend; he kept the receiver in his hand. Once he stopped dialing, we could hear the conversation taking place in the office; in effect, he was holding a live microphone in his hand. John told his staff that he would be going out of town for the weekend and would be back to the office on Monday, late morning or early afternoon. He told them to have a nice weekend and hung up the phone, never completing his call. That conversation persuaded us to surveil John Walker the weekend of 18–19 May 1985.

I told John Hodges and Henry "Hank" Bolin to have the airplane ready and be in the air by 7:00 A.M. on Saturday, 18 May. Hank Bolin, an ex–Marine fighter pilot, would fly the plane. Hodges would be the observer, keeping his eye on John's vehicle and directing the surveillance vehicles. The airplane would give us the advantage of watching John's movement from the air and keeping our ground units back out of his view.

I instructed the other agents who were to take part in the surveillance to meet Wolfinger and me at 6:45 A.M. I went home that evening wondering what tomorrow would bring. Would Jaws make his move? Would he detect our surveillance? I had told my squad many times that if we couldn't beat a private detective at this game, then shame on us. Would we catch him tomorrow? I was pumped, ready to match my wits against that master spy. I had given a talk about the FBI to my son Bob's class, at First Colonial High School in Virginia Beach, earlier in the week. One of the students asked me if I was working on any interesting cases, and I told him that I couldn't discuss current investigations—but I did have one case that might make the news pretty soon if things went the way I hoped they would. I spent that Friday evening eager for Saturday, 18 May 1985, to arrive.

11

Cat and Mouse

I had studied Walker's neighborhood. We would not be able to place any of our vehicles where we could actually see John's house, because there was no cover. If we could see his front door, he would be able to see us. All I could do was place a car at every point where John could leave his neighborhood, and let Bolin and Hodges in the plane "have the eyeball"—a surveillance term for having the subject in sight—and tell us when they saw John pulling out of his driveway.

Everyone involved in the surveillance was on time 6:30 Saturday morning. The plane was up, the secure (scrambled) radios were working, and we were in our assigned positions by 6:45. The wire-taps were still in place. We settled in to wait for Jaws to make his move.

Sometime after 9:30, Hodges told us that Jaws was cutting his grass. Later, he quit working on his yard, got into his new blue and silver Chevy Astro van, and pulled out of his driveway. We followed him to his waterfront lot at 617 West Ocean View Avenue, where we watched him work on his houseboat (also called *Jaws*). He stayed at the boat for a while and went back to his house in midafternoon. Not a very exciting day for the surveillance team, so far.

Around 4:00 P.M. the agents on the wiretaps reported that John had just made a date for the evening. Not with his fiancée, P.K. Carroll; she had to work that night, so John made arrangements to go out with someone else.

We stayed in our positions until around 5:30, when Wolfinger and I called everyone to meet to discuss plans for the next day. Needless to say, the troops were getting a little restless. We had been working this case since mid-February, had developed no evidence, had been working long hours, seven days a week, on the wires—and now we had just spent the day watching John cut his grass and work on his boat. He was having a much better day than we were. There was some bitching and moaning about whether we should come back tomorrow and watch him finish his yard work.

Of course we had to come back. Wolfie and I decided we would return to our positions at 6:45 A.M. on Sunday, 19 May, and if John didn't move by 1:00 or 1:30 P.M., we would all take the rest of the day off to go home and cut our own grass.

So we came back and were in place at 6:45 A.M.

Morale was not good. The plane was screwing itself into a tight circle in the sky above John's house. Absolutely nothing was happening. There wasn't even any good music on the radio. Around 10:00, I radioed the troops that I was going to a McDonald's on Tidewater Drive, a few blocks from John's house, to get a cup of coffee.

I pulled into the parking lot and went inside. As I went through the front door, I glanced to my right and was, to say the least, very surprised to see John Anthony Walker Jr. sitting alone in a booth, having some breakfast and reading the paper. I beat it to the men's room and nearly had a heart attack. I thought we had him under FBI surveillance! How could he have gone to McDonald's without me knowing it?

I got my coffee, returned to my surveillance position, and had a serious discussion with my cohorts about how we were the premier law enforcement agency in the world, and maybe we should pay a little closer attention to why we were out there. As it turned out, John had ridden his bicycle to McDonald's by way of a neighborhood path. The plane had not been in a position to see him when he came out of his house and got on his bike, and no one in the cars would have been able to see him leave.

A little while later, John rode his bike home and went into his house. I wondered what he was doing in there. He obviously was once again having a better day than I was.

Around 10:30, I talked with Wolfinger and then told Bolin and Hodges to set the plane down, refuel, get some lunch, and be back in the air in an hour. They had already been flying for nearly three and one-half hours, and I knew they were going to need fuel soon. The call to have them set down was one of those times when "the Man Above" was looking out for us: soon after they were airborne again, John Walker would make his move.

Bolin and Hodges were back in the air by 11:40 A.M. Everyone on the stakeout was in place, waiting for 1:00 to arrive so that they could go home. There was no activity on the telephone taps. All that had happened so far that day was John's breakfast at McDonald's.

At ten minutes past noon, Hodges announced that John was getting into his van. I reminded everyone to be alert but stay back and let Hodges have the eyeball. I didn't know whether John was just going over to work on his houseboat again, or what. The only thing I was pretty certain of was that he wasn't going to church.

John backed out of his driveway onto Old Ocean View Road and headed north toward Bay View Boulevard, a main thoroughfare a block or two from his house. He drove across Bay View into a little neighborhood and then did something I considered very unusual. Near the intersection of Old Ocean View Road and Creamer Street, he pulled over to the side of the road and stopped. He just sat in his van and looked around. He was looking to see if anyone was following him—looking for surveillance. This was not something an innocent man would do. At that moment, I felt in my gut that Walker was still an active agent, and that he was about to embark on an espionage run.

I was thankful that Bolin and Hodges had refueled a short time earlier. Now they would have enough fuel to fly to the D.C. area, if that was where John was headed. Had they not refueled, they would not have been able to fly that far, and we would have had to move our cars in much closer to John, running the risk of him seeing us.

The likelihood of our being able to follow him, undetected, all the way to D.C. without the airplane was remote at best.

After Walker satisfied himself that no one was following him, he worked his way through the neighborhood back to Bay View Boulevard and turned west. He stopped two more times, once in a 7-Eleven parking lot, and again in a gas station lot. He didn't get out of his van either time; he simply looked around. Satisfied that no one was on his tail, the man who called himself Jaws proceeded to Interstate 64 and headed west through the Hampton Roads Bridge Tunnel toward Richmond.

After we went through the tunnel, Wolfinger dropped out of the surveillance and called Jack Lowe, the Washington field office supervisor, at home. He told him we were following John Walker and it was time for the Washington agents to put their surveillance plan into effect. They had about three hours lead time to get everyone on their team assembled and in position to await our arrival. Lowe said he would notify Kolouch to get the team in position. I was praying that Walker was on his way to D.C. and not someplace else. I was well aware that he could go to Richmond, turn south on Interstate 95, and go to Charlotte, as we had heard him saying on the wiretaps. If he went to Charlotte, I was going to look mighty stupid, and a whole bunch of agents on the Washington field office surveillance team were going to be mad about being called out on a Sunday afternoon for nothing.

Wolfinger also called Dave Szady, Headquarters supervisor of the case, to alert him. Szady was out playing golf but got Joe's message. Szady called U.S. Department of Justice attorney John Dion, telling him we had Walker under surveillance and we might need his assistance. (An espionage case can have a direct effect on our foreign relations, and the case can become highly political. Only the U.S. Department of Justice can authorize an arrest and prosecution in an espionage case. The local U.S. attorney, with assistance from the Department of Justice, handles the actual prosecution of the subject of such a case.)

We followed John as he proceeded west. Walker drove in an erratic manner designed to detect surveillance. He would drive the speed limit for a while, then speed up, and then slow down to below the limit, all the while watching in his rear-view mirror for cars that did the same thing. The plane gave us the luxury of avoiding that trap. We didn't have to keep any cars close enough to John for him to see them. Hodges did a wonderful job of keeping us advised of everything John did.

As we were heading west toward Richmond, Bev Andress, who was riding with Kevin Kenneally, came on the radio and said, "Hey, Hunter, are we having fun yet?"

I said, "Not yet." We went another twenty miles or so. When John took the turnoff that connects to I-95 North toward Washington, D.C., I got on the radio to Andress and said, "Now we're having fun!"

When he made that turn north, I knew we were going to have a chance to catch a spy. I fired up a cigar. The adrenaline started to flow. I hoped Kolouch had succeeded in getting his troops assembled.

When we were about fifty miles south of D.C., I passed John's van. I was alone in my Bureau-issued Jeep Cherokee. I didn't look at him as I passed, but I could see he had on the same gold wire-rimmed glasses and dark blue short-sleeved pullover shirt with red trim that he had been wearing when I saw him earlier in McDonald's. I remember thinking, as I passed him, that this was likely to be his last day on earth as a free man.

I passed the Dumfries Rest Area. A few minutes later I heard Hodges say that John was pulling in there and someone should go in behind him, to see if he meets anyone and watch what he does. A few minutes later one of the guys came on the air and said no one saw him do anything but go into the men's room. John got back into his van and continued north. They checked the men's room after he left and determined that he had not left a package or any obvious signal in there.

Wolfinger and I conferred on our secure radios and agreed that we would go to the Washington field office, where a command center had been established to run the surveillance. Although we both wanted to be part of the surveillance, if it progressed as we hoped it would, we would need to be in the command center with Szady to help make decisions as things developed.

We arrived at the command center shortly after 4:00 P.M. The surveillance had been turned over to the D.C. agents. Wolfinger had told the Norfolk people that they could either go back home to Norfolk or spend the night here and return home the next day. They all went home. Imagine how difficult it was for them to break away from the surveillance of John Walker, after putting so many hours into the case and following him from Norfolk to D.C. They were well aware of the potential significance of the case. I have great admiration for them all and was proud to be associated with them.

As it turned out, it was a good thing they did go home, because their services would be needed again in about sixteen hours.

The command center was equipped with radios, wall maps of D.C. and the surrounding areas, and telephones. I was pleased to see Jackie Carrico working the radio and generally running the show. Jackie had been a first-office agent in Norfolk, and I knew she was top-notch.

Wolfie and I had been there a short while when Szady arrived. We were listening to the progress of the surveillance via radio. Wolfinger had spoken with Jack Lowe by car phone. Lowe was the supervisor on the scene in the surveillance. Spirits were high. Everyone in the command center was aware that we might get an opportunity to stop a serious breach of national security. We listened with great interest as John got onto the beltway around the southwestern rim of the D.C. area and then went out onto the country roads of suburban Maryland. Then, at approximately 4:45 P.M., the bottom fell out.

John was reported to be a couple of miles from River Road in Montgomery County, Maryland, when someone came on the air and said, "Does anybody have the eyeball?" Then, "We lost him!"

Wolfie and I almost swallowed our cigars. Szady went ballistic and made some remarks about how the hell a little office like Norfolk could follow John Walker for over three hours and then the "real agents" from Washington Field lose him inside of an hour. After we regained our composure, we talked about what we should do. I caught some heavy flack for not having wanted the beeper on John's van. All I could do was grit my teeth and hope we could salvage the operation. We remembered Barbara saying that when she went to D.C. with John, they always went to the drop sites in the afternoon to make sure they could find them later. Then they would check into a hotel and go back in the evening to conduct the drop under the cover of darkness.

We agreed that we should set up a "picket line" surveillance and have our people at various locations along the route where John had last been seen, hoping he would return when it got dark. We passed the word to Jack Lowe.

As the hours oozed by, Wolfinger and I sat in the command center, waiting for John Walker to return to the Maryland countryside. We clung to the hope that he and his Soviet cohorts were creatures of habit, like the rest of us, and that he would return, as he had with Barbara nearly twenty years before, to conduct his act of espionage after the sun went down.

We sent out for sandwiches, but my throat was so dry I could hardly swallow. These were the longest several hours of my life. I had a very real fear that I had blown the case by not agreeing to put that beeper on John's van. I felt like whale dung on the bottom of the ocean. Life was not good.

We waited and listened to the stony silence of the surveillance radio. That silence was broken nearly four hours later when, at a few minutes before eight that evening, Jim Kolouch and Jack Lowe, who were riding together, spotted Walker coming back into the area where he had last been seen. A cheer went up in the command center. We were right back in the chase. I took my first good breath in nearly four hours.

Wolfie and I lit up a cigar. The level of excitement was incredible as we listened to radio reports of the surveillance. Szady called John Dion, of the Department of Justice, and asked him to meet Gerald B. Richards, head of the FBI Laboratory's Special Photographic Unit, at FBI Headquarters. Gerry was a specialist in forensic photography and an expert in identifying and recognizing espionage paraphernalia and tradecraft. It would be his job to examine any package we might recover during the surveillance. It would be Dion's job to look at the evidence with Richards and decide whether to give us the authorization we needed to arrest John Walker.

Things were heating up, and the adrenaline was really pumping now. It was great watching that group of professionals working in the command center. Everyone was focused and doing his or her job. As I had said, "If we can't beat a private eye from Norfolk at this game, then shame on us." I knew we didn't need that beeper. Life was good.

Once Jaws came back, the activity became intense. A few minutes after 8:00 P.M. he was observed getting out of his van on Watts Branch Drive, near the intersection of Circle Drive and Ridge Drive, between Rockville and Poolesville, Maryland. It was the darker side of twilight. Ron McCall was flying the "Buplane"; Francis McKenzie Jr. was riding in the jump seat and had the eyeball on Jaws. No one on the ground was close enough to see what he did when he got out. John got back into his van and worked his way to Quince Orchard Road, near the intersection of Dufief Mill Road, where he pulled over. No one could see whether he got out.

When Jim Kolouch put his surveillance plan together, he had organized a search team of experienced people whose job it would be to go in behind John, searching any area where he had stopped or was observed doing something unusual. After John left the Watts Branch Drive location, the search team went in and searched the area but found nothing. When they searched the Quince Orchard Road site, they found an empty 7-Up can on the ground near a utility pole. Kolouch and Lowe went to the location and looked at the can, picked it, determined that it was empty, and put it back down. Everyone left the area.

A couple of minutes later someone came on the radio and reminded the search team to go back and get the 7-Up can because it would be used as evidence. He meant that the team should pick the can up after the surveillance was over, but the instruction was misunderstood, and they went back and got it right away. It was between 8:00 and 8:30 P.M. when John put the can down and we recovered it.

We later learned that the can was John's signal to his Soviet handler that he was in the area and ready to do business. There is no doubt that we screwed up by taking that can. If we had left it in place, the Soviet who was supposed to show up that evening would have seen it and would probably have fulfilled his role in the drama being played out before us. But he didn't take part that night, possibly because we had taken the signal can that he was supposed to see, and he left the area thinking John had not showed up for the drop. Taking the can didn't hurt the case, although it would have been a lot neater if we could have caught the Soviet in the same net we had out for John.

After John left his signal location, he drove to White's Ferry Road and turned south onto Partnership Road. About one-tenth of a mile south on Partnership Road, he pulled over to the right and stopped under a large oak tree. It was almost totally dark. McKenzie could not see whether John got out of his van. The headlights stayed on. After a minute or two, John pulled back onto the road and left the area. It was a few minutes past 8:30 P.M.

Once we felt sure that John was out of the area, the search team went in to do its job. Wolfinger, Szady, and I were in the command center, in contact by radio. We all wanted to be out there where the action was. It was very exciting listening to history being made as the case unfolded, but it took some restraint not to jump into a car and head out that way. We talked with Jack Lowe every few minutes and followed the surveillance progress on a map. The pressure was intense. If we were to succeed, everything had to go just right. Everyone in the command center and on the surveillance knew it; one little slip, and the case would go down the chute.

Jaws continued to drive those country roads. He went to the Quince Orchard Shopping Center, got gas, and sat in his van for fifteen or twenty minutes.

Meanwhile, a Soviet diplomat had been spotted. Shortly before 8:30 P.M., a late-model Chevrolet with diplomatic license plate DSX-144 was seen on Dufief Mill Road. A quick check of the plate told us the car was assigned to Aleksey Gavrilovich Tkachenko, the vice consul of the Soviet embassy, who was known to our Washington field office to be a member of the KGB. He had been assigned to the Soviet embassy in D.C. since 7 January 1983. One of our people on the surveillance recognized Tkachenko and his wife and daughter, who were in the car with him. For Tkachenko to be spotted out there, driving the same country roads as John Walker, was remarkable. Tkachenko had maintained a very low profile during his assignment to the Soviet embassy in D.C. We were surprised to see such a low-level embassy guy out there to service John, a spy of extreme importance to the Soviet Union.

Tkachenko was seen again a few moments later, still traveling on Dufief Mill Road toward its intersection with Quince Orchard Road. He was last seen approaching that intersection, about one hundred yards from where Walker had left his 7-Up can. Tkachenko was not our main interest, however. We were certainly interested in his activities, but we had to concentrate on John. We knew that Tkachenko had diplomatic immunity and that all we could do with him, if he took part in an exchange of packages or a face-to-face meeting with Jaws, would be confront him, make him identify himself, take him to our office, and call the Soviet embassy to come get him.

We didn't get the opportunity, however, because he high-tailed it out of the area and went back to his residence in the Hamlet Apartments in Alexandria. It would have been great fun for our guys to have had the opportunity to confront Tkachenko out there that evening and watch him try to explain why he was carrying over $200,000 and instructions for John's next drop. (John told me during the debriefing process that he had expected to receive over $200,000 and instructions for his next drop from his Soviet handler that night.) If we had stopped Tkachenko and taken his package from him, the U.S. Treasury would have been $200,000 richer—a little windfall for us taxpayers. I doubt that the Soviets would have lodged a protest, since that would have required them to admit their part in the Walker case.

A couple of days later, several of our guys from the Washington field office had an opportunity to examine the car Tkachenko had driven out in Montgomery County on the evening of 19 May. The entire exterior of the car had been cleaned. Even the underside, including the wheel wells, had been steam-cleaned of any evidence that the car had ever been in Montgomery County.

On 23 May 1985, Tkachenko and his family were escorted to Washington National Airport by several KGB goons. They flew to Montreal, where they boarded an Aeroflot flight to Moscow; I don't know what became of them. Several of our agents later went to Tkachenko's apartment and searched it. It was obvious that he had left in a serious hurry. There were pans of food on the stove, the sink was full of dirty dishes, and the refrigerator was still stocked. There was a "Reagan for President" sticker on a wall in one of the bedrooms—I thought that was a nice touch. And it was no surprise to find out that the ill-mannered Russians hadn't notified their landlord that they would be leaving.

At 9:30 P.M. Doug Stauffer, who was the leader of the search team, came on the radio and stunned everyone by announcing that they had found John's drop package. Until that moment, I had had no viable evidence that John Walker was an active agent for the Soviets; I certainly had nothing to take into court. The moment we found the package, I had a perfect case against him. Cheers went up in the command center, and there was near pandemonium for a couple of minutes. We had just caught John Walker in the act, exactly as I had said we would do. Wolfie and I fired up another cigar.

It was Agent Bruce K. Brahe II who actually found the package hidden in some tall grass at the base of a utility pole about twenty feet from that big oak tree Walker had parked under on Partnership Road. When he realized it was the package, he shouted "I've got it" and took off running across a cornfield with the package clutched to his chest. Stauffer was right on his heels. When they got a safe distance away, they looked in the bag and saw that it contained classified documents from the USS *Nimitz*. The documents were wrapped in white plastic and had been placed in the bottom of a brown grocery bag and then covered with items of trash. Arrangements were made to rush the package to FBI Headquarters, where Gerry Richards and John Dion were waiting to examine the contents. The trip would take about forty-five minutes.

We later determined that the utility pole where John left his package was 24.9 miles from the White House. The Soviets were allowed to travel freely, without notifying our State Department of their intentions, within a twenty-five-mile radius of the White House. They were just within their "legal" limits in this case.

Meanwhile, the surveillance of John Walker continued. He was still sitting in the Quince Orchard Shopping Center near a High's Ice Cream Store. We had two agents parked nearby pretending to be making out—one male, one female, in case you were wondering—as they kept tabs on what John was doing. They saw him turn on his dome light and check a map. He also kept looking around as though he were looking for someone.

At approximately 10:15 P.M., Walker left the shopping center and went to the intersection of Old Bucklodge Lane and White Ground Road. We couldn't get anyone close enough to see what he did there. After he left that area our search team went in but didn't find anything. After we arrested him, we learned that the Soviets were to have left their package for John behind a tree near that intersection, so he went there to retrieve his package—but it wasn't there, because Tkachenko had fled.

We had left several members of the surveillance team, including Brahe and Stauffer, hiding in the area where John had dropped his package for the Soviets, to see if anyone would come to retrieve it. No one ever showed up, of course. As we followed, John returned to his drop site twice that evening, got out of his van, and searched the area for his package. He was obviously confused: he had put his package down, and it was gone—yet he had not found the package the Soviets were supposed to have left for him. Each time he returned to search, he came within five feet of our guys lying in the bushes. One of the agents later recalled that John had a flashlight, and its beam passed right over him; John didn't notice. Our guys lay in those bushes all night and did not know until the sun came up that they had been rolling around in poison ivy. I understand that they had some very interesting cases of poison ivy in places I won't discuss here. This job does require an occasional sacrifice.

John stayed out on those dark country roads, with the FBI following along behind, until shortly after midnight, when he pulled into the parking lot of the Ramada Inn at 1251 W. Montgomery Avenue in Rockville.

Meanwhile, the package had arrived at Gerry Richards's office. He opened the package and was stunned by the simplicity of it. It was a grocery bag containing 129 highly classified documents inside another grocery bag that was folded shut, wrapped in plastic to keep it dry, and covered up with an empty Coca-Cola bottle, an empty rubbing alcohol bottle, an empty cotton swab box, some crumpled cellophane, and an unused crushed tissue. All of the items were clean; even the bottles had been rinsed and the caps put back on.

Richards and John Dion looked at the documents, all of which came from the aircraft carrier *Nimitz,* Michael Walker's current duty station. After reviewing them, Dion called us at the command center and gave us authorization to arrest John Walker on espionage charges. That call came in to us just as John was pulling into the Ramada Inn lot. It was a few minutes after midnight, 20 May 1985.

12

All Those People—My God, I Had No Idea

When Dion gave us authorization to arrest Jaws, I got on the phone with Jack Lowe and told him to take John into custody. Jack gave his guys the order, but by the time they got into the hotel, John was nowhere to be seen. The desk clerk said no one had checked in within the past hour. Reviewing the hotel register, the agents quickly determined that John had registered on Sunday afternoon around 5:30 P.M. He had given an address in Portsmouth, Virginia, and registered under the name John A. Johnson. But he had signed "John B. Johnson" at the bottom of the registration card. He had also put the correct license number of his van on the card. It didn't take a rocket scientist to figure out that our man was registered in Room 763.

Jack Lowe called me at the command center to report that John had apparently gone to his room. Jack asked me to check and find out if there really was a John A. Johnson at the address in Portsmouth, just as a precaution; we didn't want to go rousting some innocent citizen out of bed in the wee hours of the morning. I called the Norfolk FBI office and had the night clerk check the Portsmouth City Directory and telephone book. The address Walker used did not exist.

Jack had talked to Joe Wolfinger while I was checking out the address, and they decided that I should go to the hotel and take part in the arrest of John Walker. It is traditional in the FBI to have the case agent make the arrest if he is available to do so. Naturally I was champing at the bit to go out there and arrest John Walker. I asked Wolfie if he was going, and he said he would stay at the command center to make telephone calls and do other administrative stuff.

Jack Lowe sent a car to pick me up. We hustled out to the Ramada Inn and had a meeting in a room down the hall from John's. We met and discussed how we would go about arresting John. We didn't want to go crashing through his door; it was too risky. We knew he carried a gun and might come up shooting if we crashed in on him. He had been out of our view for several hours Sunday afternoon and evening, and we didn't know whether he was alone in the room. We wanted to accomplish the arrest with as little fuss and fanfare as possible. We certainly didn't want any of the hotel guests to get hurt, or even to know about it, if we could avoid it. We agreed that we would make the arrest at 3:30 that morning, while the guests in the other hotel rooms were sleeping.

But how were we going to do it? Fishing for an idea, I mentioned John's new van. He had bought it about two weeks earlier, and we had heard him bragging about it to several people on the telephone. Could we use this somehow? We checked to see whether John would be able to see his van from his hotel window. He wouldn't; he had parked on the other side of the hotel.

A plan was born. Agent Bill Wang would pose as a desk clerk. He would call John's room at 3:30 A.M. and tell "Mr. Johnson" that someone had run into his van in the parking lot. Wang would ask him to come to the lobby to deal with the problem. Jim Kolouch and I would arrest John at the elevator area down the hall, a few steps from his room. Other agents would be in position at various locations in the hotel, in the event that Kolouch and I missed him for any reason.

Kolouch and I put on white Kevlar bullet-proof vests over our shirts and took our position a couple of steps down the hallway across from the elevators on the seventh floor, so that we would be out of John's line of sight as he came from his room toward the elevator. It was a minute or two before Wang was to make his call. We knew we were about to arrest the most damaging spy in the history of our nation. We looked at each other and waited. It was incredibly exciting. The adrenaline was pumping. Yet we were both calm, ready to do our job. I'll never forget it, and I'm sure Jim won't, either.

It was very quiet in the hotel. At 3:30, we heard the telephone ring in John's room. Then we heard his door open. But he didn't come around the corner to the elevator. Kolouch and I looked at each other, wondering what John was doing. After a minute we heard his door open again, but he still didn't come to the elevator. It sounded as though he had left his room and returned, but where had he gone?

After fifteen minutes of standing in that hall, waiting to arrest John Walker, we heard his door open again. It was 3:45. This time John came around to the elevator very quickly. As he reached for the elevator button, Kolouch and I moved from our position to confront him. And as we moved, John wheeled toward us, pointing a snub-nosed blue steel Smith and Wesson .38-calibre revolver.

We had had our weapons out before John even came out of his room. For a brief time, we were in a standoff. We were six to eight feet apart. I remember looking at his revolver and seeing the bullets in the cylinder. I was paying close attention.

We told him we were FBI and ordered him to drop his weapon. He looked a bit confused, and for a few seconds I wasn't sure what he was going to do. I recall thinking that I didn't want to shoot him but was certainly prepared to do so if necessary. Kolouch would have, too. I'm sure we would have hit him; neither of us was a bad shot from that distance. Then John dropped his gun to the floor, and we took him into custody. I told him he was under arrest for violation of the espionage laws of the United States.

As we arrested him, the other agents in the hotel converged on the scene. We braced John against the wall with his feet spread. I held my gun on him while Kolouch searched him. Jack Lowe came up beside me. Kolouch emptied John's pockets, which contained a few dollars, keys, and some change. He also removed his belt and his shoes and socks. We knew that John wore a toupee. His family called it "Daddy's plastic hair," and he wouldn't let anyone see him without it neatly in place. Well, Jim just reached up and pulled that toupee off. I'll never forget the loud sucking sound it made as it came off his head. Kolouch threw the toupee to the floor. It looked something like a muskrat or a weasel lurking there. I nearly took a shot at it.

When we make arrests, we always do a complete and thorough search. We do it for the prisoners' safety as well as our own. We don't want them to have anything they might use to harm themselves or us. We do find some unusual things in surprising places. For instance, when I was working a murder case at the Norfolk Navy Base back in the early 1970s, we found a .25-calibre semiautomatic pistol in the suspect's bushy hairdo under his hat. On another case, my partner, Bob Arnold, and I found $1,500 wrapped around a bank robbery suspect's ankles under his socks. So we look everywhere for possible weapons or evidence. We don't intend to embarrass anyone. I must admit it, though: I sure enjoyed seeing that toupee come flying off John's head.

John had one other item with him. As he whirled around to face us, he dropped a standard-size manilla envelope. I can still see it floating to the floor. We took it, along with everything else John had, as possible evidence. We decided not to open the envelope until we obtained a search warrant. I didn't know it then, but the contents of that envelope would go a long way toward locking John up and throwing away the key.

When Kolouch finished his search, we took John down the hall to the room we had set up as an on-the-scene command post. I advised John of his rights and gave him a form that spelled out his rights and contained a waiver section for him to sign. John said he knew his rights and he didn't want to make any statement until he had talked to his attorney. End of interview. Once a suspect refuses to talk to the FBI and requests an attorney, we cannot continue questioning him. If we did, nothing he said would be admissible in court. (The Advice of Rights form John signed is reproduced in appendix A.)

We strip-searched John and made plans to take him to Baltimore, where we would take him before a U.S. magistrate. We were bound by rules of federal procedure to take him to the nearest magistrate in the federal district where he was arrested. Since we were in Rockville, Maryland, Baltimore was the place we had to go.

Kolouch, Lowe, and I would transport John in Jack Lowe's car. Jack would drive. Two other cars, one in front and one behind, would escort us to the Baltimore FBI office, where we would wait for the U.S. marshal's office to open around 8:00 A.M. Once the marshal's office was open, we could put John in a holding cell and leave him until time for the U.S. magistrate's hearing.

We left our hotel room around 4:15 A.M., with John in handcuffs. As we walked down the hall to the elevator, John turned to me and said, "You know, that story about my car being hit in the parking lot is the oldest trick in the book."

I just grinned at him and said, "I know. And it still works."

After we took John into custody, Jack had told all of his people they could go home. But as we left the hotel and headed for the car, we found all of Jack's troops waiting outside to get a look at John Walker; there were between seventy and eighty FBI people lined up out there. Jack and I heard John say, under his breath, "All those people—my God, I had no idea."

We strapped Jaws into the back seat behind Jack. I sat in the back with John, and Jim sat in the front. We took off. The trip took forty or fifty minutes. John never said a word. In fact, I don't think any of us did. I remember sitting there beside John wondering what was going through his mind. What was he thinking? How did he feel? What was it like knowing you had just spent your last day on earth as a free man?

13

The Wheels of Justice Begin to Turn

We arrived at the Baltimore FBI office sometime after 5:00 A.M. and took John into one of the conference rooms. Kolouch and I sat in the room with him while we waited for the marshal's office to open. Again I advised John of his constitutional rights, and again he said he understood his rights but didn't want to say anything until he had spoken with his attorney.

We took John down the hall to the processing room, where he was photographed and fingerprinted. We then went back to the conference room. I showed him a copy of a letter that had been found in the package he had left for his Soviet handler; Gerry Richards had made some copies of the letter and sent them over to me at the Baltimore office. My reason for showing it to John now was to give him some idea that we had him by the short hairs. He looked at the letter and said he had no comment; I hadn't expected him to say anything.

A while later John asked, "Who do you think I'm dealing with?" I told him we thought he was dealing with the Soviets. He responded,

"It's not the Soviets. There are some private intelligence-gathering organizations out there."

Later on, during one of the many court hearings in this case, U.S. district judge Alexander Harvey II ruled that when Walker asked us who we thought he was dealing with, his statement was an admission and I therefore should have advised him of his rights again. (It would have been the third time in less than three hours.) Since I didn't advise him, the statement was not allowed to be used against him. That was the only issue raised by the defense that they won during the entire case. It was obviously not a case-busting loss, but I would rather have won the issue.

Around 7:00 A.M. Kolouch, Lowe, and I transported John from the FBI office to the Federal Building in Baltimore and turned him over to the U.S. marshal. John was placed in a holding cell while we tended to some necessary paperwork and arranged for his hearing.

I've always noticed how much smaller the person under arrest seems to get the second that cell door clangs shut behind him. John Walker was no exception. Of course, he was small to begin with.

The federal rules of criminal procedure require a hearing for the accused as soon as possible after his arrest. Kolouch, Lowe, and I went upstairs to the office of the U.S. attorney to see if we could find a federal prosecutor to handle this case.

Initially, Yale Law School graduate Robert N. McDonald was assigned to the case, but he had to excuse himself to handle a previously scheduled court hearing. As he was trying to determine who else might be available, Michael Schatzow, a graduate of the University of Chicago School of Law, walked past Bob's office. Mike, who began his law career working for Charles Bernstein in the Baltimore Public Defender's Office, had successfully prosecuted Samuel L. Morrison, a Navy analyst, on espionage charges just a few months earlier. McDonald called Schatzow into his office and asked if he would help us. That was the beginning of a very pleasant friendship between McDonald, Schatzow, and me. We were to work many long days together preparing this case for trial. They are both extremely competent and hardworking guys.

We met with Schatzow for a couple of hours to discuss the case and prepare an affidavit to be filed with U.S. Magistrate Daniel E. Klein Jr. The affidavit briefly summarized the case that we had developed against John Walker and that would be used, along with my testimony at the hearing, to show the magistrate we had probable cause to establish that a crime had been committed and that John Walker had committed it. We also prepared search warrants for John's van and the manilla envelope he had dropped when he whirled around to face Kolouch and me. We didn't need a search warrant for the package he had left behind the telephone pole, because it was considered abandoned property, similar to trash you might place at the curb for pickup. We passed the search warrants on to members of Jack Lowe's squad who were standing by to conduct the searches.

The hearing was held that afternoon, Monday, 20 May 1985. I was the only person to testify. The magistrate was satisfied that we had shown probable cause and remanded John Walker to the custody of the U.S. marshal, without bond, pending further hearings and court appearances. Walker told the magistrate he was indigent and wanted a court-appointed attorney. Magistrate Klein appointed Thomas B. Mason, an assistant federal public defender. He would later be joined by Fred Warren Bennett, a rather emotional but likable federal public defender.

There were several members of the media present at the hearing, but nothing to compare with what was to come. Once the case went public, the media crowded every court proceeding. Representatives from major newspapers, television, and radio seemed to be everywhere. It is my understanding that after the case broke, articles appeared in the *New York Times* for thirty straight days. There would be four books written about the case (not including this one); a two-part made-for-TV mini-series movie on CBS; numerous magazine articles (my picture even appeared in *Cosmopolitan* magazine, which earned me the title of "Beefcake"); and several TV documentaries, including one made for German TV in 1995, in which I appeared along with Barbara and Laura. Even Laura wrote a book, *Daughter of Deceit,* presenting her personal version of life in the

Walker family. I still get calls for interviews about the case. In the spring of 1996, I took part in a program on the case put together by cable TV's History Channel.

The publicity about the case became so intense that John's attorneys eventually filed a motion in U.S. district court in Baltimore asking the court to hold William Baker, an assistant director of the FBI, in contempt of court for making so many statements to the media. There is no doubt that leaks to the media could have become a problem—and not only with regard to the defendant's right to a fair trial. The leaks could also have interfered with plea agreement negotiations between the U.S. government and John's defense attorneys. They might have interfered as well with ongoing investigations of others possibly involved with John in his espionage business, and with the debriefings of him once the plea agreement was reached. I recall attending a meeting with high-level Navy officials, including the attorney for the secretary of the Navy and representatives from other government agencies. We gathered at the Pentagon to discuss the case one afternoon in October. We were all reminded not to discuss the meeting with anyone. The next day virtually the entire meeting was reported verbatim in the *Washington Post.* So much for confidentiality at the Pentagon!

After the hearing, Kolouch and Lowe went home. I took a room at the Holiday Inn across the street from the courthouse, had something to eat, and collapsed on the bed. It was around 7:30 P.M. on 20 May, and I had been up since 5:30 A.M. the day before. The past thirty-seven hours had been an emotional roller-coaster ride, complete with elation, depression, excitement, and euphoria. Quite a "day." I had no problem sleeping that night! I knew, however, that the work on the case was really just about to begin.

14

K.I.S.S.

Those of us who had an opportunity to see the package John "dropped" for his handler were surprised by the simplicity of the operation. We in the counterintelligence business had expected a fairly sophisticated system. After all, this Soviet KGB operation had been successful for nearly twenty years. We had expected sophisticated radio messages, or microdots and secret writing, or the use of a rollover camera to copy documents. None of these techniques was used in the Walker operation. This was the entire protocol: John put classified documents in a grocery bag, covered them with trash, and placed the bag behind a telephone pole in the country. Maybe that was the reason the operation was so successful for so long: we had expected something more complex.

Gerry Richards, the FBI Laboratory's expert on espionage paraphernalia and tradecraft, explained Walker's low-technology system to me this way:

> When John began working for the Soviets, he was probably initially handled by the GRU [Soviet Military Intelligence], who handled agents furnishing military information, until the KGB realized how

important he could be to them. The KGB then took over the case, which was not an unusual occurrence, and ran it.

Walker was so important to the Soviets, the KGB kept his identity and the fact they had such a sensitively placed source very much compartmentalized, with only a few people having knowledge the case even existed. This caused the case to be handled by KGB people who were not used to, or schooled in, the "James Bond" types of tradecraft. They didn't have the expertise in tradecraft, and couldn't ask those who did, for fear of exposing the case. So they ran it in a very simple manner.

After the plea agreements were signed and the debriefing process was under way, John told us that his espionage procedures were always the same as they had been on the night we caught him. He said his dealings with the Soviets had been based on the KISS principle: "Keep it simple, stupid." He took great delight in telling us that, and he repeated the phrase many times over the months of debriefings.

The contents of the package were very interesting—and not simple. The bulk of the package was a stack of 129 classified documents taken from the aircraft carrier USS *Nimitz,* Michael Walker's duty station. The highest classification of the documents in the package was Secret, and all of the information contained in the documents was of vital interest to the Soviets. One of the documents was a U.S. Navy study of problems with the nuclear Tomahawk cruise missile; it included schematics of a missile defense system on the *Nimitz.* There was a paper on how the Navy would respond if a war broke out in Central America. There was a study on how American spy satellites could be sabotaged. There were other papers as well—all furnished, as I would later learn, to John by his son, Michael Lance Walker, a young Navy kid who didn't even have a security clearance!

John had included a letter to his Soviet handler in which he identified and discussed all the members of his espionage ring, in cryptic terms using letters rather than names to identify them. This was of particular interest to me. The letter read as follows:

Dear Friend,

This delivery consists of material from "S" and is similar to the previously supplied material. The quantity is limited, unfortunately, due to his operating schedule and increased security prior to deployment. His ship departed in early March and they operated extensively just prior to deployment. The situation around him looks very good and he is amassing a vast amount of material right now. His last correspondence indicated that he now has material that would fill two large grocery bags. Storage is becoming a problem. As is obvious, I did not make a trip to Europe to pick up material for this delivery.

His schedule does fit fairly well with our meeting and I plan to meet him during a port call which will give me two days to make it to our meeting. I will arrange to pick up the rest of his material and deliver it in bulk; photographing it while on the road does not seem practical. Also, the entire amount he has would be impossible to safely transport and I plan to deliver that at the schedule you will provide. I hope his ship doesn't experience a schedule change which will put me in the same situation we once faced in Hong Kong: I did not make the primary date, and we met on the alternate. So, I have a decision to make and here it is: If his schedule changes and I can not make the Primary date, I will collect the material and make the Secondary date.

Since "S" is providing a large quantity of material, the quantity of film to shoot is all is also becoming large. I have been trying to figure out an alternative method that will decrease the size of the packages to deliver. I have a super 8mm movie camera which is capable of single frame shots. There is 50 feet of film in each cassette which, unless my math is off, would consist of over 9000 frames.

I have enclosed a short sample of a document shot with the camera using different focusing methods. The first two were shot from 1.5 feet and measured: then 2 from two feet, then 2 while focusing normally. They don't look very good to me, but I thought you may have an idea on how we could make this method work.

"D" continues to be a puzzle. He is not happy, but is still not ready to continue our "cooperation." Rather than try to analyze him for you, I have simply enclosed portions of two letters I've received. My guess? He is going to flop in the stock broker field and can probably make a modest living in computer sales. He has become accustomed

to the big spender life style, and I don't believe he will adjust to living off his wife's income. He will attempt to renew cooperation
within 2 years.

"F" has been transferred and is in a temporary situation giving
him no access at all. He is having difficulty in making a career decision in the Navy. He is not happy and is experiencing family pressure with our father who is 73 and in poor health. He [the father]
married a younger woman who has a significant drinking problem.
"F" feels obligated to support them. He may come around and good
access is possible.

"K" and I have discussed your proposal and I will pass on some
extensive details when we meet. Briefly, he is involved in Carrier and
Amphibious ship maintenance planing. He would instantly recognize unrealistic repair schedules or see that ships were off their normal schedules. This may provide a basis for the information we seek.
Otherwise, he has no useful material.

So, I will see you as scheduled and hope I will make the Primary
date with no problems. I'm sure you have access to S's port schedule and can anticipate my moves in advance. I am not providing his
schedule in this note for obvious reasons.

Good luck.

For security reasons, the letter was undated and unsigned. Still,
it gave us the key to the rest of the case: the identities of the other
members of John Walker's espionage ring. When I read the letter the
first time, it was obvious to me that "S" was John's son Michael. Up
until then I had really not considered him a viable suspect as the
source of classified documents for John's espionage business. I simply did not want to believe that a father would involve his son and
expose him to a possible life term in prison. In that regard, I had
underestimated John Walker.

Two other parts of the "Dear Friend" letter were of particular
interest to me. The first was the part in which John described his
experimentation with his 8mm movie camera, concluding that he
could furnish nine thousand pictures per cassette of film if the Soviets could help him figure out how to do it right. The thought of John
(or anyone else) passing nine thousand pictures of classified U.S.
government documents to the Soviets was staggering. We were get-

ting the picture: John Walker was not just a small hole in the security network of our country, he was a leak of catastrophic proportions.

My attention was also drawn to John's comments regarding "F," in which he referred to "our father." His use of the possessive pronoun *our* was obviously a breach of security procedures, since it implied that he and "F" were brothers.

We sent a copy of the "Dear Friend" letter to Walter Price in Hyannis, Massachusetts, and he showed it to Barbara on 21 May. It was an extremely emotional and difficult thing for her to do, but she identified "S" as her son Michael, "D" as Jerry Whitworth, "F" as John's half-brother, Gary Walker, and "K" as John's brother, Arthur James Walker.

Barbara's world had caved in around her. To this day she feels guilty and responsible for the fact that her only son will be spending a major portion of his life in prison. Barbara has kept in touch with me over the years and has lived in the Virginia Beach area for some time now. She has told me many times that she never would have turned John in to the FBI had she known that Michael was involved in his father's espionage business. She has also said she would have killed John had she known he had recruited Michael. I can understand that.

During the debriefings, John said he had talked to Michael before he shipped out on the USS *Nimitz* in March 1985, and told him to tell his mother that he was involved in the espionage business with his dad. John believed that this news would prevent Barbara from reporting him to the FBI. But Michael didn't tell her, and at any rate, it was too late; she had called us five months earlier.

John made one other comment about Michael that sent chills through me. He turned to Kolouch and me one day during a lunch break and said that I had really "screwed him up." When I asked what he meant, he said, "I was grooming Michael. I had been training him to take over the business. I was going to retire. The business [espionage] was to be my legacy to my son." Kolouch and I just looked at each other in amazement. It was as though he were talking about turning the family bakery over to the next generation.

As John indicated in his "Dear Friend" letter, he was including in his package two letters that "D" (Jerry Whitworth) had sent him. Interestingly, John had cut Jerry's signature off the bottom of each letter, obviously to conceal his identity, but had left the salutation "Dear Johnny" on each one.

John would later tell us that Jerry had retired from the Navy and was no longer in a position to furnish classified documents. He said Jerry had retired once before but had quickly found that without all of that tax-free espionage money, he couldn't live the lifestyle to which he had become accustomed. So he went back into the Navy and resumed stealing the nation's secrets. John said he had fully expected Jerry to fail at his second attempt at civilian life, and thought he would go back into the Navy yet again to resume his career in espionage.

Later, the FBI Laboratory would find eighty-three of John Walker's fingerprints and sixty-three of Michael's on the contents of the drop package. They would also find John's and Jerry's fingerprints on the two letters from Jerry that John had included in the package.

On the morning we had followed John, as I sat in my car down the street from his house, I had wondered what he was doing in there. During the debriefings, I asked him what he had been doing that morning. He said that after breakfast at McDonald's, he spent the morning typing the "Dear Friend" letter to his Soviet handler and preparing his package.

15

Overwhelming Evidence

With the arrest of John, activity on the case reached a new level of frenzy. Joe Wolfinger called Jack Wagner, special agent in charge of the Norfolk office, advised him of John's arrest, and asked him to have all available agents alerted and ready to execute search warrants on John's residence, place of business, vehicles, houseboat, and airplane. He also asked that agents be sent to each of those locations to secure them—and to make sure no one had access to them until search warrants could be obtained. After Joe made that call from the command center in D.C., he took off for Norfolk, lights flashing and siren blaring all the way. He made it in record time.

During my career I have always tried to have the evidence lined up and to know the answers to every possible question before I ever approached a suspect. But this case was just the opposite. I didn't know any of the answers; John was already in jail and not talking to us. I knew we had a perfect case against him, but I didn't like having to conduct the fact-finding after the arrest. Except for our interviews of Barbara and Laura, we had conducted only one interview and one surveillance prior to the arrest!

. . .

Monday, 20 May, was a day of executing search warrants.

We were able to open that manilla envelope John had dropped when he had turned, gun ready, to face Kolouch and me. Inside, we found fourteen photographs and two pages of printed instructions for the espionage procedure John was to follow on 19 May 1985. These photos and instructions had been prepared by the KGB and furnished to John in a previous exchange of packages on 15 April 1984.

There were pictures of each location involved in John's drop activity, and a portion of a map of Montgomery County, Maryland, with all of the roads John had traveled that night highlighted in yellow; our two "necking" agents had seen him looking at that map when they were parked near him at the Quince Orchard Shopping Center. The most important part of each set of instructions was printed in red. The KGB had printed more instructions on the back of each picture. They had also drawn arrows on the pictures to indicate the various signal and drop locations. No names, not even that of the type of signal can, were mentioned in the instructions.

When Gerry Richards, our expert in espionage tradecraft, examined the contents of the envelope, he declared the photos and instructions to be the most detailed and elaborate he had ever seen in his fifteen-year career.

These are the KGB instructions John followed the evening of 19 May 1985:

For our next exchange we'll use the following sites in Montgomery County, Maryland:

To signal that I am ready to exchange I'll drop my initial can of the usual kind at a utility pole on Watts Branch Dr near its intersection with Circle Dr and Ridge Dr. The utility pole in question is the second one to the east of the intersection (The first utility pole is located right at the intersection of Watts Branch Dr and Circle Dr). My signal site will be on your right when you drive on Watts Branch Dr from Circle Dr toward Valley Dr. I'll drop my signal on the road shoulder a foot or two from the surface of the road. Check my signal after 8:00 pm.

To signal that you are available for our exchange drop your initial can of the usual kind at the bottom of a utility pole on Quince

Orchard Rd at its intersection with Dufief Mill Rd. The utility pole in question will be on your left when you drive on Quince Orchard Rd from Dufief Mill Rd toward Darnstown Rd (28) It is the first utility pole from the intersection on that side of Quince Orchard Rd. I'll check your signal after 8:30 pm

Drop your delivery behind a utility pole on Partnership Rd near its intersection with Whites Ferry Rd (107) The utility pole in question is located at a huge tree on the right hand side of Partnership Rd about 0.1 mile from the intersection of Partnership Rd and Whites Ferry Rd (Your drop point will be on your right when you drive on Partnership Rd from Whites Ferry Rd toward Sugarland Rd). Before reaching your drop point you'll pass a road sign "Stop Ahead" on your left. Going south you'll see the reverse side of that sign. Thus your drop point is located between the huge tree on your right and the stop ahead sign on your left.

I'll drop my delivery behind two trees accreted at the bottom on Old Bucklodge Lane at its intersection with White Ground Rd. The two trees are located on the right hand side of Old Bucklodge Ln when you drive on Old Bucklodge Ln from White Ground Rd toward Bucklodge Rd (117). The two trees are about 8–12 yards from the intersection and about 2–5 feet from the surface of the road. These are the first two trees from the intersection on the right-hand side of Old Bucklodge La which are accreted at the bottom and located right at the road. Pick up my delivery after 10:15 pm.

To signal that you've picked up my delivery drop your final can of the usual kind on Esworthy Terr at its second (Southern) intersection with Esworthy Rd. Drop your can on the right-hand side of Esworthy Terr (The signal site will be on your right when you drive on Esworthy Terr toward its southern intersection with Esworthy Rd). Drop it on the road shoulder about one car length from the stop sign a foot or two from the surface of the road.

To signal that I've picked up your delivery I'll drop my final can of the usual kind at a large tree which is located at the only bridge on Piney Meetinghouse Rd between Glen Rd and River Rd (190). The tree in question is located to the north of the bridge about 8–10 yards from it, on the left-hand side of Piney Meetinghouse Rd (The tree will be on your left when you drive on Piney Meetinghouse Rd toward River Rd). This is the second large tree to the north of the bridge on that side of the road. It is located right at the road. Check my signal after 11:15 pm.

Directions from Capital Beltway (495) Make a turn on to River Rd (190) and proceed west. Then turn right on Falls Rd (169), left on South Glen Rd, right on Glen Mill RD, right again on Circle Dr, right again on Watts Branch Dr, check up my initial signal, left on Valley Dr, right on Glen Mill Rd, left on Darnstown Rd (28), left again on Travilah Rd, right on Dufief Mill Rd, left on Quince Orchard Rd, drop your initial can as described above; proceed north on Quince Orchard Rd, left on Darnstown Rd (28), left again on Whites Ferry Rd (107), left again on Partnership Rd, drop your delivery as described above; proceed south on Partnership Rd, left on Sugarland Rd, left again on Darnstown Rd (28), right (almost immediately) on White Ground Rd (121), left on Old Bucklodge La, pick up my delivery; proceed north on Old Bucklodge La, right on Bucklodge Rd (117), right on Barnsville Rd (117), left on Clopper Rd (117).

The procedure John went through to accomplish the exchange of packages was very complex, even though the packaging itself was simple. No wonder he had to go out there and find all those sites during daylight! The procedure covered sixty miles and ran from 8:00 P.M. when he read the first signal until 11:15 P.M. when he was to read the last one. That made for a long day for John, considering that he had driven two hundred miles from Norfolk earlier in the day.

During the debriefing process I asked John why he had had that manilla envelope with him at the time of his arrest. He recalled that he knew something was wrong that night, but he didn't know just what. He hadn't been able to find the package the Soviets were supposed to have left for him (there wasn't one), nor, when he went back to check, had he been able to find the package he had left for them (we had it). Because he was uneasy, he didn't want to leave the drop instructions in his room while he went the lobby to see about the "wreck" of his van. He had intended to hide the envelope someplace in the hotel between the seventh and the first floor.

In the search of John's van, the most significant items we found were an empty 7-Up can, which was to have been John's signal that he had retrieved his package from the Soviets, and a Montgomery County street map, with handwritten notes and colored markings, which John used to find the signal and drop sites used on the evening of 19 May. We also found a map of the D.C. vicinity, with notations and colored markings, and a crushed 7-Up can, which could well have been the Soviets' signal can retrieved by John during his evening.

Our agents executed a search warrant and searched John's room at the Ramada Inn, in the presence of the hotel's general manager, Keith Wolling. Nothing of great significance was found. John had been traveling light that day. He had been carrying the most damaging evidence with him in that envelope when we arrested him.

16

The Motherlode

Meanwhile, in Norfolk, U.S. Magistrate Gilbert R. Swink issued search warrants for John's house at 8524 Old Ocean View Road, Norfolk; his offices at 405 South Parliament Drive, Virginia Beach; a 1977 Dodge Van Camper that John used for surveillance work in his detective business; John's personal car, a 1980 Chrysler New Yorker; his Grumman airplane; and his houseboat, *Jaws*. All of the warrants were issued on 20 May and executed that same day.

We didn't find anything of great value to the investigation in John's Chrysler, houseboat, surveillance van, or airplane. We did, however, find some interesting notations in his flight logs regarding flights he had supposedly taken and stops he had made. John's airplane had only a single engine, and it was not in good condition; it had begun to rust in spots and generally did not appear to be well maintained. When John Hodges reviewed the flight logs, he remarked that he would never have taken some of the trips in that plane that John claimed to have taken. As I recall, John had logged trips to Iceland, Mexico, and California, all long treks for a single-engine craft in questionable condition.

Later, during the debriefings, John told me that many of the notations in his flight logs were false, intended to cover up trips he had made to Washington for package exchanges with the Soviets and to satisfy his flight instructor for his annual flight certification. Since John is an inveterate liar, there is no way of knowing which entries in his logbooks were true and which were pure fiction.

Jaws, the houseboat, was not in the best of condition, either. It needed a good coat of paint. It was probably fit enough for partying and cruising the local waters, but it was no yacht by any standard.

John's business office was located on the second floor of the Kempsville Professional Building at 405 South Parliament Drive in Virginia Beach. My family and I had lived within a half-mile of the place in the early 1970s. It was modestly furnished. John had a few pictures of himself on the walls. He also had a plaque announcing his membership in an organization called the Society of Old Crows, whose membership is made up of former military experts in electronic countermeasures. His certificate of membership in the American Society of Industrial Security was hanging next to the Old Crows plaque. There is no doubt that his membership in those two organizations might have presented opportunities for John to meet and recruit people into his espionage ring, or to gain access to classified information. However, we never developed any information that he had done so. He later claimed that he had joined these groups in an effort to build up business contacts for his detective agency.

When we searched John's office space, we took all of his investigative files and business records. From these we learned that he employed a large number of Navy people as part-time investigators. I never developed information that he had recruited any of them to commit espionage, either. There was no evidence that he had, and he denied it during the debriefings. He said he used his Navy personnel to develop information on wayward Navy spouses in the divorce cases his detective agency handled.

The 8mm movie camera John had mentioned in his "Dear Friend" letter was found in his office, but we didn't find much else in the way of useful evidence there.

. . .

It was in John's house that we found the motherlode—a quantity of extremely damaging evidence. It was a two-story middle-class tract house, with white siding and some brick facade. Originally it might have had a one-car attached garage, later converted to the family room where John kept his pool table. (He later took great pride in telling Kolouch and me how he once had sex with one of his girlfriends on the pool table, her with feet snugly planted in the corner pockets.)

There were six rooms on the first floor: kitchen, bathroom, family room with bar, pool table, and an American flag, John's den/office, and a living room. The second floor had five more rooms: a bath, two bedrooms, a room used for storage, and a room set up as a workshop, with tools, electronic gear, and other supplies. A detached garage at the rear of John's property was crammed full of junk.

John's taste in furnishings ran from the functional to the ugly. He had some paintings on velvet. As I recall, some Navy-related items and pictures were hung on the walls. And he had a few photos of himself in the robes of the Ku Klux Klan.

Later, during our questioning of John, he told us that he had joined the Ku Klux Klan in 1979 at the request of a man who paid him $1,000 to do so. His job was to report the identities of other Klan members. He assumed that the man was either an FBI agent or a member of B'nai Brith. John told us he contacted his former Navy buddy Bill Wilkerson, who was the leader of the Klan, and joined. Wilkerson then put him in charge of recruiting new Klan members in Virginia.

I can tell you for a fact, if someone did ask John to join the Klan and report back to him, the man was not an FBI agent. I myself was the agent who did all of the Klan investigations in the Norfolk area at that time (and I would never have paid anyone that much money to join the Klan). I had excellent sources in all of the klaverns and had never heard of John Walker being a member of any of the klaverns around here. However, I do recall hearing a man on a local radio talk show around that time talking about the Klan and trying to recruit new members. The man gave his name as John Baxter—an alias, I would learn during this investigation, used by John Walker.

One of the many photos we found showed John and Bill Wilkerson in their Klan robes (without hoods), so I suppose it is possible that he was in a klavern whose members were military people. NIS would have been charged with investigating the KKK in the Navy. They have always claimed that they had no record of John ever working for them as an informant in the Klan.

As for reading matter, Walker had a few girlie magazines and a couple of sexually explicit paperbacks, but nothing that ever made the *New York Times* bestseller list. He had some kinky sexual devices in the nightstand in his bedroom. One, as I recall, was a round sponge object with a hole in it and a couple of tentacle-looking things sticking out in several directions. I don't know what it was, but it had been used.

The evidence we found in this house was momentous. One of the major pieces of evidence was a three-by-five card bearing the first name of each member of John's espionage ring, with code-letter designations printed beside the names. These matched the code found in the "Dear Friend" letter. The notations on the card read:

Gary   F
Jer   D
Art   K
Mike   S

During the debriefings of John, which started at the end of October 1985, he said the letter designations for Jerry, Art, and Mike had been given to him by his Soviet handler at a face-to-face meeting in Vienna, Austria, in 1984. He wrote them on the card while on the plane back to the United States. He gave his half-brother Gary the letter designation of "F" himself, after he made his recruitment pitch to him in late 1984.

We also found the same names and code letters in a journal John had kept.

The "Dear Friend" letter was found, quite legible, on the typewriter cassette ribbon from John's typewriter. He had thrown it into the trash can in his den.

. . .

We also found a sophisticated piece of espionage paraphernalia, made by the KGB and given to John within the first few months of his career as a spy. The device, which I dubbed the Russian Rotor Reader, was found in the den, along with two typewritten pages of operating instructions. Gerry Richards examined it and was able to determine that it had been made at a cost of approximately $50,000.

This electronic device, when closed, was about the size of a cigarette case. John had used it to determine the internal wiring of the rotors in the KL-47, one of the primary code machines used by the U.S. Navy at that time. These rotors performed the function of encoding messages. When John used the Rotor Reader and passed the information to the Soviets, he enabled them to make duplicate rotors and decode our messages. In fact, during the first two months of his espionage career, he sold the Soviets a manual for the KL-47 code machine, which enabled them to build one of their own.

When John started selling information to the Soviets in late 1967, the first thing he provided was a "key list" (daily code settings) for the KL-47. Soon after, on 3 January 1968, the USS *Pueblo,* an American intelligence-gathering ship positioned off the coast of North Korea, was boarded and taken by the North Koreans, allies of the Soviets. There was a KL-47 on board the *Pueblo;* the North Koreans kept it. It has been speculated (but not proved) that the *Pueblo* was taken at the request of the Soviets so that they could have the machine for which John Walker was furnishing the daily code lists. Very interesting. But we will never know—unless some Russian or North Korean who knows comes forward with the truth.

One stranger-than-fiction twist about the *Pueblo:* After John was sentenced in 1986, he was sent to the federal penitentiary at Lewisburg, Pennsylvania. When Jim Kolouch and I went to talk to him there, we chatted with one of the assistant wardens and learned that he had been on the *Pueblo* when it was taken by the North Koreans! We did not tell him that John Walker might have caused his capture and subsequent torture.

In late May 1968 the *Scorpion,* one of our attack submarines, was heading home to Norfolk after a short deployment. It was due back in port on 27 May, but the submarine never made it. Without any word or warning, it disappeared. The boat's wreckage was found in the fall of 1968 on the bottom of the Atlantic. All on board—nearly one hundred officers and enlisted men—perished. A few days later, knowing nothing of the disaster, their loved ones gathered on the Norfolk pier to await their return. The cause of the demise of the *Scorpion* remains a mystery. One theory is that it had encountered a Soviet submarine or surface ship in the area where the wreckage was later found. After we arrested John, Navy experts and intelligence people speculated that the information John had passed to the Soviets could have given them the ability to detect the whereabouts—and cause the disappearance—of the *Scorpion.* This is another intriguing, albeit unproven, theory.

Whether or not John's treachery resulted in the capture of the *Pueblo* or the loss of the *Scorpion,* I can't help but wonder what it was like in the communications center at the headquarters of the Atlantic Submarine Force (SUBLANT), where, when these incidents occurred, John Walker was the communications watch officer in charge. I can picture the scene: grim men and women working around the clock, sending out gravely critical contingency messages to the *Pueblo;* I can imagine their frantic efforts to contact the *Scorpion.* John must have been aware that he might have been responsible for both disasters.

In all of the espionage cases the Bureau investigated over the years, we had found only one other Rotor Reader. That one had been given to Joseph Helmich, a U.S. Army sergeant, by the Soviets during his espionage activities on their behalf in the 1970s. Helmich befriended Michael Walker in 1985, while they were both in the federal pen at Petersburg, Virginia.

The search of John's house also turned up calendars dating from 1978 through 1985, which had notations of every act of espionage John had committed during that period. On the calendar for May 1985, he had circled the notation "#1" on 19 May, the day we followed and caught him. That was John's reminder to himself that he was to fill a drop to the Soviets on that day. The "#1" meant that it was the first choice, or primary date, for the drop. He was always given a fallback or secondary date that he could use in the event that something happened and he or the Soviets couldn't make the primary date. As I recall, the secondary date for the 19 May drop was in early June.

The "#1" notation was written on various other dates in those seven years of calendars: those were days he was to conduct a drop exchange of packages with his handler. He had printed "FF"—meaning face-to-face, or personal, meeting—on various dates. The secondary date for a face-to-face meeting or a drop was also marked on the calendars, usually indicated by "#2."

James Milburn and Gary Heinz of the Bureau's Analytical Unit at Headquarters later came to Norfolk and went through all of the evidence with a fine-toothed comb. The work they did was extremely impressive. After they analyzed the notations on John's calendars, they were able to trace every act of espionage he committed from 1978 to 1985. It was no challenge for Milburn and Heinz; those guys are good!

In John's desk we found a Minox camera he had used to photograph Navy documents. Another Minox, model 110, was found in his workroom. The tiny Minox camera is the traditional camera of choice for spies. It is easily hidden, is simple to use, and takes excellent pictures. The KGB has given the Minox camera to spies for years. John later told us the Soviets had given him a Minox early in his career, but he wore it out and had to buy a new one.

Quite a large stash of old drop instructions, complete with pictures of the drop and signal sites, was also found in John's desk. All of the drop sites were in the D.C. area, exactly as Barbara had told us.

We found a map of Vienna, with several streets highlighted in yellow as on that map of Montgomery County included with John's drop instructions for 19 May. Accompanying the Vienna map was a page of hand-printed instructions titled "The Vienna Procedure."

These instructions had been given to John by the KGB and were used by him when he went to Vienna to meet his Soviet handler face to face. They met in Vienna because the Soviets are comfortable there, where espionage is not considered a crime and they can move about freely without fear of being caught. Vienna is the espionage capital of the world.

These instructions described a route John had to walk in Vienna before his Soviet contact would approach him. He would show up at a kitchen appliance store called the Komet Kitchen on a pre-arranged date at 18:15. He had to carry his camera bag with the strap over his left shoulder and carry a small paper bag in his right hand. He was to stay in front of the Komet Kitchen until 18:17 and then walk the route outlined on the map and in the instructions. The route was designed to take him forty minutes. At 18:55 he would come to the end of the route in front of a men's clothing store called Bazala. He was to browse there until 18:58. The Soviet contact was supposed to approach him, either someplace along the route or in front of Bazala. If the Soviet did not show, John was to come back and go through the routine on the alternate date he had been given.

John had kept some used airline tickets to Europe and some hotel receipts from Vienna that corresponded with several meetings with his Soviet handlers. We could see that he traveled in style, usually flying on Pan American Airlines. His hotel of choice in Vienna seemed to be the Intercontinental Hotel.

In the desk we also found a series of KGB instructions dealing with the following topics:

Procedure for face-to-face meeting outside the country, to be used if you need to see me urgently

Procedure for extraordinary face-to-face meeting in the country, to be used only in the case of extreme emergency

Procedure for summoning you to a face-to-face meeting

Procedure for summoning me to a package exchange

These instructions were to be used if an unforeseen situation arose, such as a change in John's Navy schedule, a need to pass information before a scheduled drop, or some major change in world affairs, such as declaration of war.

All of these instructions specified that if John needed to get in touch with the Soviets, he had to go to Washington and draw a signal, either a lipstick mark on a specific building or a lightning-bolt-shaped mark on a certain pole. He was to make his mark on a Thursday, and the Soviets would see it the next morning, which meant that they passed by the area sometime every Friday morning. They would meet or conduct their drop that evening or the next day. When the Soviets needed to call for a special meeting or drop exchange, they would send John a cryptic postcard, and he would carry out previously furnished instructions.

I was surprised that we didn't find instructions for an escape plan, giving John a way to leave the country should he find out that the FBI was on to him. John told me he had never been given such a plan and his handlers had never discussed it with him. Personally, I think John was lying. There are some things John didn't tell us, and that, in my humble opinion, is one of them. They might not have put such plans in writing, but you can bet they discussed it.

Among the items John saved from the KGB was an undated and unsigned letter that had the words "Please Destroy" printed in red at the top of the page. The letter said:

Dear Friend,

Welcome back! It's been a long time! How was the trip? What are your impressions and experiences?

Enclosed are $24,500. This includes the payment for the period of six months (June through November) plus $500 for expenses. The rest of the money we owe you will be enclosed in my next delivery together with the usual amount due by that time. I realize that you may resent this procedure, but we are doing it out of concern for your safety. My delivery is already much too voluminous and difficult to hide.

Under the circumstances we decided to split the amount in order to reduce its volume and thus the risk of an accidental exposure during the inspection at the airport in view of the new secu-

rity regulations introduced at air terminals in January. The secu-
rity has been stepped up to such a degree that I am seriously wor-
ried whether you'll be able to get safely through the inspection the
contents of this delivery. The new procedures and devices include
x-ray equipment to examine checked baggage, walk-through and
hand-held magnetometers to detect metal objects, the inspection
by hand or with the use of electronic devices of all carry-on bag-
gage (sometimes x-raying is used thus damaging the film) and
occasionally the "pat-down" of the passengers. In a few cases the
airlines for lack of equipment have purses, briefcases and pack-
ages searched, for instance in Atlanta, I suggest you have as little
metal on you as possible to pass smoothly through the magne-
tometers. Once this check is okay the rest of the screening includ-
ing the "pat-down" is performed with less care, if at all. The guards
look not only for concealed weapons, but for explosives as well and
search sometimes small packages. Therefore it is not advisable to
concentrate money in large bundles.

John later told us that he had received this letter in a drop package
in the Washington area after his return from Navy deployment on
the USS *Niagara Falls* off the coast of Vietnam in the early 1970s.
The number of aircraft hijackings had increased significantly all
over the world around that time, and airport security had been
heightened accordingly. The last thing the KGB needed was to have
its most valuable agent caught while attempting to smuggle his spy
pay home on an airplane.

On a shelf in a cabinet in the upstairs workroom, we found a stack
of Secret Navy documents, which, I later learned, John had photographed and furnished to the Soviets. The stack was about eighteen inches high and had been given to him by Michael. John told me
it was his normal procedure to photograph the documents and save
them until the Soviets told him the photographs were acceptable.
Then he would destroy the documents.

I sent all of the documents we found in John's house to the FBI
Laboratory's Latent Fingerprint Section for processing. The lab's
people were able to locate a total of 828 prints on the documents
and determine that 191 of them were John's and 520 Michael's. One

of the documents was titled "The Navy Warfare Publication Threat Intelligence Summary Naval Air Forces," or "NWP 12-8." It turned out to have Jerry Whitworth's palmprint on page 182. I can still remember taking that call at the office. It was a Saturday, and I had gone in to do paperwork. John Saunders, from the Latent Fingerprint Section, called to tell me he had found Whitworth's palmprint. That print would become a very important piece of evidence against Whitworth.

John later told us Jerry Whitworth always photographed his documents and gave him film rather than hard copies. Since John didn't actually see the information Jerry was providing, he and Jerry always discussed the contents of the film before John passed it to his Soviet handler. John liked to give the Soviets a short written report of the contents of his packages, as he did in the "Dear Friend" letter we recovered on 19 May.

During our search of the house we found another item that implicated Whitworth: a manilla envelope with notes written on it that obviously had to do with communications. Joe Wolfinger called and arranged for Steve Carter of the National Security Agency to come to Norfolk to interpret the notes. Carter confirmed that they dealt with a very sensitive military radio system, and he declared them to be so detailed and sensitive that they should be classified Secret. The envelope was then sent to the FBI lab for fingerprint analysis, and fingerprints of both Jerry Whitworth and John Walker were found on it. This envelope too would become a key piece of evidence against Whitworth. John later said he had written the notes when he was in California picking up several rolls of film of classified Navy documents from Whitworth and they were discussing the contents of the film, which he would later pass to the Soviets.

In an upstairs closet we found four rather unusual walking canes. The top section of one pulled off to reveal a knife blade about sixteen inches long. The bottom of another unscrewed and contained three clear glass test-tube-style containers; they were empty, but I suspect they were intended to conceal drugs or possibly money.

Another "cane" turned into a rifle when the ends were adjusted. The fourth cane pulled apart to reveal in the upper half a limber but potentially damaging slapstick.

Another extremely important bit of evidence we found was a sheet of paper in the desk that set out, in monthly detail, the amount of money John had paid Jerry Whitworth for his part in the espionage business. Jim Milburn and Gary Heinz analyzed the document and determined that John had paid Jerry $332,000 during the ten years he worked for him. We also found a thick book in the den that had a dollar-bill-shaped section cut from the inner pages. John used it to hide money in when he traveled to California to pay Jerry for his services.

As the investigation developed, we obtained two more search warrants for John's house. We found a fake wall socket in the den, which John apparently sometimes used to hide his map of Vienna and the "Vienna Procedure" instructions. Brother Arthur told us John had shown him the map and instructions, and had taken them from the wall socket to do so. It was empty when we found it; the Vienna map and instructions had been among the papers in John's desk. In fact, none of the material we found in the house had been purposely hidden, although many items were commingled with unrelated papers.

John had also altered a section of the front frame of a kitchen cabinet so that it opened to reveal a space where documents, drugs, money, or other items could be concealed. We didn't find that hiding place; it was discovered, almost by accident, by an Internal Revenue Service agent who accompanied my people on the last search. It too was empty.

We did some damage in the house looking for the money we thought John might have hidden. We took off all the baseboards and knocked some holes in the walls with sledge hammers. We even had Gerry Richards's crew from the FBI lab come down and x-ray the walls and furniture. We never did find any of the money we were looking for. Wolfie and I wanted to take the house apart piece by piece and excavate the yard, but the IRS wouldn't permit it. Soon after John's arrest, the IRS became involved in the case and seized all of his property, on the grounds that he had not paid any taxes on the money he earned from his espionage business— the worst crime of all! Eventually the IRS held a public auction and made a few bucks by selling many of John's personal items. They sold the house too, but John still owes the IRS at least $200,000, probably more.

17

Like Father, Like Son

Michael Lance Walker was born in Vallejo, California, on 1 November 1962. Because John was transferred every few years, young Michael grew up moving around the country with his family. It is fair to surmise that his childhood was not ideal; we know that his psychopathic, womanizing, dope-smoking father became a spy when Mike was five, and that his mother was an alcoholic.

After John and Barbara split up in 1975, Michael went to live with Barbara and the girls in Skowhegan, Maine. He started using marijuana and other drugs. He and some teenage buddies turned to burglary and were caught and put on probation—like father, like son. Mike moved back to Norfolk to live with John in 1980 and managed to graduate from Ryan Upper High School in June 1982. In his senior year he was voted "best looking" and "best dressed." He worked for John in the private investigation business and partied with his dad and his dad's women. Mike was a lot like his father and had strong loyalty to him. They smoked pot together, drank together, and talked about Mike's future. Mike loved surfing and the PI business and would have been content to do those things forever. John, however, had a different idea.

While Mike was in high school, John gave him an average of $100 a week for clothes, food, and fun. One day when they were talking about Mike's future, John said that someday he would reveal how he made his money. Mike wasn't sure what John meant, but he remembered that when he was living with his mom in Maine, she had told him John was a traitor and a spy for the Soviets.

In 1982 John introduced Michael to Rachel Allen, a student at Old Dominion University in Norfolk. John himself had hit on her, and she had turned him down. Rachel was working her way through college as a go-go dancer and waitress. She and Michael hit it off right away. They were married in December 1983, in spite of John's objections; John worried that a wife would divert Michael's attention from the espionage business.

John often talked to Michael about his own days in the Navy, encouraging him to join after his graduation and show his sisters that he was going to amount to something, even if they weren't. Mike is color-blind, so he couldn't qualify for radio or electronics school. Still, John knew there were plenty of other jobs in the Navy that would give Mike access to classified information.

As soon as we read John's "Dear Friend" letter to his Soviet handler and saw the 129 classified documents from the USS *Nimitz* in his drop package, we knew that Michael was involved. Mike was working in the Operations Administration Division on the *Nimitz* and had access to virtually all communications passing through that office. We didn't want to alert Mike that we had an interest in him, so rather than send a message to the Naval Investigative Service agent on board his ship, we discussed the problem with NIS special agent supervisor Tom Boley in Norfolk. Tom agreed to notify his counterpart in Italy and have an agent dispatched to the *Nimitz,* which was then in the Mediterranean. NIS special agent Keith Hitt got the assignment and went to the *Nimitz* to confront Michael. But first he had to get past the captain, who, I am told, was irate that he had not been "cut in" on our interest in one of his sailors. Captains of Navy ships are funny that way. Can't blame them, I guess, but the guy made Hitt's life miserable for a few minutes.

I remember another Navy captain who was really obnoxious and actually impeded an espionage investigation. When I was working on the Brian Horton case, mentioned earlier, I asked an NIS agent to contact the man in charge of the Nuclear Strike Planning Branch at the Norfolk Navy Base, where Horton worked, and get me a copy of his service record. The captain in charge was apparently terrified that his career would go down the chute if one of his men was charged with espionage, and so he stonewalled the request for Horton's record. He chastised the NIS agent for being involved in such a "non-case" and told him to go find something better to do. Eventually he backed down and gave us the records. Horton, of course, confessed and was convicted. The captain later became the military head of NIS, which was a nice ironic twist. He subsequently retired and, tragically, hanged himself in the family garage a few years later.

Aboard the *Nimitz,* on 23 May, Michael admitted to Agent Hitt that he had been stealing documents for his father. Hitt searched the area around Mike's bunk and found two boxes full of documents—about thirty pounds—that he had stolen and stored to pass to his father. I would later learn that John was scheduled to go to Vienna for a face-to-face meeting with the Soviets on 21 September 1985, and he planned to meet Michael in Naples just before then to get the documents from him.

Michael had been placed in the brig on board the *Nimitz* on 21 May, the day Hitt found the hidden documents, and was returned to the United States on 25 May. He was flown to Andrews Air Force Base. It was a breezy, sunny day. Michael came down the steps of the plane wearing a white shirt, blue jeans, and white high-topped running shoes with red laces.

As soon as he stepped onto U.S. soil, I looked him in the eye and said, "Mr. Walker, I'm with the FBI. You are under arrest for violating the espionage laws of the United States." Agents Jim Kolouch, Bill Buckley, and I took him into custody.

By this time, the media attention was incredible. There were at least seventy-five reporters and photographers at Andrews. The arrest was shown on TV and in all of the world's major media publications. I still see the pictures on TV and in various magazines from time to time.

We put Michael in the rear seat of a Bureau car. I slid in beside him, fully aware that his dad had occupied that seat just a few days before. The kid was terrified. He was a pleasant and respectful twenty-two-year-old who was definitely having a bad day. I gave him a stick of gum, and we settled back for the thirty-minute drive to the Baltimore FBI office, each of us lost in our own thoughts. I don't know what Mike thought about, but I thought about my own kids, their lives, what they were doing, where they were.

When we arrived at the FBI office, we took Michael to an interview room. He confessed to his part in his father's espionage business and gave us a twelve-page statement. His statement reads, in part, as follows:

> I joined the U.S. Navy on December 13, 1982, and am presently an enlisted man in the U.S. Navy. . . .
>
> I completed my recruit and seaman apprentice training on April 16, 1983, and was assigned to Fighter Squadron VF-102 at the Oceana Naval Air Station, Virginia Beach, Virginia. I worked in the office located in Hangar 200. I performed clerical duties which included typing letters and memos. I was also the registered mail yeoman. . . . I did see and have access to Confidential and Secret documents on a regular basis. . . . While assigned at Squadron VF-102 we were deployed on the aircraft carrier USS *America*. We returned from a cruise . . . and I told my father . . . that I had seen my first piece of classified material. . . . A month or so later my dad told me I could make money if I would take classified material from my workplace and give it to him. He told me he would pay for the material but we never discussed how much he would pay. I didn't ask him. I was shocked and afraid at what my dad was suggesting. I knew what he was suggesting was illegal. I think my father said he makes money by doing that [selling classified material] but I'm not positive. . . .
>
> About three months later, possibly November or December 1983, while at work in my office in Hangar 200, . . . I took a document classified Secret from one of the . . . burn [trash] bags in the office. The document was clearly marked Secret at the top and bottom of the front page. It was either a NATOPS [naval air training and operat-

ing procedures standardization] or a news gram. . . . I think the document had a drawing of a jet plane on the front page. . . . There were three other people in the office at the time, probably my supervisor, the administration officer, and the master chief; but they couldn't see me because the office is partitioned into sections. I took the document . . . and put it under my jacket and took it to my dad's house and gave it to him in his den. He looked at it and said it was good. He seemed pleased. . . .

I took my father approximately five more documents . . . from Squadron VF-102 before I was transferred to the USS *Nimitz* on January 31, 1984. I can only recall they were all classified Secret and were clearly stamped. . . .

Soon after I was transferred to Operations Administration [on the *Nimitz*] I began taking classified documents from the burn bags in the office. This was approximately October 1984. I removed the documents at random and put them in a burn bag which I kept in the fan room where we store the other burn bags prior to their destruction. I was in charge of getting rid of the burn bags and was in charge of the burn run schedule so it was no problem for me to keep my bag of stolen documents there. I took the documents with the intent of giving them to my father in return for money.

On approximately ten occasions between October 1984 and March 8, 1985, when the *Nimitz* deployed to the Mediterranean, I took my father stacks of classified documents which I had stolen from the Operations Administration Office. I delivered to my father a total of approximately twenty pounds of classified documents, many of which were classified Secret. The remainder were classified Confidential. They were messages, all currently classified and clearly marked, such as "rainforms" which contained information regarding Soviet submarines, U.S. Navy fleet exercise information, operations messages regarding U.S. Navy ship locations, and where the ships were going. About 80 percent of the messages were from DIA [the Defense Intelligence Agency] and contained geographical information concerning countries throughout the world. I took stacks of documents which were several inches thick off the ship in my duffel bag or in my ditty bag and gave them to my father at his house.

When I gave my father the first stack of documents from the *Nimitz* I told him I had been gathering them for a while and also told him how I had obtained them and how I stored them on board the ship before I took them off. My father was pleased and said it looked like we were on a roll. He told me to go ahead, keep it up, and kept saying "keep it flowing."

At the times I was taking the classified documents and giving them to my father there was no doubt in my mind that he was selling those documents to a communist country which I believed to be the Soviet Union.

While Michael was making his statement, I showed him the stack of documents we had recovered from his father's drop point in Montgomery County on 19 May. His response:

I recognized them to be copies of approximately one-third of the total amount of documents which I had given my father prior to March 8, 1985. . . . Each of the documents I looked at came from the Operations Administration on the *Nimitz*.

Michael Walker concluded his statement in this way:

I knew when I was taking the classified documents from VF-102 and the USS *Nimitz* that the unauthorized disclosure of them to a foreign country could harm the United States.

Michael gave us one frightening piece of news when we were taking his statement. During the time he was stealing classified documents for his father, he did not have a security clearance! In fact, the Navy never did complete a background investigation (BI) on him. Mike even brought his lack of a clearance to the attention of his chief petty officer and was told that it was OK, he had an "interim clearance" until his BI was completed. Who knows what they might have learned had they actually done a BI on him.

I gave Michael Walker's statement to the staff to be typed. The next day, 26 May, Kolouch, Buckley, and I took the typed statement to Michael at the Herford County Detention Center in Bel Air, Maryland, where he read and signed it, acknowledging it to be true and correct to the best of his knowledge. Kolouch, Buckley, and I witnessed Michael's signature on the statement.

Some time later, in the course of the court proceedings, Michael's attorney, Charles Bernstein, took me aside and told me he was impressed with the statement we got from Michael. He thought it was pretty much airtight. He said that had he argued the case in court, he could have defeated the statement Michael gave the NIS, but not the one he gave the FBI. A very unusual compliment from a defense attorney.

As Kolouch, Buckley, and I were interviewing Mike in the Baltimore FBI office, Dave Majors, the supervisor of the Foreign Counterintelligence Squad in Baltimore, called me out of the interview room to tell me that Michael's wife, Rachel, had arrived at the office, and he wanted to interview her. I told him to go ahead and to let me know what she had to say. About a half-hour later Dave told me he was convinced Rachel didn't know anything about Michael's espionage activities. He also said he had given her $50 because she was broke.

A few weeks later I interviewed Rachel in their small, sparsely furnished apartment on Cypress Avenue in Virginia Beach. She admitted knowing that Mike had been stealing classified documents and giving them to his father. She told me that she had found some classified papers in Mike's duffel bag, confronted him—just as Barbara had John—and tried to get him to stop. Her dad had been in the Navy too, so she knew that Mike shouldn't be bringing classified documents home or giving them to his dad. I remember how Rachel looked that day in 1985 when I visited her: thin, scared, and uncertain about her future. As I was leaving, she asked, "What will happen to me now?"

Other evidence we developed, especially letters passed between Mike and Rachel, left no doubt: Rachel had known what Michael was doing. Some time later I was told that Dave Majors was giving lectures to various audiences in the "intelligence community" about the Walker case and was claiming credit for solving it. This case made a lot of careers.

The case also had some twists of plot that made it seem stranger than fiction. One day, a few weeks after Michael's arrest, Joe Wolfinger received a call from a man at Evangelist Pat Robertson's Christian Broadcasting Network in Virginia Beach. He said he had a videotape of Rachel Walker performing a seminude dance, and he wanted to know if we had any objection to him selling the tape to another TV broadcasting company for $25,000. We took custody of the tape, and after conferring with the U.S. attorney, I destroyed it. My daughter Susan, who lived in Virginia Beach, later told me that she had heard talk of a group of guys in Virginia Beach who had Rachel perform the dance and videotaped it with the intention of embarrassing her by turning it over to CBN. They were upset that Michael was a spy and thought they could get back at him by embarrassing his wife.

In another peculiar twist, it turned out that Michael had a Social Security number whose first three digits were 007, the code name of one of the most famous fictional spies of all time, James Bond. Mike was amused and fascinated by this fact. He talked about it during our debriefing sessions and said it added to the excitement and mystique of being a spy.

Not long before his arrest, Mike had been chosen "Yeoman of the Quarter" for his performance on the USS *Nimitz*. The last performance rating he received was at the end of January 1985, and it reads in part:

> Assigned to Operations Administrative (OX) Division as department Yeoman. Prepares correspondence, directives and incoming/outgoing message traffic. Files outgoing messages, directives and correspondence. . . .
>
> Seaman Walker is an outstanding, alert and bright Yeoman Striker. Hard charging, completely dependable, and unhesitant in the assumption of responsibility, he has willingly volunteered for additional duty and responsibilities in order to further his professional background. A dynamic leader–self starter. Exemplary in conduct, bearing and uniform and sets the example for others to emulate.
>
> Seaman Walker is highly deserving of this 4.0 evaluation. His outstanding performance, attention to detail and ensuring each assigned task is completed correctly and in a timely manner make him a valuable asset to the division and the *Nimitz*. Seaman Walker has my strongest possible recommendation for designation as a Yeoman and immediate advancement to YN3. He is strongly recommended for retention.

Michael Walker was paid a total of $1,000 by his father for the documents he stole while "earning" that glowing performance rating. He was sentenced to twenty-five years in prison for his crimes. That comes out to $40 per year if he does the full sentence. In addition, after he was convicted, Rachel divorced him and remarried. The kid paid a high price to be like his dad.

18

Am I My Brother's Keeper?

Arthur James Walker was born in Washington, D.C., on 25 October 1934. He was the first son of John Anthony Walker and Margaret Loretta Scaramuzzo. Growing up, both Art and John had to cope with an abusive, alcoholic father.

The most disruptive periods of Art's early life came when his father went on drinking binges and battered him and John Jr. and their mother, if they were within striking range. In addition to being a drunk, the senior John Walker was a strict disciplinarian—not an unusual combination of personality traits. Inevitably, his alcoholism caused trouble in the marriage. The drinking, carousing, and abuse eventually led to divorce.

Art played trumpet in the high school band, as well as several sports. Early on, he developed a keen interest in girls, an interest that never waned. He graduated from St. Patrick's High School in Scranton, Pennsylvania, in 1952, and joined the U.S. Navy on 16 June 1953. He married Rita Claire Fritsch, his high school sweetheart, and they had three children.

After basic training at the Naval Training Center, Bainbridge, Maryland, Art went to the Fleet Sonar School at Key West, Florida, and then on to Submarine School at New London, Connecticut, in June 1954. He was assigned to several diesel subs—the *Torsk, Medregal, Carp, Gallo,* and *Grenadier*—and a few other commands during his twenty-year career.

Throughout his career Art held positions of trust in the U.S. Navy; he had a Top Secret security clearance during most of his career. On 9 February 1960 he accepted a commission as an ensign. He continued to perform well and attained the rank of lieutenant commander on 1 November 1968. In September 1968 he reported to his last Navy duty station, the Atlantic Fleet Tactical School at the Little Creek Amphibious Base, Norfolk, where he was assigned as the training aids division officer, staff duty officer, and antisubmarine warfare (ASW) instructor. Art was an expert in ASW and even taught a class on it to a group of NSA people.

During his twenty years in the Navy, Arthur was awarded three Navy Good Conduct Medals and a National Defense Service Medal. He was highly thought of as a naval officer. He retired from the U.S. Navy on 1 July 1973 and started collecting his pension. In February 1980 he went to work for VSE, a government contractor in Chesapeake, Virginia, dealing with Navy ship repair scheduling.

Special Agents Beverly Andress and Carroll Wayne Deane were sent to interview Art Walker at his residence at 5708 Chickasaw Court in Virginia Beach around 6:30 in the morning on 20 May 1985, only a few hours after Kolouch and I arrested John.

Art answered the door and invited the agents in. He expressed surprise when they told him that his brother had been arrested on espionage charges. As the questioning wore on, he maintained that he knew nothing of John's espionage activities and had never been involved in the business of espionage with him. Art agreed to accompany the agents to the Norfolk FBI office for more questioning. Andress and Deane spent several hours with him, and although he continued to maintain that he was not involved and knew nothing of John's espionage activities, they were convinced he was lying. Art agreed to return to the FBI office that afternoon for a polygraph examination.

When Art returned, as promised, he had his first session with Special Agent Barry D. Colvert, the FBI's polygraph expert, who interviewed him in preparation for the lie-detector test.

I want to take a few minutes to talk about the lie detector, or polygraph. It has been used in law enforcement since the mid-1920s and in my opinion is an extremely effective tool to use in an investigation. However, it is not foolproof, and therefore the results are not considered scientifically exact enough to be commonly accepted in court.

The polygraph measures certain physiological responses that we humans cannot easily control. Specifically, it measures the blood pressure, respiration, and pulse rate of the person being tested. A pneumograph tube is fastened around the chest to measure respiration, and a blood pressure/pulse cuff is placed on an arm. Several small cuffs are also attached to various fingers. The readings of each response are recorded on a graph by several pens, similar to an electrocardiogram.

The most important factor in the use of the polygraph is the skill of the operator. Barry Colvert, who conducted nearly all of the polygraph exams in this case, was in my opinion the premier polygraph man in the FBI. He had the gift of putting the person he was going to test at ease. He could establish a rapport before ever asking a question.

Here's the procedure Colvert followed: He would meet in a room alone with the person. Ideally, the room would have no windows and nothing distracting on the walls. They would chat for a while, just getting to know each other. Barry would then explain the procedure and ensure that the person understood what was about to happen.

He would then conduct an extensive pretest interview regarding the person's knowledge of the crime. Barry and the person being tested would formulate questions to be asked during the test. Barry would explain each question and make certain the individual was comfortable with them all. Each test would consist of five or six questions, several of which would be "control" questions, such as "Is your name ——— ?" or "Is this Wednesday?" All questions must be answered yes or no. Often at this stage of the process a suspect will realize that he can't beat the machine, and he'll confess.

Once Colvert was satisfied that the person was ready to be tested, he would hook him up to the machine and test him. When he had completed the test, he would discuss each question and the person's responses. This was another critical time when people often confessed.

Early on, under Colvert's questioning, Art's armor began to crack. When Colvert gave Art the polygraph test, he failed every question having to do with his own involvement in espionage and his knowledge of John's espionage activities. He then made some admissions about suspecting that John was possibly selling classified information; admitted that John had asked him if his job at the government contractor, VSE, gave him access to information regarding U.S. Navy ship movements; and admitted to having given John an unclassified document from VSE.

Polygraphers don't like to use the words *pass* and *fail.* Rather, they use three terms to describe the person's response to the questions: *showed deception* (he's lying;) *inconclusive* (couldn't definitively say one way or the other;) and *no deception indicated* (he's telling the truth).

In February 1997 I spoke with Barry about his recollection of Art's performance on the polygraph exams he gave him on 20 and 21 May and again on 17 and 18 September 1985. These are the questions on which Art consistently "showed deception" each time he was tested:

1. Did you provide more classified information or material to your brother than you have told me about?
2. Did you provide classified material or information to the intelligence service of another country?
3. During your service in the Navy, did you provide John Walker with classified material or information?
4. Other than John Walker, have you had personal contact with anyone representing a foreign intelligence service or the Soviet Intelligence Service?

Barry said he talked with Art after each test and actually stopped testing him after he "showed deception" on 18 September, because

Art wasn't able to explain why he had failed. Barry recalled Art's response when he specifically asked Art why he thought he had failed questions 2 and 4. Art said, "It is indeed possible that I may have had more involvement, but because of a mental block I have just forced it out of my memory. I'm not consciously aware of any other involvement, and I may have given John other documents or publications. I have a number of self-doubts about additional involvement with my brother and would like to try and eliminate this mental block through counseling with a psychiatrist and would agree to be hypnotized if it would help."

Colvert continued the questioning. Art made a few more admissions, all intended to minimize his knowledge of and involvement in John's espionage business. He took another polygraph test and again failed every question. I wish I had kept track of the number of times we asked Art why he thought he was failing the polygraph. The response—and the gesture that accompanied it—was always the same: he would thump his forehead with the heel of his hand and say, "I know it's in there!" Colvert ended that first day by suggesting that Art go home and get himself a good attorney.

Art showed up at the FBI office early the next morning. Bev and Carroll took another run at him. He made more admissions; he was getting himself in deeper and deeper but was determined to continue to talk to us. He would later admit to Colvert that he was trying to confess to knowing just enough to pass the polygraph, and hoped to convince us that he had "no real involvement" (that was Art's phrase).

Over the next several days Art continued to show up at our office. One time he stayed all day, being interviewed by Bev Andress and John Hodges. I was in the office going over paperwork on the case. John and Bev came to me several times that day to bring me up to speed on Art's latest revelations. They were talking to him in a small interview room, about seven by nine feet. It was cramped, and Art was a chain-smoker. I stuck my head in the door a couple of times to see how things were going; it was worse than any bar or pool room I had ever seen.

Sometime around 6:30 or 7:00 P.M., after Bev and John told me that Art was still jerking them around, giving half-answers and generally pulling their chains, I went into the interview room, grabbed Art by the shirt, and threw him out the door into the public hallway. I told him I was sick of his damn lies and he should go home and not come back until he was ready to tell the complete truth. But he was back the next morning before the office was even open; I saw him in the hall when I came in.

Eventually Arthur did confess enough to get himself a long prison term. He admitted that he had known that John was a spy and had been for many years.

The way Art told it, he had invested $1,000 in the bar John and Barbara opened in South Carolina, but he never made any money on it. He and John then opened a car radio shop, Walker Enterprises, which went broke in 1979. He was in debt and out of a job. Art said he and John were in John's truck, outside Charlie's Waffle House on Newtown Road in Virginia Beach, one day in early 1980. He was moaning about being broke and not having a job, and John suggested he get a job with a government contractor. According to Art, John told him he had friends who paid for classified information, and Art could make some money if he got a job with access to classified material.

Art said that soon after his talk with John, he saw an ad in the local newspaper for a job at VSE. He got the job and started working there in February 1980. His job involved scheduling U.S. Navy ships for maintenance and repair. Art admitted photographing a Confidential portion of a damage control book for the USS *Blue Ridge* in early September 1981 and leaving the film in John's desk at his detective agency. A damage control book contains information that would be used to assist a ship in surviving damage sustained in battle or in a collision. At that time the *Blue Ridge* was one of the two most sophisticated ships in the U.S. Navy.

On another occasion, Art recalled, in early 1982, John picked him up at VSE for lunch. Art had checked out a Confidential casualty report message list (a listing of casualty reports detailing ship malfunctions) for the LHA-class ships (general-purpose amphibious ships designed to be command [flag] ships during an amphibious assault). The Walker brothers drove to the parking lot of an abandoned Kmart and photographed the document in the back of John's van. Art returned the document after lunch—no problem. Art also admitted passing unclassified technical manuals and plans for some U.S. Navy ships to John.

Art said John paid him a total of $12,000 for the documents he passed but took $6,000 back in payment for the bills they had accumulated in the failed car radio business. Art used some of his money to buy a new gas barbecue grill, brakes for his car, and a new hairpiece. He kept the remaining $4,000 in his briefcase, out of Rita's view, for "happy hour money"; he needed an extra supply of cash just then, as he was having an affair with one of the women in his office.

Arthur really sealed his fate on 28 May 1985. A federal grand jury in Baltimore was hearing testimony from witnesses in the case against John and Michael. Mike Schatzow and Bob McDonald, the assistant U.S. attorneys handling the case, had subpoenaed Art's wife, Rita, to testify regarding her knowledge of John's espionage activities. (Barbara had told me that she told Rita that John was a spy, and we wanted to get Rita's recollection of what she knew and when she knew it on record before the grand jury.)

I had already testified and was in the U.S. attorney's office when I noticed Art smoking and pacing in the hall. I told Mike Schatzow that Art was there. Schatzow already knew, of course, that Art had made several admissions to us in the four or five days after John was arrested. We walked up to Art and, after Schatzow told him he did not have to say anything, had a brief conversation with him about what he had told the agents in Norfolk. Then I asked Art if he wanted to testify before the grand jury—and he said he did! Schatzow and I were stunned. Mike said he would arrange for Art to go before the federal grand jury that afternoon.

Arthur appeared before the grand jury on the afternoon of 28 May and confessed to committing espionage. Mike Schatzow would read this testimony into the record at Arthur's trial in Norfolk in August 1985. This was a first in the history of espionage investigations and trials in the United States.

Poor Arthur looked like a whipped hound when he came out of that grand jury room and had to get into the car with Rita for the five-hour drive back to Virginia Beach. I can imagine how the conversations must have gone, Rita having just learned of Art's involvement in espionage and of his many extramarital escapades. The lady was steaming! Art must have felt like a trapped rat. I bet that was some ride.

Before his grand jury appearance, Arthur had confessed quite a bit to us in Norfolk. Once we had verified some of the information he had given us, we pressed the Department of Justice attorneys to let us arrest him, but they put us off and demanded more evidence. After Art confessed to the grand jury, though, the decision was made. On 29 May, John Martin, chief of the Internal Security Unit, authorized his arrest.

I drove back to Norfolk that day, got home around 5:30 P.M., and called Wolfinger to find out what was going on. He told me that we had authorization to arrest Art and that he was getting some of the squad together to go get him. Wolfie wanted me to come in and assist in the arrest, but I begged off. I knew how hard Bev Andress and John Hodges had worked on Art's aspect of the case, and I thought they should go arrest him without me getting in the middle of it. That's what I told Wolfie. Then I hung up the phone. I spent the next couple of hours wondering how things were going and itching to be there. I spoke with Wolfie later that evening and learned that all was well. Arthur's arrest had gone without a hitch. John and Beverly, accompanied by Ed Schrader and Butch Holtz, simply picked him up at his house and took him to the Virginia Beach City Jail.

19

Arthur's Trial

The federal judicial system is divided into various districts. Norfolk
lies within the Eastern District of Virginia, a district that, because
of its no-nonsense, hardworking judges and assistant U.S. attorneys,
is known as the "Rocket Docket." Once a person is charged with a
crime in the Eastern District, he can be assured that his case will
be handled with great competence and speed. Few delays or con-
tinuances are granted. Even though John and Michael had been
arrested before Arthur, I knew that Art's trial would be over before
theirs even began.

The task of trying Arthur's case went to the Honorable Judge J.
Calvitt Clarke Jr. Judge Clarke was born in Harrisburg, Pennsylvania.
His family moved to Richmond, Virginia, when he was six years
old. His father, a Presbyterian minister, founded the Christian Children's Fund, now the largest child welfare organization in the world.
Judge Clarke attended the University of Virginia, where he earned
undergraduate and law degrees. He practiced law in Richmond for
thirty years before he was appointed a U.S. district court judge. He
had been a federal judge for over eleven years when he handled
Art's case.

Tommy E. Miller was the lead drug task force attorney in the U.S. Attorney's Office for the Eastern District of Virginia. He was designated to be one of the two prosecutors in Arthur's case. Tommy is a Norfolk native, a 1970 graduate of the University of Virginia (B.A. in government) and a 1973 graduate of the law school at the College of William and Mary. In 1974 he became a local prosecuting attorney in the Commonwealth Attorney's Office in Norfolk, where he earned a highly deserved reputation as a tough and aggressive prosecutor, and was appointed an assistant U.S. attorney in 1980.

Robert "Rob" J. Seidel Jr., one of Tommy Miller's associates in the U.S. Attorney's Office, was the other member of the prosecution team. Rob was born and raised in Alexandria, Virginia, on the outskirts of Washington, D.C. He graduated from Virginia Tech with a B.A. in political science in 1971. After taking a year off from school, he entered the College of William and Mary School of Law and graduated in 1975. He spent a year in private practice and then became a state prosecutor in the Commonwealth Attorney's Office in Norfolk, where he worked for about five years. He spent a year in the Commonwealth Attorney's Office in Virginia Beach before joining Tommy as a federal prosecutor in the U.S. Attorney's Office in Norfolk in October 1982. Throughout those years Rob built a reputation as an outstanding prosecutor and a formidable foe in the courtroom.

Tommy and Rob were both highly respected by the defense attorneys in the Norfolk area. Anyone facing them in court knew he had better be well prepared.

Preparation for the trial was an extremely intense time. The prosecution called in and interviewed every potential witness they intended to use. I worked with them. We spent many days, late nights, and weekends working to get the case ready. John Hodges, Bev Andress, and the other FBI squad members did a great job corroborating the information Arthur had given us. Of course, once he was arrested and his attorneys were appointed, we no longer had an opportunity to talk to him, so we had to try to verify every bit of information he had given us. We were quite successful. We located the damage control book; the folks at VSE reproduced a copy of the casualty report list Art had told us about; we even located the logs showing that Art had signed the documents out. We built an extremely strong case against him.

Arthur couldn't afford to hire an attorney, so Judge Clarke appointed Samuel W. Meekins Jr. and J. Brian Donnelly, a former assistant U.S. attorney, as his defense team. He was entitled to two attorneys because espionage is a capital offense.

There were only two ways Arthur was going to avoid conviction: either his attorneys would have to succeed in getting his confessions thrown out, or they would have to convince Judge Clarke that no testimony regarding John Walker's espionage activities should be allowed. They failed on both issues in pretrial hearings, and the trial was set to begin on 5 August 1985.

Just a day or two before the trial was to begin, Art's attorneys came to Tommy and Rob with an offer for Art to plead *nolo contendere* (the equivalent of a guilty plea) to an espionage charge. It would carry a life sentence, and he would agree to cooperate fully with the government in its investigation and prosecution of the other members of John's espionage ring. We liked the offer, and we advised Judge Clarke. He too was pleased, and he said he would accept Art's plea if the Department of Justice officials put their blessing on the deal.

We ran into a problem right away. Edwin Meese, the attorney general at the time, was out of the country, and we couldn't reach him. Lowell Jensen was the assistant AG standing in for Meese, but we couldn't find him, either. No one else had the authority to make the decision. We went back to Judge Clarke and explained the problem. The judge had little patience with the bureaucrats in D.C., and he expressed his displeasure over our predicament.

Jensen surfaced after a couple of hours but would not let us accept Arthur's plea. He said, "The country deserves to see an espionage trial in this case."

We informed Judge Clarke. His hands were tied. Because of the tremendous media coverage, he was concerned about finding an impartial jury.

Art was disappointed that we couldn't accept his plea and do away with the embarrassment of a trial. He decided to waive his right to a trial by jury and be tried by Judge Clarke. The trial began on 5 August and ended on 9 August.

Arthur was a pathetic figure during the trial. He was suffering, no doubt about it. One scene I'll never forget came to pass after we were finished in court on Thursday, 8 August. I was waiting for an elevator on the fourth floor of the courthouse when I heard a clanking, rustling sound coming toward me down the marble-floored hall. After a few seconds, Art Walker, former lieutenant commander, U.S. Navy, came around the corner in leg irons, handcuffs, and chains, accompanied by three U.S. marshals.

We presented all of our evidence. Agents testified about the surveillance of John the night he left his package for Aleksey Tkachenko. Gerry Richards mesmerized the audience with his expert testimony about the drop instructions John used the night we followed him. His testimony was pivotal in proving that John was indeed a Soviet agent—a crucial part of our case. If we couldn't prove that, we really had no case against Art.

Barry Colvert charmed us all with his down-home Arkansas manner but really drove the stake through Arthur's heart with his testimony about Art's confessions to him. Barry said he had asked Art if he had ever had access to higher-classified material than Confidential, and Art told him that at one time he had a Secret technical manual—but, he went on to say, "I don't really believe that I ever gave that manual to John to copy or photograph; however something in the back of my mind tells me that I at least let him have it to review." I loved it. I could just see Art thumping his forehead as he tried to answer Barry's question.

The testimony of Bruce Brahe, the FBI agent who found John's drop package, was riveting, and he had the courtroom buzzing when he answered Meekins's questions on cross-examination:

> Q. You testified that you believed there was going to be a drop of classified information to the Soviets. Based on what information was that?

A. We were briefed that a Soviet intelligence operation was in the offing; much of that information was classified. I've worked many years in the foreign counterintelligence field; I have a master's degree in Soviet studies; I'm a former Central Intelligence Service officer; I'm a former captain in the U.S. Marine Corps involving security; and when I smelled one, I knew one.

Needless to say, Brahe took quite a ribbing from me and other fellow agents after his testimony. To this day I don't think he believes he made that statement.

Bev Andress was on the witness stand for four hours testifying about Arthur's confessions. In his cross-examination, Sam Meekins attacked the credibility of her written reports (302s, in FBI parlance) on her interviews of Art, intimating that her reports were not a complete account of the interviews. I was surprised at Sam's attack and was not quite sure what he was driving at. On redirect, Rob Seidel asked Bev, "Agent Andress, would you tell us what topics were in your notes, that were not contained in your 302, that you discussed with Mr. Arthur James Walker?" Bev's response was a real ballbuster. She replied, "The only topics that I can recall discussing that did not appear in my 302s were Mr. Walker's extramarital affairs."

Meekins went ballistic, objected to her response, and asked Judge Clarke to strike it. Judge Clarke said, "You were the one that brought out that the witness was testifying from her 302, and you're the one that attempted to cast doubt on the accuracy and completeness of the 302, because you talked to her about her notes. Objection overruled."

Tommy, Rob, and I were astounded. It was a perfect example of why you should never ask a question in court unless you already know the answer. It had nothing to do with the charges against Arthur, but the incident really made him squirm.

Navy experts testified that a hostile power could use a damage control book to determine what type of weapons should be used against a particular ship to cause the greatest damage and where those weapons should be aimed; the damage control book would also reveal various engineering and technical techniques of the U.S. Navy. Other experts testified that an enemy could use the casualty reports to determine the period of readiness for each of the ships in the LHA class, and that the reports would also help an enemy predict U.S. fleet readiness. I'll never forget how Capt. Edward D. Sheafer Jr. (now an admiral), senior intelligence officer, U.S. Navy Atlantic Command, described the damage control book. Should it fall into the hands of the enemy, he said, it would be a "Bible for sabotage."

And, of course, there was Arthur's confession to the federal grand jury in Baltimore, which Mike Schatzow read into the record. To my knowledge, that was the first time an assistant U.S. attorney ever testified in an espionage trial. Art and his attorneys were whipped.

Meekins and Donnelly put on no witnesses in Arthur's defense. That was because he had no defense; we had an unbeatable case. They talked to the media on the courthouse steps every day after court, trying to minimize what Art had done and make him look like a victim of his brother John. Meekins commented, "Art might be a sap, but he's no spy." That must have made Art feel better.

On 17 June 1985 a federal grand jury in Norfolk had indicted Arthur on seven espionage-related counts. Count 1 charged him with conspiracy to commit espionage in violation of Title 18 U.S. Code Section 794(c); counts 2 and 5 charged him with espionage in violation of T18 USC 794(a); counts 3 and 6 charged him with copying, making, and obtaining documents to be used to injure the United States in violation of T18 USC 793(b); and counts 4 and 7 charged him with the unauthorized possession of information relative to the national defense of the United States in violation of T18 USC 793(e).

After closing arguments on Friday, 9 August, Judge Clarke said there would be a brief recess. He wasn't kidding; he came back in fifteen minutes and announced his verdict. I was sitting at the prosecutor's table to the left of Tommy Miller and had drawn a bull's-eye on a piece of paper. As Judge Clarke read each charge and his verdict, I penciled a dot in the bull's-eye. Tommy watched with a look of amusement and pride as the home-run verdict was read: guilty on all seven counts.

Judge Clarke set 15 October 1985 for the sentencing; at the request of Art's attorneys, he later changed the date to 12 November. Art was facing a possible sentence of three life terms plus forty years, and a substantial fine.

The author with Laura and Barbara Walker at the author's home in
Virginia Beach, 1996. *Lynn Dean Hunter*

Young Michael Lance Walker in his Navy uniform. *FBI evidence photo*

John Anthony Walker Jr. early in his career in the U.S. Navy.
FBI evidence photo

Arthur James Walker, U.S. Navy officer. *FBI evidence photo*

Jerry Alfred Whitworth and his wife, Brenda, in happier days.
FBI evidence photo

John left his last package for the KGB behind this utility pole on Partnership Road in Montgomery County, Maryland, on the evening of 19 May 1985. *FBI photo*

The contents of John's last package for the KGB. *FBI photo*

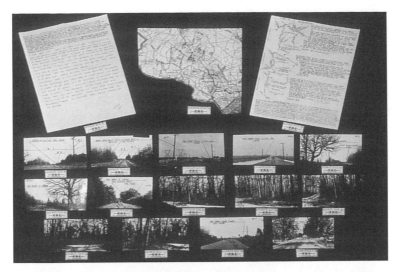

KGB dead-drop instructions and photographs used by John Walker the night he was caught by the FBI. *FBI photo*

The scene on the seventh floor of the Ramada Inn on Montgomery Avenue, Rockville, Maryland, where the author and his FBI associates arrested John Walker on 20 May 1985. Note the toupee referred to in the Walker family as "Daddy's plastic hair." *FBI photo*

John and his girlfriend, P.K. Carroll, getting ready to party.
FBI evidence photo

Michael and his wife, Rachel, getting ready to party. Like
father, like son. *FBI evidence photo*

John takes on the role of Castro. *FBI evidence photo*

John and his KKK buddy circa 1969. *FBI evidence photo*

"Rotor Reader" device given to John by the KGB to enable him to determine the internal wiring on the rotors used in our code machines. The information John obtained by using this device gave the Soviets the ability to read many of our encoded messages. *FBI photo*

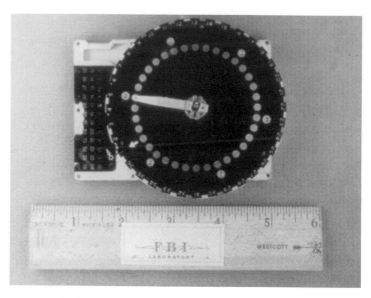

"Rotor Reader" shown with a rotor in place, ready to be "read." *FBI photo*

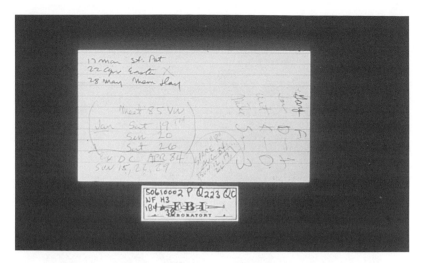

A three-by-five card found in John's den during an FBI search, on which John had written the identities of the members of his espionage ring and the date (including backup dates) of his first meeting with the KGB in 1985: "Jan Sat 19th." *FBI evidence photo*

Fake wall socket in John's den, which he used as a hiding place for his map of Vienna and his KGB meet instructions, the "Vienna Procedure." *FBI photo*

Concealment area found in John's kitchen cabinet. *FBI photo*

Aleksey Tkachenko, Soviet diplomat and John Walker's last KGB handler. *FBI photo*

The author, FBI credentials in hand, waits for Michael Walker to step onto U.S. soil at Andrews Air Force Base before placing him under arrest on 25 May 1985. *Michelle McDonald, Virginian Pilot–Ledger Star, Norfolk*

20

The Mystery of Art Walker

Art is a strange character, perhaps the most mysterious of all the characters in this case. He was highly regarded in the Navy, at VSE, and in his neighborhood in Virginia Beach. He was always well mannered, personable, and polite with me—an easy guy to like. And yet he was a lying, deceitful womanizer who betrayed his family, friends, and country. His brother John was all of those things too, but not an easy man to like. Art, in his own way, was even more dangerous than John, because he was smarter and more polished at deception than John ever was.

I was never convinced that Arthur had told us the complete truth in those interviews before his arrest. Barry Colvert and I talked about him many times. Colvert commented that outwardly Art handled his responsibilities as a father, older brother, husband, and naval officer very well, but he harbored an inner streak of rebelliousness that he acted out through drinking, gambling, and promiscuous behavior. He suggested that Art might have become involved in espionage because he feared that his wife, Rita, would find out about his debts and extra-marital affairs. The money he could earn selling our nation's secrets would enable him to pay his debts and support his affairs.

We both believed that Art had more to tell us. After Art was convicted, his attorneys counseled him to cooperate with the FBI in the continuing investigation of the case, in an effort to get some leniency when his sentencing date arrived. Our interviews of him continued after his trial.

One day, about a month after the trial, John Hodges and I picked Art up at the Virginia Beach City Jail and headed for our office in downtown Norfolk, where we had scheduled an interview with Tommy Miller and Sam Meekins. We were headed west on the expressway when I took the turnoff at Newtown Road and drove to Art's neighborhood. When we came to his house, I stopped and told him to take a good long look, because unless he gave us the complete truth, that was the last time he was ever going to see his home. Art looked and said, "Yeah." He lit another cigarette.

We did the interview and got nothing new from him. In fact, his answers to our questions were so confusing and convoluted that it was hard to make any sense of them. Even Meekins got a little rankled.

The big hang-up had to do with the extent of Arthur's involvement in espionage. Barbara had told me that when she and Art were together one afternoon in 1968, she was lamenting her discovery that John was a spy. Then Art told her that if it made her feel any better, he had "done the same thing when he was in Groton, Connecticut, only not to the extent that John did and for a shorter period of time." Barbara passed Colvert's polygraph on that question, but Art failed it every time he was asked.

I always felt that if Art had been more involved in espionage than he admitted, it meant he had done something while he was on active duty; he just couldn't bring himself to confess to having passed Navy documents to the Soviets while wearing the uniform of his country. Asked why he was failing the polygraph, he continued to thump his forehead and say, "I know it's in there." Something was "in there," that's the truth, but he never told us what it was.

A few weeks later Art requested that he be interviewed under hypnosis. He was desperate to convince us that he had told us everything. I arranged the interview, and Special Agent Richard L.

Ault, one of the six original profilers in our Behavioral Science Unit, and Lt. Col. Neil Hibler, command clinical psychologist for the Air Force Office of Special Investigations, came to Norfolk. I sat in while the colonel hypnotized Art. Then he and Ault questioned him.

The interview was very interesting and thorough; it took several hours. They asked Arthur about the day he and Barbara were together at her Algonquin House apartment and Barbara told him John was a spy. He remembered it quite vividly, down to the detail that Barbara was having her menstrual period that day. He denied telling her he had "done the same thing when he was at Groton." The colonel instructed him to answer the next few questions by raising his index finger if his answer was yes and his middle finger if it was no. Then he asked him if his name was Arthur James Walker. Art raised his index finger. Colonel Hibler asked a couple more easy questions, and each time, Art raised his index finger. The colonel then asked Art if he had been truthful with all of his answers, and Art's middle finger popped straight up. I figured that about summed things up for Art.

If Art could have had his subconscious confess for him, we would have gotten the whole story. But since it doesn't work that way, we only got the part he felt comfortable telling us.

We had done a hypnotic interview of Barbara Walker at Quantico not too long before we did Art. We did her interview not because we felt she was lying but in order to "wring her out"—that is, to get every detail from her memory about John's espionage business that we possibly could.

I had never seen a hypnotic interview before. The experience certainly made a believer out of me. Contrary to common belief, being under hypnosis does not make a person tell the truth. However, it often does enable a person to remember things he or she couldn't recall without hypnosis.

Dick Ault, Colonel Hibler, and I were seated across from Barbara. The colonel had no problem getting her "to go under." (He had no problem with Arthur, either.) At first it was difficult for me to believe that she was actually hypnotized, because she was answering the questions with such ease and lucidity. However, when the colonel asked her to describe the circumstances of her discovery that John was a spy, I was convinced beyond all doubt. She described in great detail how she went through John's desk and found the photos and instructions of the drop sites and the $1,500 in the tin box. When she finished telling us that, she became physically ill and ran into the bathroom and threw up. She had actually relived that day.

Barbara answered all of our questions with the same sharp recollection she had always displayed. When she was asked to recount the day with Art in the Algonquin House, the information she gave matched all the information she had given me before. I believe Barbara's account of the events of that day: Arthur told her he had done the same thing as John while he was at Groton. There is no doubt in my mind about that. The big question is, Why did he say that? Was it because it was true? Or was he simply trying to soothe Barbara's upset feelings so he could get her into the sack? If the latter, why wouldn't he admit it?

Barry Colvert believes, on the basis of things Art and John have said, that Art was definitely more involved in espionage than he told us. In fact, Colvert believes that Art quite probably started the whole business. I have to agree. And I always felt that John had the answer to the mystery of Art's involvement in espionage, but I never got that answer from him.

In early July, before Art's trial, I learned that Art's attorneys had sent copies of his confessions, which they had received from the prosecutors during pretrial discovery, to John's attorneys in Baltimore. On 5 July 1985 Tommy Miller and Rob Seidel filed a motion for a protective order, which read in part:

> The United States has previously provided certain discovery [material] to defense counsel. The United States has received information that counsel for Arthur James Walker have provided copies of that discovery [material] to persons not a party to this case [meaning John's attorneys]. The disclosure of that information has, within the last 3 days, hindered the over-all investigation of this case. Therefore the United States requests the court to enter an order prohibiting Arthur

James Walker, his counsel, and employees and agents thereof from copying, distributing, and disseminating any of the books, documents, photographs, [or] statements of the defendant.

Judge Clarke issued the protective order on 9 July, and Sam Meekins and Brian Donnelly signed it the same day. However, the damage was done. And it was irreversible. I had not yet had an opportunity to interview John about his espionage activities, since we were in the pretrial process with him also; he had an attorney and was off-limits to us. I would not question him until after he signed his plea agreement with the U.S. Department of Justice on 24 October 1985.

In early November, when Jim Kolouch, Bill Buckley, and I finally interviewed John about Arthur's involvement, the first thing John said was that he had read Arthur's confessions. From then on, he just parroted back to us what he had read in those confessions. That's about all he ever gave us about Art.

It wasn't illegal for Art's lawyers to give his confessions to John's attorneys, but it certainly interfered with my investigation, and it probably eliminated any possibility of learning exactly what Art had done. And, yes, John failed every question he was ever asked on the polygraph regarding Art's involvement in espionage, just like Art.

John did mention one interesting thing about the Soviets' interest in Arthur. He told us the Soviets had asked him to determine whether Art, in his job at VSE, could discover when there were changes in the Navy's DEFCON (defense condition) level—perhaps by noticing sudden changes in Navy ship maintenance or repair schedules. John's handler told him that if Art could do that, they would furnish him a hand-held device, and all he would have to do was push a button to send a signal to a Soviet satellite, indicating that our DEFCON level had changed. John asked Art, and Art said he wasn't sure that he could get such information, but maybe.

Later, during the debriefings of John Walker, we tried to get to the bottom of the Art Walker story. We doubted that we knew the truth in two important areas:

1. Was Art Walker more involved than he admits?
2. When and how did this treachery actually begin?

Discrepancies in John's story led us to wonder just who really went to the Soviets first—John or Art. John said he walked into the Soviet embassy in Washington, D.C., in late 1967 or early 1968. He told us there was a wrought-iron fence around the embassy compound when he walked in. In fact, there was no iron fence around the Soviet embassy until June 1974. However, John's description of the inside of the embassy was on the money, which seems to show that he was in there at some later time.

Barry Colvert polygraphed John eight times or so during the debriefing process. He covered the question of Art's involvement and the embassy "fence problem" on 26 August 1986.

During that session John said:

> I know you believe I'm lying about the beginning of the operation because of [my failing] the polygraph and the fence story. Let me give you a scenario: Arthur got in some type of financial trouble, probably in New York [when he was stationed at the submarine base at Groton], and became involved with a number of New York loan sharks. Art needed money desperately, and I gave him some classified documents to sell. After Art sold the documents and got some money, he became frightened and wanted to drop out. I saw no harm in selling the information to the Soviets, as the countries were not at war and would never go to war. I felt it was an easy chance to make some money, so I walked into a Soviet embassy somewhere in the world.

Barry tested John with questions based on that "scenario," and he passed.

Prior to 26 August, John always failed the polygraph when he answered no to questions along these lines:

Was Art Walker involved in any way in selling classified material to the Soviets prior to 1968?

Was Art Walker involved in any way in initiating your first contact with the Soviets?

Did Art Walker provide classified material to the Soviets before you did?

Art consistently failed similar questions.

One of the questions I asked John was whether the Soviets had ever asked him for a photograph of any of the members of his ring. John said the only one they wanted a picture of was Art, and he gave one to them. The question is, Why did they want Art's photo? Did they want to compare it with one they had from his early days as a spy, back in the early 1960s when he was at Groton? Did they want to be able to recognize him when he went to meet them in Vienna or when he filled drops for John? I'm not at all sure we'll ever know.

Arthur appeared for sentencing in U.S. district court in Norfolk on 12 November 1985. Before Judge Clarke pronounced the sentence, Art's attorneys put one witness on the stand: his wife, Rita. She looked very humble and alone, sitting nervously in the witness box dressed in a plain skirt, knitted V-neck vest, and blouse. She told Judge Clarke that Art had been a good father and a good neighbor. She recalled how he had always kept the grass cut and was willing to lend his lawn mower to neighbors. She also pointed out that Art had been president of the Community League.

After Rita finished, Judge Clarke took a brief recess to deliberate on the sentence he was about to impose. He returned in ten minutes and proceeded to chastise Arthur. He pointed out that Art had been an officer in the U.S. Navy, had held positions of trust and responsibility, and had not only participated in the espionage business with his brother John but had known about John's spying for years and should have come forward with that information. Clarke also scolded Rita for not turning John in, since she too had known of his espionage years before he was caught.

Then, having found Arthur guilty on seven espionage-related counts on 9 August 1985, Judge Clarke sentenced him to three life terms plus four ten-year terms and a $250,000 fine. The prison terms are to run concurrently.

After the sentencing Barry Colvert told me, "Bubba, if I'm ever up there for sentencing and my wife can't say anything better about me than that I let the neighbors use my lawn mower, just take me away!"

Art appealed the verdict in the U.S. Court of Appeals for the Fourth Circuit, and that court denied his appeal on 7 July 1986. He wrote a letter to Judge Clarke asking for a reduction of the sentence; the judge denied that request on 24 November 1986.

Art has been serving his sentence in the federal penitentiary near Terre Haute, Indiana, a pleasant little town in the heartland of our country. Barry Colvert and I went there twice to talk to him. We thought that maybe, after being in prison for a while, he might be ready to clear up the mystery surrounding his involvement in espionage.

The prison was built in the mid-1930s, just a couple of years after Art was born, and has been in constant use since the day it opened. The gray stone building has the usual complement of razor wire against and on top of a tall fence around the perimeter. When we drove up to the gate, we had to identify ourselves, state our reason for being there and who we wanted to see, and check our weapons.

Inside, the public area was much like the lobby of a vintage office building. There were offices down each of the two or three hallways leading away from the lobby. The hall leading into the prisoners' area was protected by a set of electronically operated steel gates manned by a guard. Those steel gates made a thunderous sound as they closed and locked automatically behind us; I don't think I could ever get used to the sound of those gates. A guard led us through the halls on our way to meet Art. Everywhere we went inside the prison, we had to be escorted by a guard.

The inmates were all over the place; those who don't have a job walk the halls. I remember one inmate in particular. He was about six five, weighed close to three hundred pounds, and had piercing eyes, a huge bushy beard, and hair down past his shoulders. He was wearing a tank-top shirt, and every inch of exposed skin was covered with tattoos. The guard said the guy was a motorcycle gang member and was doing time for multiple murders. This inmate was in the same cellblock as Arthur Walker, former lieutenant commander, U.S. Navy. Art's lifestyle had taken a drastic downward turn.

I had arranged the meeting with the warden ahead of time, so Art was expecting us. We wanted to take him some cigarettes, but gifts weren't permitted. Art looked good, except for the prison pallor. He was dressed in gray pants, matching shirt, and white tennis shoes, and he seemed glad to see us. He had taken a job in the office. His attitude was better than I had expected it to be. He missed his kids and commented that he didn't receive many letters from them. Rita was in the process of divorcing him.

Barry and I told Art that if he ever expected to get out on parole, he had to come clean with us about his espionage. He said "Yeah" and gave us that routine of thumping his forehead, saying, "It must be in there." But he didn't tell us a thing. So much for our first visit.

The second time we traveled to see Art, it was on a plane that we thought was going to go down in flames. Barry and I were in the lounge in Chicago's O'Hare Airport, waiting for a connecting flight to Terre Haute, when a tall, good-looking young lady came in and sat next to us. We struck up a conversation with her and learned that she was on the women's basketball team at a university out west. While we were talking to her we missed our flight, and so we had to take a little twelve-passenger commuter plane to Terre Haute.

I knew we were in trouble the minute we boarded the plane. Even I had to duck to keep from hitting my head on the ceiling. There were only about six passengers on the flight, and we had to sit apart from each other to distribute the weight evenly. There wasn't even a curtain between the passenger cabin and the cockpit. I don't recall a stewardess being on board; I think the co-pilot just gave us some instructions. He should have given us each a parachute.

We sped down the runway and fought our way to cruising altitude. I gritted my teeth and held on. It was like riding a bumblebee.

We had been in the air about half an hour when I began to sweat. My feet were especially hot. I asked Barry, who was two rows in front of me, if he was hot, and he said *hot* didn't begin to describe it for him. We were both sweating bullets. The other passengers chimed in with their opinions about the temperature in the plane. I reached down and felt the floor and quickly withdrew my hand and told Barry to feel the floor. It was so hot you couldn't touch it.

In a few minutes smoke began pouring out of the vents into the passenger compartment. Barry and I yelled up to the pilots that we were having a problem back there. The co-pilot came back for a look, then returned to his seat. I figured the plane must have been a coal-burner and the chimney was clogged. The pilots acted like they were used to it.

We flew on for another fifteen minutes or so as the smoke continued to surround us. I couldn't see the pilots anymore. Colvert had a death grip on the seat and was mumbling to himself. I think I heard him promise never again to talk to a pretty young thing in an airport.

The pilot finally acknowledged that we had a problem and landed at some tiny airport in Indiana. We got out and went into the terminal while the ground crew unloaded the luggage. As the pilot walked past us, I asked him what the problem had been, and he said a heat valve had stuck in the open position. We thanked him for getting us back onto the ground and high-tailed it for the car rental counter. The rest of the way to Terre Haute, we drove.

The only thing we learned on the trip was that Art's new cellmate was from Pakistan. It's a surreal picture: Arthur, day in and day out, sharing his six- by nine-foot cell—containing two bunks, a sink, and a commode—with a stranger, without benefit of a common language or culture.

Again we tried to impress Arthur with the importance of telling us the complete truth, but he just said "Yeah" and started thumping his forehead. Barry and I looked at each other and headed for the door. That was the last time we went to see Art. It was the summer of 1987.

He sent me a Christmas card that year. I wrote him a letter back and tried once more to convince him that for his own good he should just tell us the complete truth. I never heard from him again.

21

Recollections in Tranquillity

Nearly ten years had passed since the trial of Arthur Walker when I asked Judge Clarke and the principal members of the prosecution team for their recollections. I wondered what aspects of the trial were most memorable to them, and how they viewed the case in retrospect. I was also curious about what "take" each man might have on the sentencing of the Walker spies in light of the end of the cold war.

In April 1994 Judge Clarke very graciously agreed to talk to me about his recollections of Arthur's case. I asked him what the most memorable aspect of the trial was for him. He replied:

> I suppose it was the ease with which it was tried. The preliminaries to it, when the FBI or Naval Intelligence had to investigate my court reporter, my secretary, and my law clerks [to get security clearances]. . . . All of that really made me think, "Gee, this is going to be a tough proposition."
>
> But, as you know, Arthur Walker had just about confessed to everything before he ever came to trial, and so there really wasn't a big contest of facts, or anything like that, during the trial. I think the FBI, under your leadership, had done such a thorough job that the case was pretty easily presented.

Some people today feel that now that the cold war is over, leniency should be granted to some individuals previously convicted on espionage charges. In fact, even some of Arthur's former fellow Navy officers have expressed their disagreement with the sentence Art received and think he should be paroled. I asked Judge Clarke for his opinion.

"Generally speaking," he said, "without commenting on any one case, the punishment should fit the crime you did when you did it." He applied this judicial principle to the case in point: "The danger to the United States may not be now what it was at the time the crime was committed. But I would, generally speaking, reject that idea [the notion of granting leniency to the Walkers because of the end of the cold war]."

"The fact," Judge Clarke explained, "that relations have gotten better between the Soviet Union and America since that time doesn't mean that [the Walkers'] conduct wasn't endangering the safety of the United States when it occurred. And that's the crux of what they should be punished for: the jeopardy they put their country to."

In April 1994 I also spoke with Tommy Miller—now Judge Miller. He had been appointed a U.S. magistrate judge in Norfolk in 1987. I asked him about his recollections of the case. He said:

> I remember the first phone call I got. It was close to midnight, and it was in May 1985. It was Joe Wolfinger, who I barely knew at that time, since he was in charge of the FCI Squad, and which did not bring any cases to the U.S. Attorney's Office. He told me about the seizure of some goods in Maryland and said we would need search warrants for John Walker's house the next day.
>
> Personally, the reason I remember it so well is that he woke up my son, who was having a stomachache and was sleeping with me at that point. And my son, who was awakened by that phone call, promptly threw up all over the bed and me. So I spent the rest of the evening talking with Wolfinger, John Dion [of the U.S. Department of Justice in Washington], and some other people about the case, getting up to speed on it and washing clothes.

The next day we put together search warrants, which were executed that afternoon at various places.

From a personal perspective, this was the most incredibly intense trial preparation of any case I've ever had. That was because Arthur was arrested in May, had his preliminary hearing and the indictment in June, and the trial in the first week of August.

During that period of time I had to learn, from a cold start, the Classified Information Procedures Act. I had to learn what a damage control book was, a little about ship construction, and a little about a lot of things. The factual aspect of the case was actually pretty simple. The FBI did a very good job in extracting confessions from Arthur and corroborating them. There was just such a phenomenal amount that I had to learn so quickly, that I ended up sleeping about three hours a night for two months.

The night Arthur was convicted I went home, played with my kids, went to bed at seven, and woke up fifteen hours later. Totally wiped out. Didn't join the party that the agents had celebrating the conviction, because I couldn't stay awake.

I asked Tommy if he thought there was anything remarkable about the case. He replied:

Well, the cast of characters was, certainly. The Walker family could be described as a classic dysfunctional family. No one was normal, or anywhere near normal, in that group. To some extent, I felt sorry for them—particularly John's children, because of the abuse that he and Barbara had subjected them to.

Look at these people! John's business partner, Laurie Robinson— she worked in a total nude club in Washington, D.C. She danced completely naked. That, apparently, was her claim to fame as being an investigator for John Walker.

A lot of people didn't seem to appreciate what John had done, the damage he had done. They were more concerned with how this was affecting them than [with] the damage John had done to our country.

I remember after everyone was convicted, I sat down and read the classified damage assessment. All along people had been talking about what the Walker case had meant, but it didn't really hit me until a year after the case was over and I read that assessment, which was a product of considerable study and hard thought, as opposed to speculation. Frankly I was appalled at what these people had done.

Tommy recalled the many unresolved areas in Art's case, as well as John's:

> Let's deal with Arthur first. He's the one I prosecuted, talked with, and got to know somewhat. The son of a gun still has not told us the truth. He has lied about his involvement back in the '60s, as far as I can tell. He failed the polygraph test, and he lied under hypnosis. Barbara Walker passed. John Walker failed [the polygraph] also. So, I think Arthur was involved in the '60s. We don't know what damage he committed back then. He hasn't told the truth.
>
> As to John Walker, I don't think he has told the complete truth, either. I'm confident he has lied about his brother's involvement. He may have lied about other things. John attempted to destroy his entire family through the espionage business and did a pretty good job of it.

I asked Tommy to comment on his feelings regarding Art's sentence and "post-cold-war leniency":

> We still do not know the full damage done to the country by these people. I'm a believer [in] punishment as a form of deterrence, and if these people—John, Arthur, and Jerry—die in a federal penitentiary, perhaps that will deter some people from getting in the espionage game in the future. Arthur, John, and Jerry should die in a federal penitentiary. They should be shown no mercy.

Rob Seidel, the co-prosecutor of Arthur, is now executive assistant U.S. attorney in Norfolk. He spoke with me about his recollections in January 1997. Rob told me that when he looks back, it is with a sense of accomplishment: "I have a great sense of public service, to have been part of the prosecution of Arthur Walker. This case was one of the highlights of my career as a professional prosecutor." He continued:

> I got a lot of satisfaction in getting Arthur's conviction, and in having the opportunity to work with a lot of great people.
>
> Art was the first of the group to be tried, so we wanted to be well prepared, and we were. We wanted to do everything right so he'd be nailed, and he was.
>
> I remember sleeping only four to six hours a night while preparing and during the trial. We worked all hours of the day, night, and

weekends. Everyone worked as a team. The trial was flawless. I wouldn't do a thing differently if I had the case today. It was a lot of work, but frankly, our job as prosecutors was very easy: the FBI did a great job of putting the case together.

Rob recalled Art's decision to be tried by the judge, without a jury: "One of the reasons Art waived a trial by jury was that the case was so well put together, there was no defense. His attorneys could not have passed the 'red-face test' in front of a jury."

The case we presented at Art's trial was instrumental in John's and Michael's decision to plead guilty and sign a plea agreement with the government. Seidel remembered that aspect: "We were able to go back and recreate the whole background of the case: what John Walker had done, and what the FBI did. It's so rare nowadays to see a surveillance work so flawlessly. What we laid out in Art's trial, John Walker couldn't ignore."

I asked Rob what were the most memorable moments of the trial for him:

One of the most memorable aspects of the case for me was when Judge Clarke returned to the bench and pronounced multiple life sentences on Arthur. Judge Clarke talked about the fact that Arthur had been a lieutenant commander in the Navy, had known about John's espionage for so long, and had not reported it. Those comments certainly gave the sense of Art's lack of character, that he would betray his country like that.

What did Rob think about the talk of leniency for Art?

It really upsets me when I hear people calling for leniency for people convicted of espionage during the cold war. Especially when they talk about Art. There was an article by a staff writer in the local newspaper some time ago [the *Virginian Pilot–Ledger Star*, 21 May 1995] in which the writer depicted Arthur as a relic of the cold war. Nothing could be further from the truth. To say that Arthur was somehow innocently caught up in John's espionage business is ridiculous.

Before people make statements like "Art's a relic of the cold war," they need to look at the facts, and not just at some rumpled bald guy in a prison cell in Terre Haute. The reporter who wrote the story works for the local paper. It's a ten-minute walk. If he wanted the facts, he could have come in and talked to me.

Let's face it: John could not have been successful had it not been for Arthur. If he had a conscience, if he had character, and if he wasn't interested in money and selling out his country, he would have turned John in.

There's no way that a guy with twenty years' experience in the U.S. Navy, and with his background and expertise, couldn't have appreciated the significance of what he and John were doing. He's not a stupid person.

Arthur's not a relic. He's a criminal, a spy, and a liar. No, I have no sympathy. I hope he never gets paroled. People like [the Walkers] need to serve their full sentences.

I just hope, as time goes on and memories fade, that the truth isn't smothered. People need to realize these are dangerous individuals who got convicted, and all of them did a lot of damage to the country. We are just very fortunate we were not in a situation where the information they passed to the Soviets would have proved critical.

As a postscript, I remember very well the article Rob Seidel was talking about. One day in the spring of 1995, a writer for the local Norfolk newspaper called me and asked if he could come by and interview me for an article he was doing on the tenth anniversary of the Walker case. I agreed, and he showed up a few days later.

We got a glass of iced tea and went out onto the deck to do the interview. I knew I was in trouble when one of the first questions he asked was whether I thought Arthur had received a fair sentence for his crimes. After a few minutes of talking with this reporter, it was quite apparent to me that he knew nothing about the facts of the case. We spent about two hours together, most of which involved me trying to give him a factual history of the case, although he really didn't seem to be interested in the facts. It became increasingly obvious that this fellow was doing an article about how Art had been mistreated by the U.S. government. I tried to be congenial but finally told him that I had taken the same oath of allegiance to our country when I joined the FBI that Art took when he was an officer in the Navy, and he had betrayed that oath. Then I said, "I say, screw 'im." As soon as those words came out of my mouth, I knew I would see them in a prominent spot in the paper. Sure enough, when the article came out, describing Arthur as a victim and a relic of the cold war, there was my picture with a bold caption underneath: "Hunter says 'Screw 'im!'"

22

"D" Is for Jerry

On 11 May 1984, six months before Barbara Walker told us about John, the San Francisco FBI office received an envelope postmarked 8 May 1984, Sacramento, California. Inside was a letter that turned out to be an intriguing twist in the Walker case. The letter read:

MAY 7, 1984
RUS / SOMEWHERE USA

AGENT IN CHARGE / FBI
450 GOLDEN GATE AVE. / SAN FRANCISCO, CA 94118

Dear Sir:

I have been involved in espionage for several years, specifically; I've passed along Top Secret Cryptographic Keylists for military communications, Tech Manuals for same, Intelligence Messages, and etc.

I didn't know that the info was being passed to the USSR until after I had been involved for a few years and since then I've been remoreseful [sic] and wished to be free. Finally I've decided to stop supplying material—my contact doesn't know of my decision. Originally I was told I couldn't get out without approval, this was accompanied by threats. Since then I believe the threats were a bluff.

*At any rate the reason for this letter is to give you (FBI) an oppor-
tunity to break what is brobably [sic] a significant espionage system.
(I know that my contact has recruited at least three other members
that are actively supplying highly classified material). (I have the
confidence of my contact).*

*I pass the material to my contact (a US citizen) who in turn passes
the material to a contact overseas (his actual status—KGB or
whatever—I don't know). That is not always the case tho, sometimes
US locations are used. A US location is always used to receive
instructions and money.*

*If you are interested in this matter you can signal me with an Ad
in the Los Angeles Times Classified Section under "Personal Messages (1225)". What I would expect to cooperate is complete immunity from prosecution and absolutely no public disclosure of me or
my identity. I will look for an Ad in Monday editions only for the next
four weeks. Also, I would desire some expense funds depending on
the degree that my livelihood is interrupted.*

*The Ad: Start with "RUS:", followed by whatever message you
desire to pass. If your message is not clear I'll send another letter. If
I decide to cooperate you will hear from me via an attorney. Otherwise nothing further will happen.*

*Sincerely,
Rus*

The San Francisco office opened an investigation and ran an ad
in the *Los Angeles Times* on Monday, 21 May, asking "RUS" to call.
He didn't call, but another letter was received a few days later. It
was addressed the same as the first letter and was postmarked 23
May 1984, Sacramento. The second letter read:

MAY 21, 1984
"RUS" / SOMEWHERE USA

AGENT IN CHARGE / FBI
450 GOLDEN GATE AVE. / SAN FRANCISCO, CA 94118

Dear Sir:

*I saw your note today and was encouraged, however, I'm not going
to call for obvious reasons. I'll admit that my most earnest desire is
to talk to someone (like yourself) about my situation, but I feel that*

I'm unable to trust any kind of personal contact—phone included. Nor have I begun to look for an attorney. Where does that leave us or more specifically me?

I'll be very open. It took me several months to finally write the first letter. Yes, I'm remorseful and I feel that to come forward and help break the espionage ring would compensate for my wrong doing, consequently clearing my conscience. But there are other emotions: the difficulty of ratting on a "friend", and the potential of getting caught up in a legal mess (public disclosure of my involvement and a possible double-cross on immunity, assuming it was granted in the first place).

I would guess that you are conferring with higher authority and possibly other agencies. I'm wondering if my situation is really considered serious enough to warrant investigation and to give me due consideration (immunity & etc.)!

I'm going to begin looking for an attorney, which will be tricky from my view, to discuss my situation. And I will keep an eye on the LA Times, Monday editions, for any additional word/instructions from you.

It would certainly be nice for people in my predicament to have a means of confidential consultation with someone in a position of authority without the possibility of arrest.

My contact will be expecting more material from me in a few months, if I don't I'm not sure what his response will be. I'm going to come clean with him at that time (assuming no deal is made with you) and tell him I'm finished with the "business". And then get on with my life.

More info on him: he has been in the "business" for more than 20 years and plans to continue indefinitely. He thinks he has a good organization and has no real fear of being caught, less some coincidental misfortune; in that regard he feels safe also. I agree with his assessment.

Why haven't I discussed my desire to come clean (with you) with my contact and/or possibly convince him to do the same? It would be sure folly—dangerous to my health.

Sincerely,
RUS

San Francisco's efforts to identify "RUS" and to persuade him to meet with an agent intensified, but to no avail. They placed another ad in the *Los Angeles Times* and received a brief note from "RUS" postmarked 18 June 1984, San Jose, California:

FM: RUS
TO: AGENT IN CHARGE / FBI, SAN FRANCISCO

Sir:

I won't be meeting you the 21st. A letter will follow in a week or two.

The note was not signed.

The agents in San Francisco were doing everything possible to find out who was sending those letters. The letters were photocopies of typewritten pages. They had no fingerprints on them. All efforts to identify the author of the letters failed.

A fourth and final letter was received at the San Francisco FBI office, postmarked 13 August 1984, Sacramento:

AUGUST 13, 1984
RUS / SOMEWHERE, USA

AGENT IN CHARGE / FBI
450 GOLDEN GATE AVE. / SAN FRANCISCO, CA 94118

Dear Sir:

I saw your note in todays LA Times. Since my last note to you I've done a lot of serious thinking and have pretty much come to the conclusion that it would be best to give up on the idea of aiding in the termination of the espionage ring previously discussed.

To think I could help you and not make my own involvement known to the public, I believe is naive. Nor have I contacted an attorney. I have great difficulty in coming forth, particularly, since the chances of my past involvement ever being known is extremely remote, as long as I remain silent.

Yes, I can still say I would prefer to get it off my chest, to come clean.

The above notwithstanding, I'll think about a meeting in Ensenada. Funds are not the problem.

My contact is pressing for more material, but so far no real problems have occurred. I haven't explicitly told him, I'm no longer in the business.

Sincerely,

...

Although FBI San Francisco ran three more ads in the *Los Angeles Times* in April 1985, no more letters were received from "RUS."

All of the "RUS" letters were written before Barbara Walker came forward. I had no idea they existed until we opened our case on John Walker and I started sending information about him to FBI Headquarters. All of that information was given to Jim Milburn and Gary Heinz in the Analytical Unit of the Intelligence Division. In May 1985, before we followed and arrested John, Milburn and Heinz came to Norfolk to talk with us. Milburn, in his usual understated manner, told us about the "RUS" letters and said he believed that Jerry Whitworth had written them. It was a wonderful piece of analytical work, and as it turned out, Milburn was right on the money.

We called Bill Smits, supervisor of the San Francisco FCI Squad, and told him about Milburn's theory, and he finally began to show some interest in covering the leads I had been sending them. Within a day or two they had determined that Jerry Alfred Whitworth and his wife, Brenda Reis, were living in Davis, California.

For reasons unknown to me, San Francisco, under Smits's leadership, did not keep me informed of what they were doing in the investigation of Whitworth. Occasionally agents in the larger FBI offices would develop an attitude that they were closer to the action, worked bigger and more important cases, and were the "real agents" in the FBI, as opposed to the guys like us in the smaller offices. There was no way a little place like Norfolk could have any work that would compare in importance with theirs, and we couldn't possibly know how to work a complicated case. Bill Smits displayed those attitudes in spades.

In late 1985 Jim Kolouch, Bill Buckley, Mike Schatzow, and I took the evidence we had in our case to San Francisco to aid in preparations for Jerry's trial. I clearly recall going into Smits's office to meet him. He didn't even look up from what was obviously some very important paperwork. Thank goodness his attitude didn't rub off on Agents John Peterson and Bob Griego, the two guys most responsible for putting together the case against Jerry.

. . .

Jerry Whitworth was born in a farmhouse in Sequoyah County, Oklahoma, on 10 August 1939. He apparently never knew his natural father and didn't get along with his stepfather. He was raised by his mother and his grandmother.

At Jerry's trial, Thomas Francis Bennett, master chief petty officer, U.S. Navy, testified regarding Jerry's naval career. The following summary of Jerry's duty assignments is culled from the transcript of Bennett's testimony.

Jerry Whitworth joined the Naval Reserve on 17 September 1956, at age seventeen. My understanding is that a reserve enlistment was usually for a period of six years, with two years on active duty, then two years of weekly or monthly meetings, then two years in inactive reserve status. Sometime during the period when Jerry was supposed to be attending meetings, he missed too many and as punishment was placed on active duty. He was sent to the Great Lakes Naval Training Center for two weeks and then to the USS *Bon Homme Richard* as a storekeeper.

After two years of active duty, Jerry could have been released back to reserve status. Instead, he reenlisted for four years and transferred to the naval training unit at Alameda, California. Two years later he reenlisted for six years, with the guarantee that he would go to Radioman's Class A School in Maryland, a six-month school. He graduated in April 1966, in the top 25 percent of his class.

From "A" School he went to Company Air Control Squadron in San Diego and in February 1967 was transferred to the Tactical Control Squadron. In April 1967 he was promoted to radioman second class and went to Radioman Class B School in San Diego for nine months of intensive electronics training. He graduated fifth out of nine students.

Jerry then attended a five-week Computer Systems Technician Controller School, where he learned to test and repair communication systems. After graduation he transferred to the USS *Arlington,* a communications ship, as transmitter supervisor. He stayed there until 1969. In April 1969, when he was promoted to first-class petty officer, he was transferred to the USS *Ranger,* an aircraft carrier out of Alameda. He was supervisor in charge of facilities communications in 1970, when he asked for shore duty and extended his enlistment for eight months to get it.

He went to Petty Officers Leadership School and then to Radio Class A Instructors School, and became an instructor in "A" School at the San Diego Naval Training Center. This is where he was in 1971, when he met John Walker.

Walker was transferred to the USS *Niagara Falls* out of Alameda in December 1971. John and Jerry became friends. According to John, this is when he began to evaluate Jerry as a possible recruit into the espionage business. Jerry and John kept in touch while they were on their separate assignments, and they saw each other when they could.

Jerry volunteered for a new naval communications outpost on Diego Garcia, an atoll in the Indian Ocean, where he was put in charge of the Technical Control Center. He stayed there two years, came back to the United States, and was discharged in June 1974.

Meanwhile, John received a commendation at the naval training center for simplifying the handling of communications security (COMSEC) training material and for developing a COMSEC control and accounting system for a cryptographic system used at the center known as the KI-1A. He photographed the technical manual for that very system and sold the film to the Soviets.

Jerry stayed in the San Diego area after his discharge, and he and John got together several times during the summer of 1974. It was during this period, when Jerry wasn't even in the Navy, that John Walker recruited him as a spy.

After four months of civilian life, having been recruited by John, Jerry reenlisted in the Naval Reserve. A month later he left the reserves and reenlisted in the regular Navy for four more years. He went directly to a five-week Satellite Communications School. After his graduation in February 1975, he stopped in Norfolk to see John. During this visit they finalized their agreement to be partners in espionage. John paid Jerry $4,000 in advance to solidify the deal.

After SATCOM School, Jerry was sent back to Diego Garcia, where he filled the billet of a senior chief petty officer, even though he was only a first-class PO. His duties were to ensure that naval satellite communications were conducted correctly. He was the supervisor of the communications area and had access to everything having to do with communications. It was at this duty station that Jerry began photographing classified encryption key lists and other valuable information for John Walker.

In June 1976 Jerry was transferred to the USS *Constellation,* an aircraft carrier, where he became the supervisor in charge of facilities control. He had total control and responsibility for ensuring that all of the on-board communication systems ran correctly. He was responsible for protecting the cryptographic material and for destroying outdated material. He had almost unlimited access to information and material of tremendous value to our enemies. He was promoted to chief petty officer in October 1977 while on board the *Constellation.*

In August 1978 Jerry was transferred to the USS *Niagara Falls.* He held the same position John had held a couple of years earlier on that ship: they both served as chief radioman, leading chief, and COMSEC custodian. The COMSEC custodian was the only person on the ship allowed to be in the code vault alone. As a supply ship, the *Falls* had to have information regarding the schedules, whereabouts, and status of all of the ships in the fleet that it serviced. Those requirements made it necessary to carry more crypto information than most of the other ships in the fleet.

This assignment was productive for John and Jerry, as it gave each of them opportunity to steal nearly 100 percent of crypto key and other valuable material. They each received $4,000 to $6,000 per month from the KGB during their tours on the *Falls.*

After his tour on the USS *Niagara Falls* was over, Jerry requested shore duty and was sent to the Naval Communications Center at Alameda, where he served as chief petty officer in charge of the Naval Training Communications Center (NTCC). Once again he had access to a wealth of cryptographic material. He was promoted to senior chief petty officer in May 1981 while at the NTCC. He had considered retiring in 1980 but changed his mind—most probably so that he could receive his promotion to senior chief and increase his monthly retirement income. Once he got the promotion, he was obligated to stay on active duty another two years.

While assigned to the NTCC, Jerry served a couple of temporary assignments at the Naval Communications Station at Stockton, California, where he assisted in installing a new communications system and trained people to operate it. He completed his tour of duty at Alameda and finished his career on the aircraft carrier USS *Enterprise,* where he once again was the chief radioman on board. In October 1983 Jerry Whitworth retired from the Navy without telling John Walker.

My theory about why Jerry wrote the "RUS" letters in 1984 is that he had a stash of stolen documents in his residence and passed photographs of them to John on a piecemeal basis after his retirement until he began to run out of them. He knew that his espionage income was coming to an end, so he started to try to figure out ways to avoid ever being prosecuted. What better way than to turn on your partner and "rat him out" in return for immunity from prosecution? I don't think Jerry would have ever written those letters had he stayed in the Navy and been able to continue selling out his country.

During the debriefings of John Walker in late 1985, I asked him to describe his recruitment of Jerry. John said he began to consider recruiting a partner in his espionage scheme in late 1970 or early 1971. He planned to retire from the Navy in July 1976 and wanted to have someone in place who could furnish him classified crypto material so that he could continue his lucrative espionage business.

He explained that everyone in the Navy who held a security clearance had to undergo an updated background check every five years. When he (Walker) had come due for an update in 1970, he felt he couldn't pass a background check. By then he had been in the espionage business for three years, and Barbara was getting drunk and telling friends and relatives what he was doing. He felt certain that his activities would be discovered during a background investigation and that he wouldn't be able to pass the test of investigators digging into his lifestyle. So he falsified the document that indicated that the background had been done. John had a rubber stamp made to match the "real" one used to show that the National Agency checks had been completed, stamped his own paper, forged his superior officer's signature, and put it in his own personnel file. No one noticed.

John figured he couldn't get away with falsifying another security clearance document and he wouldn't get through a real update, so he planned to retire in five years, when his next update came due.

The way John tells it, he began to consider recruiting Jerry as a spy within three months of meeting him. John and Barbara were having marital problems, and he was not spending much time at home. While they were in "A" School, he and Jerry went sailing every weekend they could. John learned as much about him as he could; he was looking for weaknesses in Jerry's character. Jerry told him he had been divorced for three years but hadn't told the Navy so that he could continue to collect quarters allowance. John and Jerry also smoked pot together. John quickly learned that Jerry was willing to ignore or bend the rules. They talked a lot, and John repeatedly steered the conversation to crime and the law so that he could study Jerry's reaction.

John decided to try to recruit Jerry after they saw *Easy Rider,* a 1969 movie about two friends who commit a crime and go on a motorcycle trip together using the proceeds. When John asked Jerry what he thought about the movie, Jerry told him he would be willing to commit a crime if the stakes were high enough. John told me, "That's when I knew I had Jerry—because he had larceny in his heart."

In late summer 1974 Jerry was out of the Navy and John was just off the USS *Niagara Falls.* It was then that John decided to make his pitch to Jerry, and he took him to their favorite restaurant, Boom Trenchard's Flare Path Restaurant at Lindbergh Field in San Diego. They sat at a table in a secluded part of the place, out of earshot of the other patrons. John told Jerry he was interested in using him in something illegal—even discussing it was illegal. If Jerry wanted to hear about it, John would tell him; if not, he would never mention it again, and that would be it. As John tells it, Jerry was excited and wanted to hear more. Then John made Jerry swear a blood oath that he would not turn John in if, after hearing what John had to say, Jerry didn't want to get involved. Finally, John told Jerry he had been selling classified material for a number of years, he had made a lot of money, and he wanted Jerry to join him in the business.

Jerry asked who the buyers were, and John told him he wasn't sure, but they were allied countries such as Israel, or private organizations like Jane's. They discussed various aspects of his espionage business, such as the money to be made, the small risk of being caught, and how one went about stealing the material. Jerry was excited at what he had heard. John said Jerry was proud to be asked to work with him.

That was the start of a nine-year period during which Jerry Whitworth and John Walker furnished so much critical U.S. defense information to the Soviets that, according to Vitaly Yurchenko, a highly placed KGB officer who defected to the United States in mid-1985, the Soviets would have annihilated our navy inside of two weeks had we gone to war.

Within a few days of John's arrest, the contents of the "Dear Friend" letter we had found in John's package became public. The media frantically tried to find out who "S," "K," "F," and "D" were. With the arrests of Michael and Arthur, the identities of "S" and "K" became known, but "D" remained a mystery for a couple of weeks while San Francisco tried to gather enough evidence to persuade the U.S. Department of Justice to allow them to arrest Jerry.

After a period of intense investigation, San Francisco received authorization to make the arrest. They made arrangements through an attorney for Jerry Whitworth to turn himself in on 3 June 1985, and the identity of "D" was revealed to the world.

23

Were Others Involved?

By 3 June 1985, five months after the case was opened, we had all four major players in jail. That doesn't mean we were sitting back basking in the glory of it all; not by a long shot. I had miles to go before this case was over.

John's arrest dissolved the need for discretion and stealth. Now it was time to talk to the man's friends and associates.

First on my list was "F," John's half-brother, Gary Walker. Gary was assigned to a helicopter squadron at the Norfolk Naval Air Station, so he wasn't hard to find. After a quick but thorough investigation of his background, we interviewed and polygraphed him and were convinced that he had never played a part in John's espionage activities. Later, during the debriefings, John told us he had tried a very soft recruitment approach on Gary not too long before his arrest. He recalled one day when he and Gary were talking about finances. It was obvious to John that Gary was having a rough time. John told Gary he had a way to make some money, but it was illegal; Gary should let him know if he was interested. Gary never asked to hear more about the scheme. John said he designated Gary as "F" in his "Dear Friend" letter and put the information about him in the letter to "puff up" the size

145

of his spy ring. He wanted to give the Soviets the impression that he had Gary under development, when in fact he didn't.

When we searched John's house after his arrest, we found two documents that referred to someone designated as "A." We questioned John extensively regarding the identity of "A," and he said he wasn't certain who he had meant. He emphatically denied that there ever was anyone called "A" in his espionage ring. One of the documents—a calendar, as I recall—contained the notation "Meet A." John said that in that instance he thought "A" stood for his brother Arthur. The other reference to "A" was on a page of notes found in John's den. John's explanation was that he himself was "A" in that instance; he would occasionally refer to himself as "A" when making notations regarding his espionage business.

A few days after we arrested John, a bizarre story appeared in the Norfolk newspaper. A woman named Roberta K. Puma said she had gone to Rockville, Maryland, with John in the spring of 1977 and, following written instructions and photographs he gave her, put a plastic bag by the side of a country road after dark. Puma had a master's degree in English from Old Dominion University and was a freelance writer.

When we talked with Roberta Puma, she told us her story. She had met John in the mid-1970s and had managed an apartment house he owned in the Willoughby section of Norfolk. One day John approached her and offered to pay her $500 if she would go to northern Virginia with him and help him with something he was working on. She thought it over and a couple of days later told him she would go.

They drove to Rockville, the same town where Walker's parents had been married in August 1934. They checked into the Ramada Inn, the same place we were to arrest John eight years later. Then they went out into the country. John gave her some written instructions and pictures with arrows pointing to areas where she was to look for soft-drink cans. (She saved these instructions and photographs and later gave them to us.) After they made the dry run and John had taught her what to do, they rented another car.

When it got dark, John gave Puma a walkie-talkie and told her to drive his car. He took the rental. Puma said she ran through the procedure as instructed, placed the plastic bag—she said she had no idea what was in it—by the side of the road, and went back to the hotel. John met her there later. He wanted to spend the night, but she insisted that they go home, so they drove back to Norfolk.

John dropped her off and gave her an envelope containing her pay. When Puma opened the envelope, she found $1,500 in it. The next day, when she called John and told him he had overpaid her, he came and took back $1,000.

A short time after the episode in Rockville, John asked Puma if she would be willing to spend some time in jail for $10,000; he didn't say what she would have to do for the money. When she told him no, he increased the amount of jail time and money. She told him she wouldn't go to jail for any amount of money.

Puma said she had gone to the newspaper after hearing of John's arrest in order to get her story out into the open so that others who might have been used by him in the same way would come forward. She said she felt betrayed and angry that John would have put her at risk by getting her involved in his illegal activity.

John later told us that Roberta Puma's story was true. He considered her to be stupid and spoke about her in a disparaging way. He said he used her to drop his package for the Soviets because he thought the FBI was on to him. He had come home one evening, a few days before his scheduled drop, and discovered that the window in his den was open about two inches. His immediate thought was that the FBI had come in and searched his desk. He went through his things and nothing was missing, but he still felt uncomfortable about the situation. He asked Puma to go with him and had her fill the drop while he hid nearby and watched to see who came to get the Soviets' package. As he watched, a car stopped and someone got out and grabbed the package. When he felt that it was safe, he went and got the package the Soviets had left for him.

After giving it further thought, John said, he decided that it wasn't FBI agents who had opened his window and gone through his desk;

it was the young daughter of his father and stepmother, who had been visiting him.

In 1975 John began dating Mamie Patsy Marsee. She worked as a secretary at the Armed Forces Staff College at the Norfolk Naval Base. The Staff College is a highly regarded military training school where the best and brightest military officers from all branches of our military services, as well as officers from the services of the NATO countries, hone their skills in preparation for advancement through the ranks.

John was introduced to Patsy Marsee by a woman who had worked for him at his previous duty assignment in the Navy, not long before he and Barbara separated. Patsy was definitely John's type; she loved to party and didn't ask too many questions.

Patsy always maintained that she didn't know that John was a spy, although she did say that one day he asked her what she thought about selling classified material to the Soviets, saying it would be easy to get into it. When she asked him about the large amount of money he always had, he told her he had connections in the Mafia and was involved in the amusement machine business—jukeboxes, pinball machines, and the like.

One of Patsy's tasks at the Staff College was to type the students' term papers. These were usually unclassified papers on theoretical military matters, although occasionally something did involve classified material. She would take the papers home to proofread, and she let John read them. Occasionally they would talk about them. She claimed that she never gave any of the papers to John to copy but admitted that there were times when he might have had an opportunity to make copies.

Patsy traveled extensively with John. In the late summer of 1977 he arranged to fly her to Casablanca to meet him. That evening he made an excuse to her about having some business to tend to and went out. In fact he was going to meet with his Soviet handler; it would be their first face-to-face meeting in ten years.

John's instructions from the Soviets for this meeting included some spycraft that sounded like something out of a bad movie. He was to stand on a certain street corner in Casablanca with a *Time* magazine in one hand. His contact would greet him with "Didn't I meet you in Berlin in 1976?" And John was to reply, "No, I was in Norfolk, Virginia, that hectic year." John had received a delivery of several rolls of film of classified material from Jerry in Hong Kong a day or so before, which he passed to his KGB handler. In her statements to us, Patsy claimed that she did not know what John did while he was out that night, nor did she notice the odd rolls of film or the extraordinary amount of cash John had when he returned from his meeting. He had been paid $25,000 for material he furnished in a previous dead drop.

Patsy also went with John to visit Jerry and Brenda Whitworth in California several times. She said John and Jerry always spent some time alone together during those visits. John confirmed that he and Jerry would conduct their spy business during those times; Jerry would hand over film he had taken of classified materials since their last meeting, and John would pay him for the material he had previously given.

John and Patsy went on extensive trips in his single-engine plane. They went to Central America, Peru, Mexico, and California—all pleasure trips, according to John, except when they would visit Jerry Whitworth. Patsy recalled going to Washington with John on several occasions but denied ever taking part in drop activities with him.

John and Patsy broke up in 1981, when, according to him, she started demanding more of a commitment than he was willing to give. He said he considered Patsy to be in the early stage of recruitment when they broke up. He denied ever having used her in any of his espionage activities.

Barry Colvert polygraphed Patsy Marsee on 24 and 29 May 1985. She failed all of the questions relevant to her knowledge of or participation in John's espionage activities, hired an attorney, and was not available to us for further interviews.

June Laureen Robinson went to work for John at his detective agency in Virginia Beach in 1982 and became his business partner when his original partner, Phil Prince, pulled out of the business a short time later. They were a perfect match. She had worked as a nude dancer in a bar in the D.C. area and had been married for a short time to a man from Iran.

Laurie had had some minor scrapes with the law, but no major problems in that regard. She was a tall, slender brunette and had obviously been quite attractive in her prime. But life had apparently been hard on her, and when we interviewed her, she was starting to show the wear.

Laurie traveled to the D.C. area with John on a couple of occasions that they both said had to do with their detective business. Barry Colvert put Laurie on the polygraph on 19 June 1985, and she too failed all of the relevant questions, got a lawyer, and became unavailable for further interviews regarding her knowledge of or participation in John's espionage business. Twelve years later Colvert said he could still remember how intolerable Laurie smelled when she left the room after the test.

Pamela Kay "P.K." Carroll was in her early twenties when she went to work for John at Confidential Reports, around the same time as Laurie did. She was a slender blonde with blue eyes and a perky personality. She had been in the Navy and worked shore-patrol duty in Norfolk before her enlistment ended. P.K. quickly became romantically involved with John and eventually moved in with him. She left the detective agency in 1984 for a job with the Norfolk Police Department but continued to be John's lover until we arrested him.

P.K. also traveled extensively with John, including trips to visit the Whitworths in California. She was still in her first year as a probationary officer when we arrested him. She was fired for having given John information from police files. We interviewed her preliminarily, but she quickly hired an attorney and never was available to us for extensive interviews or polygraph.

Another of John's paramours was Jimi Elizabeth Thomas Muscovak. She met John in the late 1960s, within a year or so after he began his spy career. Jimi was a student at Old Dominion University at the time and loved to smoke, drink, and party. She was just what the doctor ordered for John. He was, of course, still married to Barbara at the time. Jimi later married and divorced a Navy buddy of John's.

After John's arrest, Jimi said she had had no idea John was a spy. She said he had explained his abundance of cash by telling her he was in the Mafia, a revelation that didn't bother her in the least. Jimi said she traveled with John on occasion, and she recalled a trip to Baltimore in 1968 or 1969 during which John left her alone at their hotel for several hours while he went out on business. John later confirmed that he had taken Jimi to Baltimore, where they stayed at a Holiday Inn that had a revolving restaurant on the top floor. He left Jimi at the hotel while he went out and filled a drop with the Soviets. After he returned to the hotel, he and Jimi went out and visited the strip joints not far from the hotel.

Jimi, a single parent of a young daughter, eventually she got her doctorate from ODU in school administration. She worked for me briefly in the City of Virginia Beach Public School System's antidrug program after I retired from the Bureau. From what I could tell, her approach to life hadn't changed much since the days she was sleeping with John Walker.

After the books on this case started coming out and Jimi's role as one of John's lovers became known, she reassumed her maiden name, Jimi Elizabeth Thomas. At this writing she is shaping young minds as a teacher at a middle school in Virginia Beach. Apparently she moonlights as a roofer. One evening in November 1997, after a hailstorm had damaged many roofs in our neighborhood, there was a knock on our door. My wife answered, and a woman offered to inspect our roof for damage. She left her business card; it was Jimi Thomas.

A special federal grand jury was convened in Norfolk in January 1987 to examine what John's associates, other than those already arrested, knew about his espionage activities and to question whether he had money squirreled away somewhere. P.K. Carroll, Patsy Marsee, Laurie Robinson, Rachel Walker, and John and Barbara's daughter Margaret Walker were among those called to testify.

Nothing of any significance was learned from them during the grand jury process; there were no "smoking gun" revelations. But I did get a chance to talk to Margaret after her testimony. I hadn't met her before but was well aware that she was angry at the FBI. She had in fact told Agent Kevin Kenneally to get lost when he tried to interview her shortly after we arrested her dad. I ran into her in the courthouse hall after she left the grand jury room. We chatted for a moment. I asked her why she had never warned John that the FBI was on to him, since Barbara had told her during that ten-day April visit.

Margaret said, "Number one, I never really knew that my father was a spy. Number two, I figured if he had been, it was a long time ago. And number three, I figured you would never be able to prove it. So I just didn't tell him."

I really couldn't blame Margaret for being upset with us and with life in general. Look what happened to her when the Walker case broke: Her dad went to jail; her brother went to jail; her uncle Art went to jail. Her fiancé, a Navy lieutenant, dropped her like a hot potato. And within a few weeks she was fired from her job.

As we went through the records confiscated during the search of John's detective agency, we realized he had quite a number of Navy enlisted men and women on his payroll as part-time investigators. Was he using them in any way to assist him in his espionage business? The Naval Investigative Service, under Supervisory Special Agent Tom Boley, did a good job helping us locate and interview them. No information was ever developed that led me to believe that any of those people were knowingly involved in John's treachery. However, if they had happened to mention something useful to John, or to show him something he thought he could sell to the Soviets, he would have used it.

John said that he never used his Navy employees for his espionage business, but that he did use them to obtain information regarding other Navy people he was investigating in divorce or insurance fraud cases.

I can say with utmost confidence that we arrested and convicted all of the major players in John's espionage ring. I base my certainty on the fact that John Walker kept extensive notes and journals, KGB photos and instructions, and other data covering his entire espionage career. In the evidence recovered in the drop package and through the searches of John's properties, there were extensive references to each of his ring members—Jerry, Art, and Michael—and no mention of anyone else. If there had been anyone else involved with John, he would have had a record of it. History may prove me wrong, but I don't think so.

On the other hand, I think it is quite likely that John used others to help him from time to time, as he did Roberta Puma. We may never know about all the people he used.

I find it hard to believe that people close to him, like P.K. Carroll, Patsy Marsee, and Laurie Robinson, didn't have an inkling of what he was up to. P.K. was a police officer. She lived with him. Are we to believe that she lived in John's house but never saw any of the classified documents or KGB instructions, never asked John about the source of his income, and had no idea what he was doing?

Laurie Robinson was John's confidante. He loved to impress her. They traveled to D.C. together. Why did she fail the polygraph?

Patsy Marsee was John's steady girlfriend. She had a security clearance, had been briefed regarding the handling of classified material, and worked for the military. Yet she took work home with her and made it available to John. I find it hard to believe she didn't know what he was doing for the six years they were together. She too failed the polygraph.

All of that said, we never had enough evidence to consider bringing charges against anyone other than the four major players. Even if P.K., Patsy, and Laurie knew what John was up to, that doesn't make them participants in his espionage scheme.

I do have to note that none of these people ever came to the authorities about John. It seems that so many of John's friends and relatives just didn't have the character to come forward and tell the truth.

24

N.I.S.

During my twenty-three years of contact with the Naval Investigative Service, I reached the conclusion that it was one screwed-up outfit. In part this is because of the way it was set up: the NIS was an organization of civilian investigators led by military officers, and this created a whole set of problems. First, NIS agents primarily investigated crimes involving Navy people. This was an awkward arrangement, since the head of NIS, a naval officer, had a less-than-impartial interest in what happened "on his watch." Second, NIS agents worked under the command of military officers who had no experience in investigations. To make matters worse, these officers often seemed to have their own agendas. In general, naval officers seemed to have little respect for NIS agents. They were often uncooperative and showed more interest in protecting their careers than in seeing justice done. The end result was that NIS agents had no real authority and very little latitude in working cases.

Since they were military-led, NIS agents had to drop everything and respond posthaste if a local Navy officer called to report some problem in his outfit. No matter how important the case the agent was working on at the time, if that call came in, he had to drop everything and respond. It was nearly impossible for an NIS agent to focus on a case long enough to resolve it. It was maddening to watch. When I wasn't aggravated with them, I felt sorry for those agents.

Another serious flaw in the NIS system was the agent training—or lack of it. NIS agents had far too little training. In fact, new agents were often put on the street conducting investigations before they had received any training at all. It just didn't work. What training they did receive was inadequate. Many of the agents seemed to have no sense of how to conduct a logical, thorough investigation.

I clearly remember one case I worked with NIS. It involved working with a civilian employee of the Navy in a matter that is still classified; the subject of the case isn't important here. Since the case involved a matter of interest to the Navy, NIS had to be involved. The civilian had agreed to help us out, but NIS regulations required that he be polygraphed before his cooperation could be accepted. Well, the poor guy kept showing deception on the polygraph tests given by the NIS polygraph examiner. After a couple of hours, the examiner finally got the man to admit that he had fondled his dog when he was a young boy and was too mortified to admit it during the first hours of testing. I was embarrassed for the guy—and upset with the NIS examiner for asking "lifestyle" questions that had nothing to do with the matter at hand. The man was offering to help us out, not train the Navy K-9 corps. Not long after that experience, NIS stopped asking "lifestyle" questions on polygraph tests in cases like that one.

The FBI had primary jurisdiction in the Walker case. In other words, we were the lead investigative agency and were in charge of the investigation. As soon as we determined that Michael Walker was still on active duty, we were required to bring NIS into the case.

We emphasized how important it was to maintain the integrity of the discreet investigation we were conducting. NIS supervisor Tom Boley did a good job of keeping his troops under control until the case broke. We pressed for and got NIS's agreement not to conduct any investigations or interviews without clearing them through us first.

Boley also did a good job of arranging for Agent Keith Hitt to get the information he needed to confront Michael on board the USS

Nimitz without going through the usual communication channels, which would have probably alerted Michael to our interest in him, since he worked in the *Nimitz* communications center.

I must say, however, that in other ways NIS lived up to my greatest fears during the Walker investigation. An example: One day their agents came into our office with a list of approximately two hundred people they had identified as having probably known John in the Navy. Dan McNally, my liaison man with NIS during the investigation, picked out a name from the list and asked what connection the man had with Walker. The NIS agents explained that he was a naval officer and had attended a cocktail party where John was present many years ago; they wanted to go find and interview the guy. I told McNally it sounded good to me; they should locate and interview every person on the list and then advise us of the results. They never turned up a single piece of useful information. A colossal waste of time.

After John and Michael Walker signed the plea agreements, NIS liaison Alan Sipe came to Baltimore for the debriefings. He was present at most of the sessions we had with John and Michael. Alan was a decent guy; I liked him. But one day we had a problem. We had interviewed Michael a number of times. He failed several questions on the polygraph regarding whether he had ever accompanied his dad on a dead drop and the extent of his wife's knowledge of his espionage activities. Jim Kolouch and I wanted to interview Michael without Sipe being there. It was nothing personal; it had simply been our experience that sometimes Navy guys had a hard time being completely relaxed and candid when an NIS agent was present. Perhaps they feared the "naval authority" NIS represented. We just wanted to give Michael a try with only two FBI guys present.

Sipe went ballistic and insisted on being in on the interview. We had quite an argument about it. Finally I told him that *we* would be doing the interview; he could sit outside the room, and I would report our results to him as soon as we were finished. He was really hot, but I didn't let him into the room. He never spoke to me again. Michael didn't give Kolouch and me anything new, either.

That was not a good day, but the crowning glory to NIS's part in the Walker investigation was yet to come.

It arrived in the person of a Navy enlisted man, Petty Officer Second Class Daniel Rivas Jr. Rivas had worked as a part-time investigator for John Walker at his detective agency in Virginia Beach for about a year, until the spring of 1984, when he was fired after being convicted in a court-martial for bugging the office where he worked at the control tower of the Norfolk Naval Air Station. I never completely understood why Rivas bugged the office, but I think he did it to see if he could get some embarrassing information on his bosses, who were giving him a hard time. For some reason he seemed to expect John to testify on his behalf, but John didn't, and he was found guilty. Since Rivas was in the Navy, it became the job of NIS to locate and interview him about his association with John. After his conviction, Rivas was transferred to Okinawa. NIS caught up with him there in late 1986.

By that time John and Michael had signed their plea agreements with the Department of Justice. John F. Lehman Jr., secretary of the Navy, was quite upset over the terms of the agreements. Secretary Lehman felt that the Department of Justice had let the Navy down and had negotiated a poor deal with the Walkers. Lehman's attitude flowed down through the Navy and into NIS. After all, ultimately they worked for Lehman. They were hell-bent on finding out something about John that we in the FBI didn't know, and possibly bringing additional charges against him. Rivas was just what they were looking for.

NIS brought Rivas back to the United States, and over the next couple of months he told them several astounding stories about John Walker. One such story was about the murder of a Navy enlisted woman named Pamela Kimbrue. She was a messenger who was killed in the wee hours of the morning on 25 March 1982 as she was delivering classified messages from the Breezy Point Communications Center on the Norfolk Naval Air Station. She was found in the back seat of her car, which had run off a ramp into the water not far from the com center. She had been beaten, sexually assaulted, and nearly strangled to death, but she had died of drowning.

A dark ski mask was found in the back seat of her car. Rivas told NIS that John Walker had told him that he (John) was responsible for Kimbrue's death and that he had unintentionally left Rivas's ski mask in her car. Rivas also said he had seen Kimbrue at John's house.

When NIS came to me with that story, I nearly choked on my cigar. I told them it didn't make any sense to me; they should put Rivas on the "box" (polygraph) right away and concentrate on people Kimbrue had worked with as suspects in her murder. I told them I didn't think John had the "heart" (criminal jargon for nerve) to murder anyone. On 26 June 1996 NIS arrested and charged one of Kimbrue's former co-workers, Richard H. Whittle, with her murder. He pled guilty and is now in prison.

Based upon information provided by their man Rivas, NIS tried to make a case against John for murdering another Navy enlisted woman. In the spring of 1983 Carol Ann Molnar's body washed up on the beach not too far from where John kept his houseboat in Norfolk. She had been shot. Molnar had worked in the same office at the Armed Forces Staff College as Patsy Marsee. She also danced in a couple of bars in the Ocean View section of Norfolk, where John went from time to time. Rivas told NIS he had seen John and Molnar together in a bar in the D.C. area. To my knowledge, that case has never been solved. No information was ever developed to tie John Walker to the murder.

One Saturday morning in early 1986, Joe Wolfinger called me at home and asked me to go to the NIS office with him to listen to a tape recording Rivas had given them. The tape turned out to be a recording of some disjointed conversation Rivas had had with Laurie Robinson, John's partner in the PI business, a day or so before.

It made very little sense and was of no value to the investigation of John or anyone else. There was some mention in the conversation of classified documents, and it was obvious that Rivas was trying to get Laurie to talk about them. It sounded to me like she had figured out that Rivas was taping their conversation. Rivas told NIS he had seen classified documents in Laurie's house. Once more I pressed NIS to put Rivas on the "box," but they continued to encourage his storytelling. I can only assume that they were under tremendous pressure to come up with something to pin on John.

Rivas told them one bizarre story about making a waterproof box for John so that he could hide valuables underwater in the Chesapeake Bay not too far from where he kept his houseboat. He also told them about a "safe house" John had in Ocean View, where he would debrief people he had rescued from cults. And then there was the story about John contacting him from jail, asking Rivas to help him escape. The list of revelations from Rivas seemed unending.

Then the NIS people called Wolfie and me to their office to look at a "classified message" from Michael to John "found" by Rivas. When we arrived, they told us Rivas had called them and told them he had found a Secret Navy message stuck in a chain link fence on the Navy base. He had asked them to meet him there early that morning, which they did. The NIS showed us this supposed Secret message. I don't recall the topic of the message, but it was obviously not a legitimate Navy message. Anyone with an ounce of sense could have told that it was a fake.

Once more Wolfinger and I told them to polygraph Rivas and stop wasting our time with his stories. They finally agreed, and Rivas blew the test off the charts. He ended up confessing that he had made up all of the stories he had told NIS, and that he himself had typed the "classified" message from Michael to John. They charged him with 111 counts of furnishing false information in an official investigation. One hundred eleven counts!

I do want to say that although some of the NIS agents I met couldn't have found their ass with both hands and a map, the majority of them were decent people, and they wanted to do a good job. It wasn't their fault they were working for a screwed-up outfit. My understanding is that now they have a top-notch organization. According to Rob Seidel, they now do a great job, and some sorely needed changes have been made. I hope so. The NIS employees—and we taxpayers—deserve it.

25

A Proffer, Preparations, and the Vienna Procedure

The summer of 1985 was hectic. The case took on a life of its own when we arrested John and Michael. We had to conduct as detailed an investigation into the activities of John, Michael, and Arthur as possible. This meant identifying and interviewing all of the Walkers' associates regarding their knowledge of the Walkers and their relationships with them. I set leads out for other FBI offices by telephone and followed my calls with a teletype, rather than a letter or airtel, as was normally done. When I was out of town or so busy that I couldn't do it all, Joe Wolfinger or other squad members pitched in to get the job done.

That was also the summer of our intense preparation for Art's trial (which took place in August) and the investigation of Jerry Whitworth out in California (of which I tried to keep abreast, with little success).

And, of course, John, Michael, and Arthur pursued all of the lawful remedies available to persons immersed in the federal criminal justice system. We had the federal grand jury in Baltimore for

John and Michael on 28 May and the grand jury for Art on 17 June. After each was indicted, there was an arraignment, at which time each one had the opportunity to enter a plea of guilty or not guilty. Each pled not guilty and was held without bond.

There were court hearings in Baltimore as John's and Mike's attorneys attempted to win various motions challenging our case. Similar hearings were held in Norfolk for Arthur's case. I was present at many of the hearings for John, Michael, and Arthur. None of the defense attorneys won a significant battle. We had built an airtight case against the Walkers.

Other interesting aspects of the story were unfolding. One of the reasons Barbara had turned John in was to help Laura get her young son Christopher back from her ex-husband, Philip Mark Snyder. It worked. Soon after John's arrest was announced to the world, Laura contacted Pat Robertson's Christian Broadcasting Network regarding her plight; she had become a born-again Christian. The folks at CBN were sympathetic. Laura came to Virginia Beach and met with officials of CBN, who wanted to interview her on the *700 Club* show.

Laura spoke with one of CBN's attorneys about getting Christopher back. Her main problem was that she didn't know Snyder's address. She called Mike Schatzow in the U.S. Attorney's Office in Baltimore and lied to him, saying she had lost the address, when in fact she had never had it. Mike gave her the address, and the CBN attorney arranged for her to have a car and $500. In mid-June, Laura and a friend drove to Lanham, Maryland.

The next morning they waited outside Snyder's apartment and watched as Christopher came out to play. They snatched him right out of the play area and headed back to Virginia Beach. Christopher was five years old at the time. It is my understanding that neither Laura nor Snyder had been given legal custody of Christopher after they separated; Snyder had just taken him, so Laura took him back.

Laura kept her part of the agreement and was interviewed on the *700 Club* within a day or two of their arrival back from Lanham. She met and was photographed with Pat Robertson. CBN got her an apartment in Virginia Beach and gave her a secretarial job, which she held for a couple of years. She worked hard, eventually got her nursing credential, and is working in that field today. Sadly, her home life hasn't fared as well. She remarried, had a daughter, and divorced. She remarried yet again not too long ago.

John was lodged in the Baltimore City Jail for a short period of time after his arrest. Later he was transferred to a cell in the Montgomery County Detention Center. Since there are no federal prisons in most U.S. cities, federal prisoners who are not out on bond awaiting prosecution are housed in local jails until their trial in federal court. The U.S. Marshals Service has contracts with many of the local jails and pays them an agreed amount per day to house federal prisoners. John was immensely disliked by his fellow inmates in the Baltimore and Montgomery County jails. I have been told by prison authorities that child molesters and spies are the two categories of criminals most hated by prison inmates.

Not long after he arrived at the Montgomery County Detention Center, John started working on a plan to escape. He discussed his plan with his cellmate and talked to his daughter Margaret about cashing in his life insurance policies to help fund his plot. He also called Laurie Robinson, his former business partner, and tried to get her to contact Dan Rivas to assist in his escape. John allegedly was willing to pay Rivas $200,000 for his help. The plan never really got off the ground. Instead of contacting Rivas, Robinson called us, as did John's cellmate. The plan disappeared in the wind. Security was tightened around Mr. Walker.

In late June, Fred Bennett, John's attorney, made his first approach to Assistant U.S. Attorneys Mike Schatzow and Bob McDonald about a possible plea bargain for John. He might plead guilty and offer information in return for leniency in Michael's sentencing. We were ready to go to trial and had great confidence in our cases against them, but we also knew we needed to get John's account of the military information he had been selling to the Soviets for nearly two decades. The government always has to do a damage assessment after a spy is arrested, and generally speaking, not much of one can be done without the spy's cooperation.

On 2 July 1985 Fred Bennett brought John in to the U.S. Attorney's Office in the Federal Building at 101 W. Lombard Street in Baltimore so that John could make a proffer—a sample statement of the information he had to offer so that the government could evaluate his sincerity, his honesty, and the quality of his information before agreeing to any kind of deal, which normally involves granting some leniency in sentencing.

This was the first opportunity we had to talk to John since his arrest on 20 May. The interview was conducted in a rather plainly decorated conference room on the eighth floor. As I recall, it contained an average-sized conference table, seven or eight chairs, and photographs of the attorney general (then Ed Meese) and President Ronald Reagan.

John, Fred Bennett, and Tom Mason, another of John's attorneys, sat on one side of the table. Schatzow, McDonald, Special Agent Barry Colvert, and I sat across from them. The ground rules for the interview were agreed upon. We were not allowed to ask any questions about what material John had sold. Nor were we to ask to whom John sold his information. The reason for those restrictions was that if John made admissions regarding those two topics and a plea agreement was not reached, the information he had given could then be used against him in a trial. Bennett did a good job of protecting his client's rights. John was expected to tell the truth and was to submit to a polygraph exam after the interview. He was somewhat nervous, but not overly so, and seemed to enjoy the attention he was getting. He had brought a folder of papers with him, something he would do every time we had a debriefing session with him in the future. The papers he carried were notes he had made to himself regarding his recollections of his spying activities, Navy assignments, and so forth.

The first question I asked John was when and how he got started in the espionage business. He responded with a cock-and-bull story about meeting a taxi driver in Norfolk one day in 1968 or 1969, when he was at the cab company looking for a part-time job. The cabbie allegedly told John he might be able to connect him with some people who could help him. A couple of weeks later John supposedly got a call and met two guys in a bar in Norfolk. They represented a private intelligence service, which he couldn't name, and were interested in information regarding Soviet ships. John said he met with the two men a few more times. He said he told them the kind of information he could get and agreed to work for them. They supposedly gave him pictures of drop locations, maps, written instructions on how to make drops, and dates he should deliver material in the D.C. area.

John said he was given instructions in the use of a Minox "spy" camera during his first year of gathering information for the intelligence service. He identified Jerry Whitworth, Art Walker, and Michael Walker as the other members of his espionage ring and said he had made about $50,000 per year during his career as a spy.

During one of our interviews, Art Walker had told us that John had taken their mother, Margaret Walker, to Italy one year. They went on to Vienna, where John had a face-to-face meeting with his Soviet handling agent. Art said John told him he got paid at that meeting, put some of the money in a money belt, and had their mother bring it through customs into the United States for him. Now I asked John about that. He denied having used his mother. He said he brought the money back into the United States himself.

During his proffer, John said he could identify all of the U.S. Navy communication systems he and his comrades had compromised, but his attorney would not permit him to do so at that time.

After an hour and a half, it was time for John to go with Barry Colvert and take the lie-detector test. Two hours later John and Barry emerged from the testing room. John was visibly shaken. Barry told us John had failed the test. Fred Bennett was devastated. So ended John's first attempt to manipulate the legal process with lies.

Barry told me later that he would never forget how John had slumped in his chair after he looked at his polygraph charts and realized he hadn't "beaten the box." Barry said John actually had tears in his eyes when he said, "You know this means I'll die in prison, don't you?" For the time being, the plea agreements were off.

. . .

We continued to prepare for John's and Michael's trials. Mike Schatzow asked me to arrange a flight over the route John had driven during his package drop on 19 May. Mike wanted to fly over the route so that he could get a good perspective of what our agents had seen John do that day. On a blazing hot day in late August, Mike, Bill Buckley, and I met Agent Frank McKenzie at a small airport in Montgomery County, Maryland.

McKenzie flew the Cessna. Buckley sat beside him. I got in behind McKenzie, and Mike sat behind Buckley. When Mike wasn't looking, I reached up and directed all of the air-conditioning outlets in our part of the plane onto myself. The temperature was approaching 100 degrees before we took off.

As we flew over John's route, McKenzie told us what John had done the day we followed him. I watched as Mike began to sweat. As we neared the end of John's route, Mike was turning an ugly green. He asked if anyone else was hot. I said I wasn't hot; in fact I needed a sweater. That's when Mike noticed that all of the AC vents were blowing on me. He muttered a few obscenities at me and demanded that we land. I had to buy him a beer to calm him down.

In mid-September, William "Buck" Farmer, the assistant U.S. attorney from San Francisco handling the prosecution of Jerry Whitworth, sent us word that he, his boss Joseph Russoniello (the U.S. attorney for the Northern District of California), Bill Smits (supervisor of the Foreign Counterintelligence Squad in the San Francisco FBI office), and Gerry Richards (supervisor of the Special Photo Unit in the FBI Laboratory) were going to Germany and Austria at the end of the month. The purpose of the trip was to attempt to obtain hotel records in Vienna, where John had stayed during some of his face-to-face meetings with his Soviet contact. They also wanted to visit the Minox camera factory in Geissen, near Munich, and to take photographs of certain points along the streets in Vienna where, according to the "Vienna Procedure" instructions, John had to walk when meeting his contact. They wanted to obtain evidence in preparation for the trial of Jerry Whitworth. Wolfinger and I agreed with their reasoning but took exception to the tone of the announcement from San Francisco, and to the glaring omission of the lead investigator in the case, me, from the list of travelers. After a few phone calls, Wolfie was able to have me added to the list.

FBI agents cannot just hop on a plane and go conduct investigations in other countries. We have agents assigned as legal attachés— "legats," in Bureauspeak—acting as liaison with the local and national police agencies in the major cities around the world. Normally, if an agent in the United States needs an investigation conducted in a foreign country, he sends a request to FBI Headquarters, and a supervisor there forwards the request to the appropriate legat. In this case we had to contact our legats in Bonn (West Germany) and Bern (Switzerland) and ask them to apprise the appropriate authorities in West Germany and Austria of our impending arrival and of the reason for our trip.

One Sunday afternoon at the end of September, Gerry Richards and I rendezvoused at Dulles Airport, near Washington, and flew nonstop to Frankfort, West Germany. Buck Farmer and the rest of our contingent met us there, and we began a memorable ten-day stint in Europe.

Our FBI legat from Bonn met us, and we went on to Munich, where we met with officials of the Bundeskriminalamt (BND), the West German equivalent of our FBI. I gave them an unclassified briefing on the Walker case in their headquarters, which was in the same building Hitler had used when he met with Himmler and his Gestapo cronies during World War II. I spoke in the same briefing room Hitler had used. The building was an impressive place, old and solidly built. As I spoke to the group through an interpreter, I could feel the presence of those men who had planned and played out horrific acts against humanity in that very room.

We were guests of the BND at a very nice afternoon luncheon. I sat next to a high-ranking BND officer who asked me what books he should read to get some understanding of politics in America. The question set me back a second or two. I recommended Carl Sandburg's biography of Abe Lincoln and Theodore White's book, *The Making of a President.*

We needed to talk to one of the officials at the Minox camera factory in Geissen, not too far from Munich. Bill Smits had served in our legal attaché's office in Bonn and spoke German, so he was our official interpreter and driver on the trip. We borrowed a car from the legat's office in Bonn and started out for Geissen.

Everything was going along quite according to plan until we got a few blocks from the Minox plant. Smits stopped at an intersection and then proceeded. As he entered the intersection, a man in a Volkswagen "bug" came from our left, hit the front end of our car, and literally took it off. None of us was injured. We were lucky Smits hadn't pulled out farther into the intersection. If he had, the VW would have been in his lap or mine.

We all got out and surveyed the scene. The VW driver was Turkish. His wrist was slightly injured. He didn't speak German or English, so we couldn't communicate with him at all. A local resident called the police. I watched in amazement as a couple of neighborhood women came out with brooms and dustpans and swept up the debris. They had the street completely cleaned up before the police even arrived. We rented a car, met with the Minox official, and returned to Munich later that evening.

As luck would have it, Oktoberfest, which is always held during the first two weeks of October in Munich, was just beginning. We went as guests of the BND. They were gracious hosts and had reserved a table in one of the several huge tents that are set up on the midway each year. Each tent held thousands of people and was filled with row upon row of picnic-style tables. The inside perimeter of each tent was lined with a multitude of delectables: rotisseries laden with chickens, sausages, oxtails, and many other traditional German goodies.

Each tent had a center stage for bands and entertainers. After a few hours of drinking, people from the audience often joined the band on stage. Joe Russoniello was an outgoing guy with political ambitions and had told us soon after he joined us in Germany that he hoped to be governor of California some day. Throughout the trip he gave his business card to any of the locals who would accept it, which I considered rather strange. After we had been in one of the tents for several hours and the crowd had achieved a certain level of "looseness," we had the master of ceremonies introduce Russoniello to the crowd as the future governor of California. The crowd roared its approval. Joe loved it and didn't seem the least bit fazed or embarrassed. I suppose any recognition is better than none. Gerry Richards and I looked at each other and shook our heads in amazement.

Each tent had its own staff of waitresses who served the crowd of thousands in a very efficient manner. The beer came in one-liter mugs, and each waitress carried six mugs in each hand. True, they were strong, full-figured women, but it was still astonishing to see them working their way through the crowd carrying twelve liters of beer and never spilling a drop. One of the BND men told us that the competition to get a beer concession in one of the tents is fierce. He pointed out a line about an inch from the top on each mug and said that the beer, not the foam, must come up to that line. If it doesn't, people will complain and the vendor will lose his privilege to sell beer in the tent, a very substantial financial loss.

When the bands played traditional German songs, it was clear to me that patriotism was not dead in Germany. The crowd would raise their steins in the air and sing and sway in unison. The hair on the back of my neck stood up as I remembered the many news films I had seen of Hitler working the crowd into a frenzy during World War II.

On Friday of our first week, we moved on by train to Berchtesgaden, a wonderful historic town in the Bavarian Alps. We stayed in the Hotel Demming, a small, comfortable family-run hotel on a mountainside almost directly across from Hitler's "Eagle's Nest" retreat at Obersalzberg. While in Berchtesgaden, we took a boat tour on Lake Koenigessee, a lake surrounded by incredibly beautiful mountains of exposed red marble and white granite. St. Bartholomae Chapel, a twelfth-century monastery, sits at the base of the white granite east face of Watzmann Mountain, which at nine thousand feet above sea level is Germany's second highest mountain.

Our next stop was Vienna—a bustling place full of intrigue, with a startling mix of architecture ranging from the ornate centuries-old to the stark, glassy modern. We stayed in the Hilton International, where John Walker had stayed on occasion as he sold our secrets.

We walked John's "Vienna Procedure" route, the one he followed when he met his Soviet handler in a face-to-face meeting. Gerry Richards took pictures of each street sign and various other locations along the route. We were able to obtain copies of some hotel records from the Hilton International, which showed that John had been there. Then we paid a visit to the American embassy to talk with a member of the State Department, as we had done in the other cities we visited. It was pretty much a courtesy call, just to meet an official and let him know we were in town and generally outline what we would be doing.

I recall sitting across the desk from a man who identified himself as the minister-counselor of the embassy. We gave him a short, unclassified briefing on the Walker case. I remarked to Gerry Richards after we left his office that the guy was awfully aloof and didn't seem particularly interested in what we had to say. I found that to be very unusual; everyone else we had talked to was extremely interested in the case. Several years later I figured out the reason for the man's attitude: he eventually came under heavy FBI scrutiny as an espionage suspect himself and resigned from the State Department in 1990. Although we were unable to put a prosecutable case together against him, if our suspicions were correct he was working for the Soviets as we spoke to him that day in October 1985. The man was Felix Stephen Bloch. I still have the business card he gave me that day in his office.

It truly was an incredible trip in every respect—great food, incomparable beer, gorgeous scenery, haunting history, and perfect weather the entire time. Skies were clear and bright blue each day. Temperatures were in the low 70s. The only rain we encountered was a light sprinkle on our way to the Vienna airport as we began our trip home, which made it a little easier to leave.

26

A Deal Is Struck

John and his attorneys were watching very closely as Arthur went to trial in Norfolk in August 1985. I mentioned earlier that a large part of the case against Art involved our proving that John was a spy for the Soviets. And we did that splendidly. John's fate was sealed, and he knew it.

Since there was no guarantee that a plea agreement would be reached, we continued to prepare for John's trial, which was scheduled to begin on 28 October. Michael's trial would follow right after. Mike Schatzow, Bob McDonald, Jim Kolouch, Bill Buckley, and I spent hours going over the evidence, preparing witnesses for their testimony, deciding the order of their appearance in the trial, and attending to the details of what was shaping up to be the biggest espionage trial since the Rosenbergs.

We often found ourselves in the U.S. Attorney's Office at ten or eleven o'clock at night, after having worked all day with the witnesses and evidence we intended to use. At the end of those days we would occasionally stop for a beer at a local spot, but more often we all went home and collapsed into bed.

"Home" for me at that time was the Hilltop Inn on Security Boulevard, an inexpensive motel not far from the Baltimore FBI office. I would much rather have stayed at a place in the Inner Harbor area of Baltimore near the U.S. Attorney's Office, but the rates for the hotels in that part of town were much more than the U.S. government per diem would cover. I finished many late evenings in my room heating a can of soup with one of those electric gizmos you plug in and put into the soup to heat it. My "cooking" more often than not was accompanied by loud music, courtesy of a crew of construction workers who were staying in a neighboring room while working on a local project.

I spoke to Mike Schatzow on 5 September 1997 and asked him what he remembers about the plea-bargaining process with John's and Michael's attorneys.

"There really was no negotiating to speak of," he recalled. "John and Michael were both dead in the water and didn't stand a chance in a trial." He continued:

> Bob McDonald and I never thought we would have any problem proving the case. It was overwhelming. We had some concern with the possibility of some classified information being disclosed in court, but it never really became a problem because neither Fred Bennett, John's attorney, nor Charlie Bernstein, Michael's attorney, ever brought it up.
>
> There was a great deal of interest from the agencies in the intelligence community to debrief John regarding how and when he got started in the espionage business and, of course, what information he sold the Soviets. The folks in San Francisco also put a great deal of pressure on us to strike a deal with John, because they needed him as a witness against Jerry Whitworth.
>
> Fred Bennett came to McDonald and me, in terms of what could be done for John, or, if we couldn't deal on John's sentence, would we give Michael a break. He knew they were both going to jail.

That's how and why the plea agreements came about. We were ready and willing to go to trial. The government certainly could have refused to discuss a deal until after John's trial. In fact, the bargaining process often never happens until after the defendant has been convicted. Then the discussions focus on how much of a break the government is willing to recommend to the judge at sentencing time in return for the defendant's cooperation and testimony against his partners in crime.

Bennett approached Schatzow and McDonald a month or so before John's trial was scheduled to begin. They notified the folks at the Department of Justice. In an espionage case, the attorneys in the Internal Security Section at U.S. Department of Justice Headquarters—in this case, John Martin and John Dion—must give their blessing to any plea agreement. I'm sure Attorney General Edwin Meese and Secretary of Defense Caspar Weinberger, as well as other high-level officials, were involved in the approval process.

Even though a plea bargain was in the making, we had to continue our preparation for trial. Getting ready for trial and trying to put together an agreement acceptable to all parties was a nerve-wracking combination. One day it would look like no agreement would be reached, and the next day it would look like a done deal. At times it was difficult to focus on trial preparation.

The suspense ended when an agreement was reached and signed by all parties on 24 October 1985. The terms of John Walker's agreement required him to plead guilty to attempted delivery of national defense information to a foreign government and unlawful receipt of national defense information in violation of Title 18 U.S. Code Sections 794(a) and 793(c). The maximum penalty for the "attempted delivery" charge was life imprisonment and a fine of $250,000. The maximum penalty for the "unlawful receipt" charge was ten years' imprisonment and a $250,000 fine.

John was also to plead guilty to conspiring to deliver national defense information to a foreign government during the period 1968 through 1985, in violation of T18 USC 794(c). The maximum penalty for that offense was life imprisonment.

Nowhere in our espionage laws is it specified that the foreign government receiving our defense information has to be an enemy of the United States for the act to constitute espionage. Jonathan Pollard is an example of a person who was convicted of providing U.S. national defense information to a friendly country, Israel. He too was sentenced to life in prison.

In addition to the guilty pleas, John agreed to cooperate with the government by (1) fully and truthfully responding to all questions about his knowledge of espionage and espionage-related activities, or any other topics put to him by federal law enforcement authorities and other federal government officials; (2) cooperating completely with federal government authorities in any matter in which his cooperation was deemed relevant; (3) submitting to polygraph examinations conducted by a representative of the government; and (4) testifying fully and truthfully before any grand juries or trials of cases at which his testimony may be relevant.

In return for John's complete fulfillment of all of his obligations in the agreement, the government agreed to (1) bring the nature and extent of his cooperation to the attention of the court at the time of sentencing, and to dismiss all other counts of the indictment against him; (2) recommend the maximum sentences, as set out above, to run concurrently, with no fines recommended; (3) not charge John with any other violations of federal criminal law for his involvement in espionage, espionage-related activities, or violations of the federal income tax laws prior to the date of the agreement; and (4) not to recall John into the U.S. Navy or subject him to court-martial or prosecution by the Navy for his involvement in espionage.

The agreement also stated that if John failed "in any way to fulfill completely each and every one of his obligations under this agreement, then the government will be released from its commitment to honor all of its obligations to him . . . and will be free to prosecute him for perjury, false declaration, false statement and/or obstruction of justice, and to prosecute the counts of the indictment that would otherwise have been dismissed at sentencing."

The agreement would also be breached if Michael failed to fulfill completely all of the obligations in his plea agreement, which required him to cooperate fully and completely with the government in terms similar to those of his father's agreement.

Michael was to plead guilty to five espionage charges as follows: (1) conspiracy to deliver national defense information to a foreign government; (2) attempted delivery of national defense information to a foreign government; (3) unlawfully obtaining national defense information; (4) unlawful retention of national defense information; and (5) unlawful transmission of national defense information. The charges were in violation of T18 USC 794(a) and (c) and 793(b) and (e). The maximum penalty for count 1 was life imprisonment. For count 2 it was life and a $250,000 fine. Counts 3, 4, and 5 each carried a maximum sentence of ten years and a $250,000 fine.

The government agreed to bring the extent of Michael's cooperation to the attention of the court at the time of sentencing and to recommend a sentence of twenty-five years on counts 1 and 2 and ten years on the other three counts. It would also recommend that the sentences on all five counts be imposed and served concurrently, which in effect gave Michael a sentence of twenty-five years' incarceration.

Now all Mike Schatzow and Bob McDonald had to do was persuade Judge Alexander Harvey II to accept the plea agreements. He had a reputation for being a hard-nosed administrator of the law and not particularly fond of plea bargains. Mike and Bob succeeded.

The Walkers appeared in court on Monday, 28 October, the day John's trial had been scheduled to begin. In due process, they would be charged, be questioned by the judge, and enter their pleas. Sentencing would take place a year later.

The proceedings were held in the ceremonial courtroom on the first floor of the U.S. Courthouse in the Edward A. Garmatz Federal Building at 101 W. Lombard Street in Baltimore. The courtroom was packed with media, Walker family members, courtroom sketch artists (since no TV or cameras were allowed), and spectators.

A hush fell over the courtroom as the U.S. marshals brought in father and son to stand before the court. Schatzow, McDonald, and I sat at the prosecutors' table on the front left side of the room. John and Michael were seated beside their attorneys, on the right side in front of the bench. John had the characteristic smirk on his face during the proceedings. Mike looked more solemn; I think he was scared stiff.

Judge Harvey spoke at length to John about his constitutional rights, his right not to plead guilty, and his right to a trial. He questioned him about whether he understood his rights, whether his plea was voluntary, and whether he was actually guilty. He explained what the consequences might be if John's plea was accepted by the court. When it was necessary for John to answer a question, he did so in a calm, clear, high-pitched voice. He did not hesitate when the judge asked how he pled. He simply said, "Guilty." I must admit, I had a great feeling of pride and satisfaction at that moment.

The judge went through the same routine with Michael. His demeanor was the opposite of his father's. The gravity of his crime and the years in prison that lay ahead of him had obviously sunk in. When he had to respond to the judge, he slumped in his chair and spoke in a whisper. His plea, "Guilty," was barely audible.

Schatzow then read before the court a thirty-seven-page statement of facts summarizing our case against John and Michael. I watched John's face the entire time, and he never changed his expression or said a word to his attorney.

When Schatzow finished, Judge Harvey commented that it wasn't his policy to sign plea agreements that set out the sentences he must give the defendants. However, he said, he was satisfied that there were "exceptional circumstances" in this case, and he accepted the agreements. The judge pointed out that the information John could provide about his years of espionage was of incalculable value to the federal government, and he thought the interests of the public would be served by the agreement.

Not everyone was happy about the plea agreements, however. On Tuesday, 29 October, Secretary of the Navy John F. Lehman Jr. issued a scathing statement to the media, claiming that the agreement with John Walker sent the wrong message to the American public and to the Navy. He was adamant: we should not have made a deal with John. Mike Schatzow, who is not bashful, responded to the media that the agreement was "no deal" for John but was a deal for the country. If Lehman was right, asked Schatzow, why had his superiors authorized the agreement? Mike ended with a comment to the effect that Lehman's statement was just the kind of crap that made the people working out in the field happy they weren't in Washington.

Within a couple of days Secretary of Defense Caspar W. Weinberger made a statement to the media. He had talked to Lehman about the agreement, he said. The newspapers quoted his statement: "Secretary Lehman now understands that he did not have all the facts concerning the matter before he made injudicious and incorrect statements with respect to the agreements." That was a very unusual public rebuke of a high-ranking official by his superior.

I had no negative feelings about the agreements. John certainly didn't get any deal. He pled guilty to two charges that carried life sentences. Even if he had gone to trial and been found guilty, which he would have been, he couldn't have been sentenced to more than life in prison. The law at that time did not apply the death penalty to the crime of espionage in peacetime. The "life without parole" punishment we have today did not exist at the time John was in court. It's true he became eligible for parole after serving ten years, but so did Charles Manson and Sirhan Sirhan. Just because his name comes up on the list doesn't mean he's going to get out. Also, there is no mandatory release date with a life sentence. Personally, I don't think he'll ever walk among us again. Nor will Art or Jerry Whitworth.

The "deal" for Michael gave him a break of a couple of years. If he had gone to trial, he would have been convicted, no doubt about that. But he might not have received a life sentence, or he might have received less than the twenty-five years he agreed to in his plea bargain. His "deal" made him eligible for parole in eight years, rather than the ten it would have been if he had gotten life.

Then what is he going to do? What will he put on his résumé when he's looking for a job? "Experienced spy, will travel"?

27

Debriefing a Spy

Traditionally, debriefings are coordinated by the case agent. However, the ink on the plea agreements was hardly dry when Bill Smits notified us that an entourage from San Francisco, led by Assistant U.S. Attorney Buck Farmer, would arrive in Baltimore on 28 October to begin the debriefing of John Walker. It was another of Smits's teletypes that basically said, "Move aside, boys, and let the real investigators take over."

Joe Wolfinger contacted FBI Headquarters and got the matter resolved: I was to coordinate the debriefings and be the FBI liaison man with the other government agencies involved. The process would begin at the end of October 1985 and continue until November 1986.

On the morning of 30 October, John Walker and Fred Bennett arrived at the U.S. Attorney's Office in Baltimore to begin the long-awaited disclosure of his career in espionage. Assistant U.S. Attorneys Mike Schatzow, Bob McDonald, and Buck Farmer and Farmer's associate Leida B. Schoggen were assembled in the eighth-floor conference room. FBI special agents Robert F. Griego of San Francisco, H. William Buckley of Baltimore, James L. Kolouch of the Washington Metropolitan Field Office, and I were also there. This was to be the first of many interviews of John for which we should have rented the local stadium.

It had always been my policy not to have too many people present during an interview. Two, or three at the most, is enough. The more people present, the greater the possibility that the interviewee will become confused, get distracted, or—as happened in John's case— play to the crowd. On more than one occasion I expressed my displeasure with the participating agencies for sending so many people to the interviews. However, I was overruled. The case had become extremely political. I was very much aware that we shouldn't ruffle any feathers at the other agencies.

John entered the room carrying his folder of notes and papers and wearing that characteristic smirk. He took a seat across the table from me, and I introduced everyone to him. He was a bit nervous but surprisingly calm.

I asked him to whom he had sold his country's most tightly held secrets and how he had gotten into the espionage business. This is the way he told it:

He had sold classified information, Top Secret cryptographic material in particular, to the Soviets for nearly eighteen years. His life was a disaster at the time he contacted the Soviets "in early 1968." (Barbara contends it was late 1967.) The bar he had opened near Charleston, South Carolina, was losing money; he was having severe financial problems; and Barbara, who was still in South Carolina with the kids, was pressuring him to bring the family to Norfolk.

He was the communications watch officer on the staff of Commander, Submarine Forces Atlantic, at the Norfolk Naval Station. He and several other sailors on the mid-watch were sitting around the office one day, discussing, as they sometimes did, how much the Soviets might pay for the crypto material they worked with every day. He thought about that conversation for a day or two, and a couple of days later he stole a SPECAT (Special Category) Top Secret key list for the KL-47 crypto system, one of several systems used by the U.S. Navy to communicate with its various commands and ships at sea, including our ballistic-missile submarines (SSBNs).

It was the end of his midnight shift. He simply took the key list and went to his quarters on the base. After a few hours' sleep, he got up and drove to Washington, D.C.

When he arrived, he looked up the address of the Soviet embassy in the phone book, got a map of the city, and determined where the embassy was. He parked his car a couple of miles away, took a cab to the vicinity of the embassy, got out about a block away, and walked past the front of the building one time. He turned around and went back and entered the embassy compound at the vehicle entrance. He had the key list inside his shirt. It was around 4:00 or 5:00 P.M. on a weekday.

A man was closing the gate of the fence as John came through. He told the man that he wanted to speak to someone in security. The man seemed a little confused but took him inside to the receptionist, where John repeated his request. In a few minutes a man came up and introduced himself as a security person. John showed the man, who never identified himself by name, the key list and asked to speak to him in private.

They went down a hallway and into a small room, where the Soviet asked him his name. At first John told him his name was John Harper, but when he couldn't produce any identification in that name, the man refused to deal with him. He demanded a picture ID, which I suspect startled John, since he was used to being in charge and controlling the people with whom he dealt. John said he wanted to sell some classified crypto information, and gave the man his Navy ID card and the key list. The man took them and left the room for about fifteen minutes. I'm sure he showed the items to someone else as well as took pictures or made copies of them while he was out of the room.

He returned with another man, and they discussed the kind of information John could provide. John told them he could furnish cryptographic material on a regular basis and asked how much it was worth. They said it depended on the quantity and quality of the material.

John had taken his "watch bill" (Navy work schedule) with him. They used it to schedule their next meeting, which was to take place three or four weeks later. He was instructed to park in a certain spot in front of a Zayre's Store in Alexandria, Virginia, and at a precise time of the evening go into the store. He was told to carry a *Time* magazine, walk around the store for a short while, and go back outside. His contact would be in the store and would follow him out and approach him.

John said he was told to memorize the instructions for the next meeting, but he was too nervous and had to write them down.

He was in the embassy approximately two hours. The embassy people asked him a number of questions, including what his duties were in the Navy, what access he had to crypto and other classified information, what his duty station was, what his marital status and family situation were, and why he had come to them. John said he answered all of the questions truthfully.

He was instructed to prepare a list of the information he had access to—known in the espionage business as a "shopping list"—and bring it to the next meeting. He was also told to copy as much classified information as he could to bring to the meeting, but to be careful. He told the Soviets he expected at least $3,000 or $4,000 per month for the information he could provide.

After they completed their business, he was paid between $1,000 and $3,000—he couldn't remember the exact amount—in fifty-dollar bills for the key list. He was required to sign a receipt.

When it was time to leave, the Soviets gave John a long overcoat and a wide-brimmed hat and told him to put them on. He got into the back seat of a car, with a Soviet on each side of him. They told him to duck down and pull the hat down over his face. Then they left the embassy compound and drove around Washington for about an hour.

When the Soviets were satisfied that they had not been followed, they took back the coat and hat and put John out. He was a few blocks from the place he had parked his car. He drove back to Norfolk and went to work that night on the midnight shift. Although he was late for work, no one asked him where he had been, because he was the boss. And that, according to John, was the beginning of his eighteen-year career as a spy for the Soviet Union.

John later told us that his personal life was so screwed up and he was so depressed that his initial act of espionage was an "alternative to suicide." He said he fully expected to be arrested within two weeks.

We talked to John every day for a couple of weeks. After the first two or three days, the debriefings were moved to the Baltimore FBI office. We met in a small conference room devoid of any decor. There was nothing to distract John or interrupt his concentration. Several agents from the Baltimore office picked him up at the local county jail each day and brought him to the office. They said that every morning, as they led him to the car, the other inmates would shout at him, saying things like "Tell them everything, all you know, before we kill you." He obviously caused quite a stir at those small local jails, and he seemed to love it. In fact, when he was in the Baltimore City Jail after his arrest, he gave several press interviews. During one of them the reporter asked how he was doing, and he declared quite proudly that he was a celebrity and was doing fine. I couldn't help thinking that John's histrionics were his way of coping with his untenable situation.

A typical day of debriefing started around 9:00 A.M. and ended at 4:00 P.M., since we had to get John back to the jail in time for the evening meal. When we broke for lunch, sometimes we would eat in the room with John, but usually we went elsewhere, mainly to get away from him. John got a brown-bag lunch provided by the jail. On occasion, if he had the money, we would get him something from the local sandwich shop. One day when he didn't have any money, Jim Kolouch lent him $10. He made John sign a receipt for it, which broke me up. I don't know whether John ever paid him back.

John always brought his folder of notes and papers with him. He would write down the names of the people interviewing him each day. Occasionally he took some notes. If he seemed to be having difficulty remembering certain details, such as how many face-to-face meetings he had with the Soviets or the locations of his dead drops, we would give him assignments to work on in the evenings or over the weekend.

We went over all the evidence we had found in his house and had him explain each item. Experts in cryptography from the National Security Agency and naval officers schooled in submarine warfare, communications, intelligence, and security came in to question him. He responded well to most of them, although he clearly disliked some of them, and none of them liked him.

One naval officer was particularly disgusted with what John had done. He told him at the beginning of the interview that he was repulsed by him, that he was there only because he had to be, and that he didn't even want to be in the same room with him. That's not a good way to start an interview. John bristled and started giving curt yes/no answers to the man's questions. After about ten minutes I stopped the interview and asked the officer to talk with me in private. I explained to him that none of us wanted to be in John's presence, but he would not get any useful information from him if he continued with his current approach. I then had a talk with John and assured him that the officer would change his attitude for the rest of the interview.

We completed the interview, although the tension was evident the entire time. I couldn't blame the Navy man. Sometimes John Walker made me sick, too. But I don't think he ever knew it. No matter how repulsive he was, I treated him with respect. The heavy-handed approach had rarely worked for me during my career, and it certainly wouldn't have worked on John. As Barry Colvert said, "You catch more flies with honey than you do with vinegar."

The day the Navy's security expert came to talk to John about how he had been able to steal our navy's highest secrets was one to remember. The man asked John for his opinion about Navy security, and John responded, "Hell, Kmart has better security than the U.S. Navy." He seemed to delight in saying things that would rile his interrogators. He obviously enjoyed sparring with them and ate up the attention he was getting. I think it was during that interview that John first said he was the best damn spy there ever was. He repeated that quite a number of times.

John went on to tell the security officer that he had had no problem stealing classified information while in the Navy; he never even came close to getting caught. He explained that he always positioned his desk so that his back was to his office door. Then, if he was photographing a document with his Minox camera and heard the doorknob turn, he could just slide the document into the middle desk drawer. When he photocopied documents he always put a cover document over the one he was copying to hide it. Jim Kolouch reminded me recently that John had a word of caution about photocopying documents: "When you do this shit on a copy machine, you better be damn sure you know how to clear jams in a hurry."

John said he usually just put the documents in his briefcase and took them home; in twenty years, nobody ever checked his briefcase. As an approved armed forces courier, he would occasionally wrap the documents like an ARFCOS shipment and take them from the ship or the base that way. John said he figured he had it made, as long as he didn't get caught at a dead drop. That, he said, was his worst nightmare.

In mid-November 1985 the U.S. Marshals Service took John to San Francisco, where Buck Farmer and his associates were preparing for Jerry Whitworth's trial. John was to testify against Jerry. They grilled him about his career as a spy and about Jerry's recruitment and his involvement with John. Farmer wanted to make certain he had gone over every possible detail in preparing John for his testimony against Jerry.

John lived in the jail at 611 Broadway in Oakland during his stay in California. Art and Michael joined him there a short time before they testified on 14 and 19 May 1986. Although they were not in the same cell, they were in the same cellblock and had some opportunities to sit around and talk over old times.

Michael later told us it was during their stay in the Oakland City Jail that he told his dad that he had found religion, as do many facing adversity. He suggested that John should do the same. John said he wasn't interested but told Mike keep it up because it would make him look good at parole time. John never did anything without figuring the angles.

Jerry's trial got under way on 24 March 1986. The jury was sworn in, and Buck Farmer and Tony Tamburello, the opposing attorneys, gave their opening statements. In typical California fashion, the trial was a grand production. I'm sure it was the most elaborate, revealing espionage trial in our history. Farmer called approximately 170 witnesses, including Barbara, Laura, Michael, and Art. He put on literally hundreds of pieces of evidence.

The show-stopper, however, was John's testimony. He took the stand on 28 April and finished testifying on 8 May. He laid his own espionage career bare, as well as Jerry's.

John appeared to be quite pleased with himself. I've always thought that when John learned about the "RUS" letters, which Jerry had written in an effort to turn John in and avoid prosecution, he made a vow to do all he could to see that Jerry got his fair share of the punishment.

Jerry's trial ended on Friday, 11 July 1986. On 24 July the jury returned and pronounced him guilty of seven espionage charges and five income tax evasion charges. In an unusual step, federal district judge John P. Vukasin Jr. said he would not require that the usual presentence report be prepared on Jerry. He said, in effect, that he had heard all he needed to hear about Jerry's life, character, friendships, employment, and background. He stated, "The Court finds that there exists sufficient information in the record to enable the meaningful exercise of sentencing discretion."

On 28 August at ten in the morning, Judge Vukasin sentenced Jerry Whitworth to a total of 365 years in prison and imposed a $410,000 fine. Over the ten years during which he stole national security secrets, Jerry was paid $332,000 by John Walker. Jerry will not be eligible for parole until he reaches the age of 106. I've always said that if he lives to see parole, I'm going to meet him at the gate of Leavenworth.

John and Michael were returned to Baltimore after their testimony, and the debriefings continued. We interviewed Michael several times. He had already told us just about everything in his confession. Most of our debriefings of him were efforts to get him to remember everything he had given John and to clear up how much his wife, Rachel, knew.

All during the debriefing process I stayed on at the Hilltop Inn, where a tuba player had taken a room across from the construction crew, and went home to Virginia Beach on weekends. I got to know every crack in the 240 miles of roads between home and Baltimore during that time.

When we were well along in the debriefing process, we began to form a pretty clear picture of John Walker's spy routines. We were surprised when John told us that after his face-to-face meeting with the Soviet in Alexandria, they never met again until August 1977; for a period of ten years, his only contact with the KGB was through package dead drops, or "exchanges," as they called them. John described that long period of no meetings with his handler: "I was taking Spy 101 by a correspondence course in drop notes."

John said the dead drops all took place in the D.C. area. The KGB told him the FBI didn't work on weekends, so for several years they had their exchanges on Saturday evenings. Then, giving him no explanation, they switched to Sunday evenings.

John said his procedures were always the same, although the drop locations were different. In eighteen years they never used the same location more than once. John would go to D.C. either by car or by plane, always arriving in mid- or late afternoon. Sometimes he flew his own Grumman four-seater. If he took a commercial flight in the United States, he always used an alias, usually John Harper or John Baxter. Most of the time he drove his own car or van.

As soon as he arrived in D.C. he would drive to the drop area and check it out to make sure he could find it, and the signal spots, later that evening when it was dark. He would then check into a hotel, relax for a while, have something to eat, and go out in the evening to conduct his acts of espionage—just as Barbara had told us they did when she went with him in 1968.

He delivered information to the Soviets an average of every two or three months from the beginning of his spy career until Jerry stopped producing for him in 1984. After that, his drops fell off to two a year, with one face-to-face meeting a year. His face-to-face meetings were usually held in Vienna, and the contact was the same Soviet who had met him in Casablanca in 1977. In all, he conducted approximately thirty drops and had thirteen face-to-face meetings with his KGB handlers. To say he was an active spy would be an understatement; the average spy passes information to his handler once or twice a year.

John seemed especially proud of his production of classified material for the Soviets during his stint as communications officer on the USS *Niagara Falls* at the height of the war in Vietnam. He was in charge of the security of the cryptographic key material and bragged that he had been able to provide 100 percent of it, including "reserve on board," which was the key to be used in the months to come.

John said he was paid an average of $50,000 per year by the KGB and made a total of between $1 million and $1.5 million. But what had happened to the money? We had several discussions with John about this. He said he spent it all. We went over an extensive list of things he said he had spent it on; we actually doubled each figure he gave us, and we still couldn't account for between $300,000 and $500,000. Once, after days of no satisfactory answers about what had happened to all of the espionage money, Jim Kolouch looked at me and said, "Interviewing John is a real ego-buster."

John always got nervous and defensive when we talked about the money. He said many times that he was "not the type to put it in a plastic pipe and bury it." Actually, that may be exactly what he did. Although he passed the polygraph, I am convinced that the money question remains unanswered.

The KGB had warned John to be careful when spending the money. They told him to keep it in a safe-deposit box rather than a checking or savings account. He was told not to flash his money around or spend it lavishly. He followed these instructions to some extent, but according to friends and associates he always seemed to have unlimited funds.

He kept a safe-deposit box at a Bank of Virginia branch at 865 East Little Creek Road in Norfolk. We were able to show that he visited the box after each meeting or exchange with the Soviets. The box contained ten 100-ounce silver bars valued at $6,140 when we searched it on 21 May 1985. The IRS got them.

John told us he told Jerry and Michael to use a simple code when they wrote to him about their gathering of material. They referred to the documents and photographs as "souvenirs" or "photography." We found several letters from them to John that contained those words. Jerry also used the term *scuba diving* to refer to espionage activities in some of his letters to John, early in his spying career. In 1974, after he had photographed his first documents at the Navy communications outpost in Diego Garcia, he wrote, "I made my first dive today," meaning that he had begun collecting information for John to pass to the Soviets.

After Jerry began supplying material, John would meet him at various locations to pick it up. They usually met in California, though a couple of times Jerry brought his film to John in Norfolk. John also met Jerry in Hong Kong and Manila to pick up deliveries while Jerry was deployed. John always timed his meetings with Jerry for a few days before he was to make a drop or meet his handler. John's trip to Casablanca, for example, followed a rendezvous with Jerry in Hong Kong.

The material Jerry brought typically consisted of six to eight rolls of Minox film, each roll containing thirty-six exposures. John said that when he and Jerry met they always talked about the contents of the film Jerry had brought. Jerry would describe what was on it, and John would take notes; sometimes Jerry would write the notes. (When we searched John's house we found several pages of notes that turned out to be notes he and Jerry had written during one of their meetings.) Later, John would write a "Dear Friend" letter to include in his package for the Soviets. This letter—just like the one we found in John's package on the night of 19 May 1985—would briefly explain what the package contained.

John never actually saw any of the pictures Jerry took of the documents; he simply passed on the undeveloped film. How, then, did he know that Jerry was providing high-quality classified information? John answered that question for us when he said that the Soviets were always very pleased and paid him handsomely for the information. He was certain they would not have done so had it not been of interest or value to them.

Our sessions with John went on day after day. Some days we felt that we were doing pretty well, getting a lot of useful information from him. Other days we weren't so sure.

In the beginning of the interview process, John seemed eager to discuss anything except his upbringing and home life; he refused to discuss those topics, maintaining that they had nothing to do with his espionage. As time went on, though, another subject came up that he didn't want to talk about. The Navy and NSA guys started to ask questions that led him to reveal that he had given the Soviets tactical information that could have gotten some of our boys killed in Vietnam; and at that point, John started to back off. It was obvious that he didn't want to admit to having given the Soviets this information. It was also obvious that he had done it. For example, while on the USS *Niagara Falls* as communications officer, providing advance keying material to the Soviets, John enabled them to read our messages as our ship captains received them. The ship was off the coast of Vietnam at that time. He gave them our "in country" code. Who knows how many of our missions met with disaster because John Walker's deceit tipped the enemy off in advance?

I lost my cool only once during all of John's debriefing sessions. It was after Art's sentencing. Over two or three days John had commented repeatedly that he thought Art had gotten a raw deal and it wasn't fair. After about the tenth time, I just looked in his eyes and let loose with "Listen, asshole, Art was an officer in the U.S. Navy. He committed espionage. He was caught, confessed, and was convicted. He got exactly what he deserves, and I don't want to hear any more of your shit about it."

John's arrogance, his self-righteous attitude, and his foul mouth wore on all of us. In retrospect, I see how closely he fit the personality profile of a psychopath, as explained to me by Dick Ault: by force, or trickery, or charm, psychopaths take whatever they happen to want, without guilt, remorse, or any signs of conscience. For example, he had a rationale for being a spy. He said, "I really didn't harm the country. Lots of people do it [spy]. In fact the material I gave them probably avoided World War III, because the information was so good the Soviets were convinced we were as strong as we said we were. That's why they never attacked us, and never will."

Some days, when John was being particularly obnoxious—usually after he had repeated that he was the best damn spy of all time—I would ask him, "John, where are *you* going at the end of the day? We're going out for beer and pizza." Several times Kolouch, Colvert, and I told him that after he was sentenced he would be sent to the federal pen in Marion, Illinois—a place known for its severe conditions, where everyone is locked in his own cell twenty-three hours a day. That irritated him. In fact, after one particularly unpleasant day when we told him that, I received a call from his lawyer, Fred Bennett. Bennett asked me not to say that to John anymore, since it was really upsetting him.

We visited John at Marion twice in the next several years.

28

Presentence Happenings

In the months prior to Judge Harvey's sentencing of John and Michael, the debriefings were my main focus, but some other interesting things were happening.

I had received several calls from reporters and writers who were interested in the case. The most persistent was a writer named Howard Blum. He was interested in interviewing me at the earliest moment so that he could get his book on the market. I kept telling him I would not be able to talk to him until after the Walkers' sentencing, which was set for 6 November 1986.

On 27 August Mr. Blum called and asked me for an interview. I told him I couldn't do it and suggested that he might want to hold off on his book for a while, since he didn't have the whole story. He called again within a week. We talked in generalities about the case for a minute, and he expressed an interest in whether Art had been more involved in espionage than had been made public.

He presented his own scenario about Art's involvement and asked for my comments. I told him I couldn't answer or comment at that time. I also told him I might write a book about the case someday, from my own point of view. He said, "What point of view could you possibly have?" I told him I didn't know; I was just the case agent. He said, "Man, I would like to get you drunk and get the real story out of you."

When I told him it would never happen, he said, "Oh, that's OK, I'll just make it up."

I replied, "I know you will, Howard. I've read some of your stuff." When his book, *I Pledge Allegiance . . . : The True Story of the Walkers, an American Spy Family,* came out in 1987, I saw that he had been true to his word: he did make it up. The book is replete with inaccuracies and visions. He should have given it the same title he gave his first book of fiction: *Wishful Thinking.*

As the sentencing date approached, there was some discontent, mainly on the part of Navy authorities, with the results of the debriefings. Neither John nor Michael had passed all of the poly-graphs. There was some suspicion that they had not been totally forthcoming, as called for in their plea agreements. I'm certain some heated discussions took place at higher levels as to whether the agreements should be set aside and John and Michael go to trial on all charges.

Within a week of the sentencing date, while those discussions were taking place, John was planning another escape attempt.

He was being kept in the Cecil County Jail, outside Baltimore, during the final stages of the debriefing process. He befriended an inmate he thought was due to be released within a week. John asked this inmate if he would help him escape after he was released—for a fee, of course. The inmate agreed, listened to John's plan, and then told a sheriff's deputy that he needed to talk to the FBI. We sent a couple of agents to see him, and he told them John's plan. It went like this:

As soon as the man was released from jail, he was to get a gun and a car. John would contact him to set a date for the escape. On the agreed date, the man was to park in the emergency-room lot at the local hospital around 6:00 P.M. In the meantime, John would feign a diabetic attack—he does have diabetes—and would have to be taken to the emergency room by ambulance. The man was to watch for the arrival of the ambulance and then wait close by. Upon being taken from the ambulance, John would suddenly recover. He and his sidekick would overpower the deputies and take off in the sidekick's car.

The inmate asked John what they would do if the deputies transporting him put up a struggle. John told him he would grab a gun from one of them and shoot them.

One major problem with the plan was that the inmate didn't own a car. When he told John this, John called his elderly mother in Scranton and weaseled $1,500 out of her to buy the man a car. He told her he needed the money to buy a computer so he could write a book about his career as a spy. Mrs. Walker, who could ill afford to part with $1,500, sent the money to the inmate's girlfriend, as instructed by John, since the inmate himself wasn't allowed to have that much money in jail.

Needless to say, we kept in close contact with this inmate, and with the help of Sheriff John DeWitt and his deputies, the grand escape never happened. Instead, John was transferred to the U.S. federal penitentiary at Lewisburg to await his sentencing.

I never asked the inmate what his girlfriend did with the $1,500. He wasn't actually released from jail; he was transferred to some other location to serve his time. Over the next several years he called me from several different southern jails, usually in an attempt to con me into getting him transferred to a jail closer to his home or more to his liking.

29

The Sentencing

After all of the high-level conferring and squabbling about whether to void the plea agreements or not, the decision was made to proceed with the sentencing. I agreed with that decision. The sentencing would take place in the U.S. district court in Baltimore at 9:30 A.M. on 6 November 1986.

The cast of characters gathered in the courtroom a few minutes before 9:30 that morning. Bob McDonald and Mike Schatzow were the attorneys for the government. Jim Kolouch, Bill Buckley, and I were among several FBI agents present. I sat at the prosecutors' table with McDonald and Schatzow.

John was accompanied by his attorney, Fred W. Bennett, federal public defender. Attorneys Charles G. Bernstein and Ellen Lipton Hollander were present with Michael. John didn't look quite as smug as he usually did. Mike looked smaller than ever; he looked like death warmed over.

The courtroom was packed, and the tension was high. Barbara, Laura, and Margaret Walker were there, as was Michael's wife, Rachel. As I recall, Margaret and Rachel didn't sit with Barbara and Laura; they were angry at them for blowing the whistle on John.

The courtroom became quiet as a church when it was called to order. Judge Alexander Harvey II took his place on the bench. It was obvious that he was in a very somber mood and wouldn't suffer fools lightly. After hearing from the attorneys for both sides and ensuring that everything was in order and everyone was ready to proceed, Judge Harvey was ready to get on with the sentencing.

Here is the court transcript of what was said:

JUDGE HARVEY: Mr. John Walker, would you please rise. Mr. Walker, before the Court imposes sentence, is there anything you would like to say to me, in mitigation of punishment or otherwise?

JOHN WALKER: Your Honor, I have reviewed the sentencing memorandum prepared by my attorney. Based on that and the remarks that he has made here in court, I just want to say that he has summarized my feelings adequately and there is nothing that I could add to them here in court.

JUDGE HARVEY: The Court has for sentencing United States of America versus John Anthony Walker, Jr. There are two cases here, Criminal Numbers H-85-0309 and H-85-0532.

Approximately one year ago, Mr. Walker, you appeared before me in this court and tendered pleas of guilty to three separate espionage charges brought against you in these two cases. The plea agreement between you and the government was reached under Rule 11(e)1(C) of the Federal Rules of Criminal Procedure, whereby if the pleas were accepted by the Court, the Court would impose the recommended sentences. The sentences recommended in your case were concurrent life imprisonment terms and a concurrent ten-year sentence.

At the rearraignment proceedings held in this Court on October 28, 1985, I accepted your pleas and the provisions of the plea agreement. I concluded that there were exceptional circumstances in this case and that substantial reasons supported the sentencing recommendations made by the United States Attorney and agreed to by you and your attorney. In my opinion, the most significant aspect of the plea agreement was your consent to cooperate fully with the federal law enforcement authorities, to supply information in your possession relating to your extensive espionage activities over a period of many years, and to testify in a related prosecution.

During the past year, you have undertaken to fulfill your commitments under the plea agreement. You have been debriefed on numerous occasions, and you have submitted to many polygraph examinations. Moreover, you have testified over a period of seven days in April and May of this year in the Whitworth trial in the Northern District of California. According to the Assistant United States Attorney who prosecuted that case, your testimony was valuable.

Mr. Whitworth was convicted in the California case on numerous counts charging espionage and related crimes, and he now has received a lengthy sentence.

Your brother, Arthur Walker, who was a member of your ring, was convicted in the Eastern District of Virginia last year and has been sentenced to life imprisonment.

Although the government has expressed concern as to the truthfulness of certain of your responses to questions put to you, the government has not moved in this case to set aside the plea agreement that was reached. It is therefore now my duty, Mr. Walker, to impose sentence.

Although the sentence is fixed, pursuant to the terms of the plea agreement, there are a few comments which I would like to address to you at this time. I have had an opportunity to review the presentence reports in this case. I have reviewed the sentencing memoranda and exhibits, and I have listened to the attorneys and you here in court this morning.

In my opinion, Mr. Walker, your espionage activities have caused tremendous harm to the national security of this country. While in the Navy, as a warrant officer and thereafter, you provided important national defense information of an extremely sensitive nature to the Soviet Union over a period of some 18 years. Your motive was pure greed, and you were paid handsomely for your traitorous acts. It has been estimated that over this 18-year period, you have received from the Soviet Union approximately $1 million in cash.

Throughout history, most spies have been moved to betray their country for ideological reasons. You and the others who participated in this scheme were traitors for pure cold cash. Whether this says something about today's society and its values, I leave for the sociologists to determine.

In reviewing the details of this offense and your background, I look in vain for some redeeming aspect of your character. When one considers the facts, one is seized with an overwhelming feeling of revulsion that a human being could be as unprincipled as you.

Certainly everyone who has ever worn a uniform of the armed services—and I served my country overseas in combat during World War II—must feel utter contempt and disgust that a serviceman could bring the ultimate disgrace to the uniform that you have.

You showed your stripes early. When you needed money for your failing bar in Charleston, South Carolina, in 1966 and 1967, you suggested that your wife turn to prostitution. Shortly thereafter, you decided that more money could be made by betraying your country. To increase your earnings from espionage, you enlarged your operation and recruited members of your own family. It made no difference to you that your own flesh and blood would be exposing themselves to extreme risks by engaging in these traitorous activities.

Your brother is now serving a life sentence. Your son is a young man who will be spending most of the next 25 years in a federal prison. Your daughter Laura, to her everlasting credit, refused to join you when you sought to recruit her. Your good friend Jerry Whitworth will be spending the rest of his life in federal prison.

None of this apparently mattered to you, so long as the cash was coming in. You, a 20-year Navy man, have betrayed your country and sacrificed your family so that you might enjoy luxuries such as an airplane, a houseboat, cars and a sailboat.

In spite of what has been said here this morning by you and your attorney, you do not seem to appreciate the enormity of these grave crimes. In my opinion, you have shown no genuine remorse for these despicable acts which continued for so many years.

There have been suggestions that you could be released on parole within 10 years. It is difficult for me to believe that any parole commissioner could ever agree to an early release for you, and I shall do everything in my power to see that this does not occur. Indeed, I will prepare and submit to the parole commission my AO-235 report, which will strenuously recommend that you not be released on parole at any time during the rest of your life. I shall send a transcript of my remarks today to the parole commission.

The sentences are as follows:

Under Count 2, Criminal Number H-85-0309, I sentence you to the custody of the Attorney General for confinement in such place as he deems proper for imprisonment for the remainder of your natural life.

Under Count 5, I sentence you to the custody of the Attorney General for confinement in such place as he deems proper for a period of 10 years, concurrent with the sentence imposed under Count 2.

In Criminal Number H-85-0532, I sentence you to be committed to the custody of the Attorney General for confinement in such place as he deems proper for imprisonment for the remainder of your natural life, such sentence to be concurrent with the sentences imposed in Criminal Number H-85-0309.

In addition, I impose a $50 special assessment on two of these counts, for a total of $100.

As to the other counts in H-85-0309, Mr. McDonald?

MR. MCDONALD: Your Honor, as I said before, the government moves to dismiss Counts 1, 3 and 6 pursuant to the plea agreement.

JUDGE HARVEY: The government's request will be granted.

MR. BENNETT: Can I be heard briefly in one regard, Your Honor?

JUDGE HARVEY: Wait until we are finished with the other defendant. You may be seated, Mr. Walker.

Mr. Michael Walker, would you please stand.

Mr. Walker, let me give you an opportunity to say anything that you would like to say in mitigation of punishment or otherwise.

MICHAEL WALKER: Your Honor, I have nothing to add to counsel's statement.

JUDGE HARVEY: Very well. This is the sentencing of Michael Walker in the first case, Criminal Number H-85-0309.

Mr. Walker, you have heard what I have just said in sentencing your father. You have likewise entered into a plea agreement with the government whereby this Court, on acceptance of your pleas, is required to impose sentences aggregating 25 years imprisonment.

During the last year, you have likewise been undertaking to fulfill your commitments, and I am satisfied that you did. Unlike your father's case, there is at least something that can be said on your behalf. You, unfortunately, looked up to your father. As an immature 21-year-old, you were easily led into these traitorous activities. You were paid very little for taking the risks you did. It should be apparent to you that it was your father who profited from using you in the manner that he did, and that you received very little in return for these risks. Because of your age, and the fact your father recruited you, I approved this plea agreement whereby you would receive 25 years rather than the life sentence.

However young you were, Mr. Walker, you were nevertheless an enlisted serviceman in the United States Navy, from which you have now been dishonorably discharged. Your duty was to defend your country. You chose to betray it. One does not need much maturity or education to understand that being a traitor is perhaps the ultimate of all crimes. It is therefore appropriate that you receive this lengthy term of imprisonment, and I will likewise recommend to the parole commission that you not be paroled at any time during your 25-year term. The sentence is as follows:

Under Count 1, I sentence you to the custody of the Attorney General for confinement in such place as he deems proper for a period of 25 years.

Under Count 2, the sentence is 25 years concurrent.

Under Count 3, the sentence is 10 years concurrent.

Under Count 4, the sentence is 10 years concurrent.

Under Count 6, the sentence is 10 years concurrent with the sentences imposed under the other counts.

The aggregate sentence is 25 years incarceration.

In addition, the Court imposes, as required by law, a special assessment of $50 for each of these five counts, or a total of $250.

The Court will recommend confinement in the federal correctional institution in Petersburg, Virginia.

There are no other counts in that indictment?

MR. MCDONALD: No, your Honor.

JUDGE HARVEY: Did you have something else, Mr. Bennett?

MR. BENNETT: Yes, your Honor. We have listened carefully to your remarks in connection with the imposition of the sentence of Mr. Walker. We think your indication on the record and what you intend to do in connection with the AO-235, in which you are going to indicate to the parole commission in writing and with a transcript of these proceedings that Mr. Walker never be released from prison during his natural life, is inconsistent with the spirit and intent and substance of the plea agreements in this case in regards to the Court's obligations.

As your Honor is aware, he would be eligible for parole consideration under federal law in 10 years. We think that this, in effect, literally amounts to an amendment of the plea agreement, providing for a life sentence with no parole.

Now, I know it is not binding on the parole commission, but we think that your Honor's indication that you are going to recommend in writing that he never be released from prison is inconsistent with an 11(e)1(C) type of agreement.

JUDGE HARVEY: You can think what you want, Mr. Bennett. That is what I will do.

We now stand adjourned.

The courtroom was abuzz with the crowd's reaction to what they had just witnessed. All of the Walker women were crying. The reporters streaked for the courthouse steps and began jockeying for position to question the attorneys.

I watched as John and Michael were led away by the U.S. marshal. An American tragedy had just come to an end. I don't know if Michael appreciated the enormity of it. John certainly did, but he couldn't let himself admit it, or he would have had to exit from the nearest eighth-floor window. I had kept my eyes on his face during the entire court proceeding, and his expression never changed, not even while Judge Harvey was chewing his ass for being such an aberrant human being. That half-grin that appeared on his face when he was in an uncomfortable situation did change some when the judge told him he was going to recommend that he never get out of prison. I could read his thoughts at that moment. I'm sure he thought the judge was being very unfair.

When Judge Harvey announced that court was adjourned, Mike Schatzow turned to me and said, "Bob, I just want to shake your hand and thank you for the job you did. This was the most perfect case I ever had as a prosecutor." I really appreciated that. I knew how hard everyone had worked on the case and accepted Mike's praise on behalf of all of the people in the FBI who were involved.

After the press conference, which was attended by reporters from the major TV networks, newspapers, and magazines from around the world, all of us who had been involved in the prosecution went to lunch. If my memory serves me correctly, we went to Sabatino's, a favorite spot of ours in the Little Italy section of Baltimore. The pressure was finally off, and we let our hair down a bit.

. . .

I had the good fortune to interview Judge Harvey in his chambers on 20 November 1997. The judge looked extremely fit, was quite personable, and was a very impressive man. I remembered his statement at the sentencing and asked him to tell me a bit about his background.

Judge Harvey was born in Baltimore in 1923. He was a member of the Yale Class of 1945. However, his college days were interrupted by a stint in the U.S. Army Field Artillery with the Seventy-first Infantry Division during World War II. In 1945 he was a first lieutenant serving in France, Germany, and Austria as an observer in spotter planes gathering information on enemy troop movements. He flew over seventy missions and earned an Air Medal with one cluster (thirty-five missions were needed to qualify for the medal). He volunteered for pilot training and returned to the United States for Flight School in late 1945. His plans to become a pilot were cut short when the war ended, and he was discharged in the spring of 1946.

Judge Harvey returned to Yale and graduated in 1947. He went on to Columbia Law School and obtained his law degree in 1950. After a few years in private practice, he became assistant attorney general of the state of Maryland. He was appointed a U.S. district judge by President Lyndon B. Johnson in 1966, a job he describes as one of the best a man can hold. Judge Harvey startled me when he said he had been interviewed as a candidate for director of the FBI after J. Edgar Hoover died in his sleep in 1972.

I asked Judge Harvey if he had actually submitted the AO-235 forms on John and Michael to the parole commission, as he said in the sentencing hearing he would do. He responded that he did submit them, on 19 November 1986; he didn't think he recommended that Michael not be released on parole on his AO-235. The judge then commented that John's attempted enlistment of his children in his espionage business was one of the most horrible aspects of the case, as far as he was concerned. He furnished me a copy of John's AO-235 (see appendix B). He recalled that the head of the federal parole commission came to see him after he received the recommendation. They discussed the case, and the commissioner agreed that John should not be released on parole, saying he would see to it.

I asked Judge Harvey what he thought about the idea of showing leniency toward the Walker gang and releasing them early, now that the cold war was over. His response was quick and to the point: "The idea is ridiculous and patently absurd."

30

Damage Done

The damage done to the security and national defense interests of the United States by the John Walker espionage ring is incalculable.

I mentioned before that six months after we arrested John, a high-ranking KGB officer named Vitaly Yurchenko defected to the United States. At that time he was the highest-ranking KGB officer ever to defect. One of his jobs in the KGB had been to try to determine why some of the KGB's operations went south. In that regard, he had to analyze why the Walker case blew up. They didn't believe that Barbara had turned him in; they thought that possibly one of their own people had screwed it up, so Yurchenko reviewed the case file.

He told us John Walker was considered the number 1 agent the KGB had ever had. He said John gave them the ability to read over one million military messages over the years. (Jim Kolouch recently reminded me that when John heard that figure he said, "A million is an understatement.") Yurchenko said John Walker provided so much information that a special building had to be built in Moscow to house the analysts who worked on the material. He also said John had walked into a Soviet embassy and "volunteered," as he had told us.

Yurchenko noted that two of Walker's handlers had received the highest awards given by the Soviet government: Yuri Linkov got the Order of Lenin Medal and Vladimir Gorovoy the Hero of Russia Medal. Boris Solomatin, the KGB resident (top officer) in the Washington embassy at the time Walker "volunteered," was promoted to deputy chief of intelligence and awarded the Order of the Red Star. John Walker himself was made an honorary admiral in the Soviet Navy.

Not long after John's arrest, Adm. James D. Watkins, chief of naval operations, commented to the press that some of the information John had passed to the Soviets had given them "a leg up on understanding U.S. submarine practices and procedures to help them in their counterstrategy." He credited John with having given the Soviets the information they needed to improve their submarine construction technology to compete more effectively with ours. In fact, after this case revealed the extent of John's treachery, our Navy men began referring to a new class of Soviet submarines as the "Walker class."

I can't summarize the damage John caused any better than Rear Adm. William O. Studeman, director of naval intelligence, did in his affidavit to Judge Harvey prior to the sentencing of John and Michael. Admiral Studeman said:

> The ultimate vulnerability of cryptosystems and all procedures designed to protect sensitive information lies at the human level. The importance of the individual spy cannot be overestimated. . . .
>
> John Walker not only provided the Soviets with details related to cryptologic and key [lists], he also provided classified documents which included information on communications architecture, future communications systems, and other military topics . . . [such as] future plans, ship locations and transit routes, military operations, intelligence activities and information, weapons and sensor data, naval tactics, terrorist threats, surface, subsurface and airborne doctrine and tactics, and similar information which could prove of incalculable value to hostile powers.
>
> [Encrypted] communications will invariably reveal classified technical information, intelligence data, intelligence surveillance activities or information critical to the United States in making decisions concerning the security of the nation or its foreign policy.

If a hostile power were able to obtain our decrypted communications, it would be able to adopt counter-measures, frustrate foreign policy, and insert misleading data into the information collection process. . . . Disclosure of specific data can lead to harmful results, both for the specific collection activity involved, and for similar activities conducted worldwide by U.S. forces and other agencies of the government.

With regard to Special Category (SPECAT) information, Admiral Studeman said:

Frequently it is necessary to transmit information which is of such a degree of sensitivity that its disclosure must be limited to only those individuals with an absolute need to acquire this Special Category (SPECAT) data. The Walker espionage ring was, on several occasions, in a position to have access to SPECAT communications.

Some examples of operations that are planned and executed through SPECAT channels are:

a. COVERT MILITARY OPERATIONS. . . . [Disclosure of such information could jeopardize] the United States' ability to conduct missions vital to the national defense and to world peace. The risks involve not only potential damage to the foreign relations policies of our government, but also danger to the lives of the personnel involved.

b. COUNTERINTELLIGENCE OPERATIONS. . . . Disclosure of SPECAT communications concerning such operations allows hostile intelligence services to develop countermeasures and techniques to render these operations ineffective.

c. HUMAN INTELLIGENCE (HUMINT) OPERATIONS. . . . Disclosure of any information relating to HUMINT operations . . . can lead to loss of the source, personal harm to the agent and the insertion of false and misleading information. . . .

d. EMERGENCY ACTION MESSAGES (EAMs) AND PROCEDURES. . . . [EAMs] are part of the procedural mechanism by which we ensure that nuclear strike capabilities will never be exercised by error. . . . [These] procedures and safeguards in the hands of a hostile power can reveal sufficient data to allow a first strike with the assurance that their opposite numbers have not yet been authorized to execute nuclear war. . . .

John Walker's commission [as chief warrant officer] led to dramatically greater exposure to other types of national defense information.

. . . [His position as communications watch officer at SUBLANT] enabled him to reveal emergency procedures for nuclear war planning, thus permitting him to significantly affect the nuclear deterrence value of U.S. submarine forces. . . . [As communications officer on the USS *Niagara Falls* he was] the custodian for all "key," which gave him unlimited access to reserve crypto materials . . . which permits the spy to provide his principals with keying material long before it will be used. This, in turn, can allow a hostile force to prepare in advance to receive the encrypted transmissions and . . . to read those transmissions as they are being transmitted.

Admiral Studeman also submitted an affidavit to Judge Harvey summarizing his thoughts on the spying activities to which Michael had confessed. Here are some of his comments:

Michael Walker's treachery produced exceptionally valuable information for the Soviet Union and represents a serious threat to the war-fighting capability of the United States Navy. . . . Many of the documents taken by Michael . . . concerned technical details of the Navy's most modern weapons systems used aboard the NIMITZ. This included not only offensive weapons, used in combat . . . but details of defensive systems with which the 5,000 men aboard the NIMITZ could detect enemy forces and defend themselves from attacks. . . . [The] Soviets were given valuable insights into US tactics and procedures for naval and air warfare. . . .

. . . Michael Walker transferred to the Soviets information on the procedures attendant to the use of nuclear weapons by naval forces.

. . . [He] passed to his father for the Soviets planning information identifying possible military targets in potentially hostile foreign countries. This information, if revealed to the target nations, would enable them to anticipate US attacks and dramatically increase expected casualties among US units.

. . . Information obtained by Michael Walker . . . described US capabilities to avoid or delay engagement by Soviet forces . . . , [enabling the Soviets to] upgrade their capabilities and thereby improve their ability to engage US vessels at a place and time of their choosing. . . .

. . . [Other] documents taken by Michael . . . described US Navy capabilities to identify unknown vessels and determine hostile from friendly forces. This information can assist [the Soviets] in development of countermeasures to our identification process and can enable the [them] . . . to employ deception techniques to disguise the true identity or mission of their forces.

. . . Among the most damaging disclosures from Michael Walker's espionage is information relating to US command and control procedures. . . .

. . . In the aggregate, the information given to the Soviets by Michael Walker helps them to anticipate our actions and what force our commanders are allowed to use. Thus forewarned, they can deceive our forces or gauge our posture to achieve surprise.

Now you know why I don't have any sympathy for Michael. He caused great harm to our country and put service men and women at incredible risk. He was a little John Walker in espionage training pants.

In a striking summary, Studeman described the devastation of national defense plans by John Walker's espionage ring:

The cumulative effect of [John Walker's] broadly based disclosures was to give the Soviets in-depth knowledge of U.S. national defense plans, policies, logistics data, force levels and tactics. This gave the Soviets an immense advantage in developing their own national defense plans. More important, it gave the Soviets an ability to make almost real-time tactical decisions because they knew the true strength of our forces, their plans for combat, the details of our logistic support and the tactical doctrine under which our forces operated. As acknowledged by Vitaly Yurchenko, this knowledge can mean the difference between victory and defeat in war. John Walker's espionage activity over almost two decades provided the Soviets insight into the very heart of this country's political/military objectives.

(For the complete text of Admiral Studeman's affidavit, see appendix C.)

John Walker made many startling remarks during our interviews, but now that the scope of his access is known, one comment of his stands out as truly chilling.

We were gathered in the conference room at the U.S. Attorney's Office in Baltimore. It was the first interview after the plea agreements were signed. In answer to my questions, John told us we had identified and arrested every member of his espionage ring and admitted that he had sold our secrets to the Soviets.

I then asked, "How badly did you hurt us? What did you give them?"

John looked across the table at me with a stunned expression, as though he hadn't expected that question, then said, "Oh my God, I'll never be able to remember everything I gave them. It went on too long. There was too much."

He sat back in his chair for a second and then leaned forward, looking at me. He spread his arms out before him. "I'll tell you this. If it was within my grasp," he said, stretching his arms as far apart as he could, moving his fingers in a grasping motion, "you can color it gone. Because it's gone."

There is no doubt in my mind that for once, he was telling the absolute truth.

31

Afterlife

During the time when we had the wiretap on John's phones, we overheard him talking to friends about how he liked to visit the Yorktown battlefield. I had been there often and found it curious that it was one of John's favorite spots, since it is where a decisive battle of the American Revolution was fought—a battle that in effect gave birth to the nation John chose to betray.

Some time after the case closed, I went to the Yorktown battlefield and spent a day there gathering my thoughts. I reflected on the Walkers, mother, father, brother, and son, and where they had gone since sentencing. What would life in the federal pen be like for Michael? For John? And I wondered about the repercussions of the Walker case. What would the implications be for the criminal justice system and the national security systems, the Navy's in particular?

Legal changes were made. In 1985, life imprisonment was the maximum punishment allowed for espionage in peacetime. Soon after the arrests of John, Michael, Art, and Jerry, there was a groundswell in the military and Congress to pass a law making the death penalty applicable to military personnel convicted of espionage in peacetime. William F. Buckley wrote a column in which he made a strong argument for the death penalty for espionage. The law, publicly supported by high-level officials including Secretary of Defense Caspar Weinberger, Senators Strom Thurmond and Bob Dole, and Attorney General Edwin Meese, was passed.

I am not in a position to know the extent of the changes in security the Navy made because of the Walker case, but I do know that there were some. The number of people with security clearances was reduced, and it became a little more difficult to get a clearance. The Navy also started to require that many more people in sensitive positions take a polygraph exam. I'm sure there have been many more changes I don't know about.

I do recall late February 1988, when I went to the Norfolk Navy Base to give a briefing on the case to a group of NIS agents at their request. The briefing was to be given in a building in the CINCLANTFLT compound, one of the most secure areas of the base. You'll recall that John worked there when he started his espionage career.

I had never before experienced any problem getting into the buildings on the compound, but things were different now. When I arrived at the building a young sailor was standing watch on the quarterdeck, where people had to sign in to enter the inner area of the building. She asked me who I was and where I wanted to go. I showed her my credentials and explained that I was an FBI agent there to give a briefing to NIS. She asked if I had a security clearance to hear the briefing. I told her I was *giving* the briefing, and that I had a Top Secret clearance along with a couple of other special clearances.

She asked to see copies of my clearance. I explained that FBI agents aren't required to carry documentation that verifies their clearances. By that time one of the NIS guys had arrived, and I explained that I was having some difficulty getting in to hear my own briefing. The problem was finally resolved by someone there calling FBI Headquarters to verify that I did indeed have the necessary clearance. Whew, that was close. I almost didn't get to hear my own briefing.

. . .

What has become of the major players?

Arthur Walker is in the federal penitentiary in Butner, North Carolina. Jerry Whitworth is in Leavenworth.

Barbara Walker is a recovering alcoholic, holds a steady job, and is an attentive grandmother to her three grandchildren. She carries a heavy burden of guilt about her son's incarceration.

After his sentencing, Michael was sent to the federal correctional institution in Petersburg, Virginia. Soon enough I received word that he had been involved in an escape attempt. The warden took immediate action and transferred Michael to the federal pen in Lewisburg, Pennsylvania. There are six levels of federal prison security. Petersburg is a level 3; Lewisburg is a level 5. So Mike went from a medium-security joint to a tighter, more secure place, occupied by more violent folks. After he got there, he had to pay protection money to a group of prisoners to assure his safety. His mother sent him the money.

He is still at Lewisburg but was placed in a less dangerous section of the facility several years ago. His parole was denied on 6 August 1997, for the second time. He will have to serve at least sixteen years and four months. I spoke to his mother recently, and at this writing, Mike is scheduled to be released from prison on 28 March 2000.

Pete Earley, author of *Family of Spies: Inside the John Walker Spy Ring,* the most accurate of the books published on this case, called me in September 1996 to say that he had received a letter from John asking him if he could help him find out how to get Michael to Russia when he gets out of prison.

John was initially sent to Lewisburg, but because of threats on his life and his plan to escape from the jail in Cecil County, he was sent to the federal correctional institution at Marion, Illinois, the only level-6 prison in the system. When Alcatraz was closed, Marion took its place. Most of the prisoners in Marion are locked in their cells twenty-three hours a day. The place has been in "lockdown" status since 1983 when the inmates rioted and killed two guards.

In October 1988 Barry Colvert and I went to Marion to interview John. The prison is in a remote area in the southern tip of Illinois.

To say it is an imposing place would be an understatement. The prison is approached by a drive through gorgeous landscaping. You think you are entering the grounds of a wealthy estate—until you get close enough to see the fifteen rolls of stainless-steel razor wire stacked up against the fence. Then there are the gun towers, and the deterrent system of poles and cables designed to prevent any escape by helicopter.

Barry and I were given a tour of some of the areas inside the prison. Everything looked freshly painted. It was absolutely spotless.

Inmates are kept in individual eight-and-a-half-by-seven-foot cells. They sleep on concrete slabs with thin mattresses, and their meals are passed to them through a space in the bars of the cell door. They each have a television set, and they spend their time watching TV, sleeping, reading, and dreaming of better days.

We watched the guards prepare to take a prisoner to the gym for his hour of exercise. He backed up to his cell door and put his hands out behind him through the space where the food is passed. A guard put handcuffs on him and told him to step away from the door. The door was unlocked, and two guards went in and brought him out. They put leg irons on him. A third guard ran a metal-detector wand over his body. They then walked him, a guard on each side and one in the rear, to the exercise area. The prisoner was placed in a holding cell adjacent to the "gym," the leg irons were removed, and the guards came out. He was told to back up to the space in the bars of the door, where the guard took the cuffs off. The electronic lock on the door to the exercise area was then opened, and the prisoner went through.

We were taken to a cellblock where the most dangerous of all the prisoners were held. These inmates didn't even get the hour a day in the exercise area. As we were about to enter the cellblock, one guard got in front of us and one behind us, as well as one on each side. I looked at the men in those cells as we passed. A few uttered obscenities at us, but most of them either just looked or looked away. They were more like caged animals than men. It was appalling to see human beings having to live that way. Don't misunderstand; I didn't feel sorry for them individually. I was moved by the circumstances—

the sad truth of what people do to other people—that lead them to places like that.

We also got a look at K-Unit, a seven-man unit in the basement where Marion holds the country's most notorious prisoners. The unit is separate from the rest of the facility. The inmates there never get out to exercise; they never associate with anyone else. Each inmate has a two-hundred-square-foot cell with his own shower and TV.

John Walker was there. Jonathan Pollard was in the cell next to him. They didn't like each other and didn't speak. Joseph Franklin, who had murdered an interracial couple in Wisconsin, bombed a synagogue in Tennessee, and killed two black joggers in Utah, was also there. Billy Bryaer, the killer of two FBI agents in Washington, D.C., was there; Barry and his associates in our Washington field office had arrested him. Edwin Wilson, a former CIA guy who sold weapons to Libya, was there, too. Later, after John was transferred to Atlanta, John Gotti would get his cell.

Barry and I were put in an interview room. A couple of minutes later John was brought in. The handcuffs and leg irons remained on him during the two-hour interview. He was wearing that irritating little grin when he came in. He seemed to be faring pretty well, and he hadn't lost much, if any, of his arrogance.

A couple of times during the interview we remarked on how small and cramped the room was. Barry—who is six four and weighs 230 pounds—and I barely had room to move on our side of the table. The place was tiny and uncomfortable. At the end of the interview John stood up and said, "The next time you come out here to talk to me, let me know ahead of time, and I will arrange a better interview room. We [the inmates] run this place, you know!" Barry and I just watched as the guard led him away.

John stayed at Marion for many years. Eventually he was transferred to the federal prison in Atlanta. Barbara called me in November 1996 and told me that John's diabetes had worsened and he had been transferred to the federal hospital prison in Springfield, Illinois. I suspect he will remain there until his days are over.

. . .

On Memorial Day 1986 I went to the Chrysler Museum in Norfolk to see an exhibit of photographs taken at the Vietnam Memorial in D.C. It was a very moving experience for me. I went and sat in my car for a while. I couldn't get rid of the vision of some American boys being ambushed and dying over there because John had given the enemy the ability to know that those kids were coming.

In 1994 the FBI arrested Aldrich Ames, a longtime CIA employee with access to extremely sensitive information about the identities of Soviets who were spying for the Agency. Many people have asked me how the Ames case compares with John Walker's.

I have no personal or inside knowledge of the Ames case, but I can still say that the two cases were quite different. Walker furnished crypto information revealing some of our most closely held secrets for nearly twenty years. He was the Soviets' trump card in the event that we went to war. Ames identified Russians who were betraying their country, which caused the deaths of several of those traitors. Walker put our entire Navy at risk and is believed to have caused the deaths of unknown numbers of our men in Vietnam. Which was more devastating? You decide.

Postscript: A Chat with the Adversary

In the spring of 1998 I had an opportunity to talk with retired KGB general Oleg Kalugin. We met in a restaurant in Washington, D.C., within sight of the Capitol Building, and spent two hours together.

Since his retirement in 1990, General Kalugin has been living in the D.C. area with his wife and grandson. He works for Intercon International, USA, with offices in D.C. and Moscow. He has written a book, *The First Directorate,* in which he describes his career in the KGB and speaks his mind about the communist system of government. This has made him, as he puts it, "not especially popular over there politically."

I was particularly interested in talking with the general because he was the supervisor of the Walker case in the Soviet embassy in Washington for the first three years of John's espionage career. Because of his handling of the Walker case, he was awarded the distinguished Order of the Red Star and became the youngest KGB officer to be promoted to general in the postwar history of the organization.

I asked Kalugin about the espionage career of John Walker from the KGB perspective. Here are some of the things he told me:

John Walker came to the Soviet embassy late one afternoon in the fall of 1967. Kalugin was upstairs talking with his good friend, KGB resident (officer in charge) Boris Solomatin, when Yakov Bukashev (true name Lukasevics, according to Kalugin), the embassy security officer, called and asked that someone come down to talk to a possible new "volunteer"—spook slang for a citizen who comes forward and offers to sell his country's secrets. Solomatin went downstairs. Kalugin stayed upstairs. Although he was to supervise the case for the next three years, he never met John.

Solomatin brought the documents John was offering upstairs to show to Kalugin. There were several classified documents, and a "code card" was mixed in with them. As soon as he saw the code card, Kalugin knew that this was a legitimate "volunteer."

John stayed in the embassy a couple of hours. He was paid several thousand dollars and received instructions for the next meeting. He was given a topcoat and large-brimmed hat and placed in the back seat of an embassy car. A KGB man sat on each side of him, and they drove out of the embassy compound. It was almost dark when they left the compound. They drove around for a while, then put John out within walking distance of his car.

Yuri Linkov was John Walker's first KGB handler. He chose the drop sites and prepared John's written instructions for the dead drops. Kalugin went out and personally approved the drop sites until he was convinced that Linkov could do a competent job of site selection in such an important case.

John had several handlers over his nearly twenty-year career. They all knew his name, but he would not have known their names. If any of them did give him a name, it would have been an alias.

John was given a KGB code name, but General Kalugin couldn't recall what it was. He noted that very soon after John came to the embassy, Solomatin started referring to him as "Number 1." It stuck. From then on, that's what John was called by the few KGB officers who knew of his existence. General Kalugin described John Walker as the number 1 agent in the history of the KGB. He said, "He was much more valuable than Ames. Especially if war had erupted."

When I asked General Kalugin if the KGB had shared any of the information John furnished with North Vietnam, he replied, "Oh, yes. Some information was shared with North Vietnam. It was sanitized and mixed in with information from other sources."

I asked if the information John furnished caused the Soviets to ask the North Koreans to seize the *Pueblo* in January 1968, in order to gain access to the KL-47 code machine. Kalugin didn't think so. Looking at the timing, he didn't think they would have developed

John's information sufficiently by the time the *Pueblo* was taken to have caused the seizure of the ship; if the seizure had happened a year later, though, John's information would definitely have been the reason. Kalugin added that the *Pueblo*'s capture "helped [the Soviets] tremendously" in understanding the information John was giving them, as it gave them access to the KL-47 and they could decode our messages with it.

I asked the general about the extent of Art Walker's involvement in espionage for the Soviets. He replied that Art had not been involved with John during the time he supervised the case. As far as he knew, Art had not dealt with the KGB prior to John's visit to the embassy in 1967. He also said it would not have been unusual for John's handler to ask for a picture of Art, since they tried to obtain a photo of each agent for their files. He could not explain why John's handler never asked for a picture of Michael Walker or Jerry Whitworth. Kalugin added, "Of course we had a picture of John— from his visit to the embassy. There was a camera behind the mirror in the room. Also, we had copied his Navy ID, which he had shown to us."

During the time General Kalugin supervised the case, John was not given an escape plan to use in the event that he came under suspicion, but the general said it is possible that he was given one at some point in his career. Moreover, if John or any member of his espionage ring was released from prison and wanted to defect, he would be welcomed in Russia. As the general put it, "We take care of our friends."

When I asked about Felix Bloch, the former U.S. State Department man in Vienna who came under intense scrutiny by the FBI as a suspected Soviet spy, the general smiled and said, "I can only say that your suspicions were well founded."

I couldn't resist asking what he knew about Glenn Michael Souther, a suspected Soviet spy from Norfolk who fled to the Soviet Union after being interviewed by the FBI in 1985. The general said he had never met Souther and had no firsthand knowledge of the case, but Boris Solomatin had told him that he had recruited Souther in Italy, after he came to the Soviet embassy in Rome and inquired about Soviet ideology and life in the Soviet Union. Souther was in the U.S. Navy at that time. Kalugin said Souther eventually defected and was welcomed in the Soviet Union, where he served as a military consultant. He committed suicide a couple of years later.

I found General Kalugin to be very gracious and straightforward—a man with a good sense of humor. Two years my senior, he looked fit and in good health. I'm sure he was a formidable adversary during the cold war. Fifteen years ago I would never have believed that one day I would take him to lunch, within sight of our nation's capitol, laugh with him, and talk about old times in the spy business. Strange bedfellows.

Appendix A.

Advice-of-Rights Form Signed by John Walker

DEFENDANT'S EXHIBIT NO. ___7____

CASE NO. __H 85-0309__

IDENTIFICATION: ___15 AUG 1985___   **ADVICE OF RIGHTS**

ADMITTED: ___15 AUG 1985___

John Walker   **RIGHTS**   *Ramada Inn, Room 250*
          Place *Montgomery Co. Md*
          Date *May 20, 1985*
          Time *3.54*

Before we ask you any questions, you must understand your rights.

You have the right to remain silent.

Anything you say can be used against you in court.

You have the right to talk to a lawyer for advice before we ask you any questions and to have a lawyer with you during questioning.

If you cannot afford a lawyer, one will be appointed for you before any questioning if you wish.

If you decide to answer questions now without a lawyer present, you will still have the right to stop answering at any time. You also have the right to stop answering at any time until you talk to a lawyer.

WAIVER OF RIGHTS

I have read this statement of my rights and I understand what my rights are. I am willing to make a statement and answer questions. I do not want a lawyer at this time. I understand and know what I am doing. No promises or threats have been made to me and no pressure or coercion of any kind has been used against me.

Signed _____

Witness: _Robert W. Hunter SA, FBI Norfolk Va 5/20/85_

Witness: _James L. Kolouch, SA, FBI, Washington DC 5/20/85_

Time: _13:58 William H. Wang SA. FBI. Washington D.C. 5/20/85_

John Anthony Walker Jr had the form read to him by SA Robert W. Hunter and stated he understood his rights and would sign the form. He then read the form, stated he did not want to waive his rights but would sign the form.

219

Appendix B.
No-Parole Recommendation Filed by
Judge Alexander Harvey

AO 235 (Rev. 8/85) Report on Committed Offender

United States District Court

_____ DISTRICT OF ____MARYLAND_____

REPORT ON COMMITTED OFFENDER

DEFENDANT NAME	DOCKET NO.
Walker, John Anthony, Jr. (a/k/a JAWS)	H-85-0532

OFFENSE	SENTENCE
Conspiracy to Deliver National Defense Information	

PROBATION OFFICER ESTIMATES OF PAROLE GUIDELINES
(To be completed by Probation Officer)

Severity Rating	Salient Factor Category	Guideline Range
8	10	100+

I. INFORMATION RELEVANT TO PAROLE DECISION-MAKING   ☐ No Comment

A. Referring to the probation officer's estimate of the parole guidelines given above, do you believe the time served by this defendant should be:

☐ Within the Guidelines

☐ Below the Guidelines (If so, how far below: _____months)

☒ Above the Guidelines (If so, how far above: xxxxxxxmonths) Indefinite—do not releas on parole.

If you checked "Below" or "Above", please indicate your reasons for such assessment in sections 1-3 below by identifying factors that in your view should bear on the parole release decision:

1. Aggravating and/or mitigating circumstances surrounding the offense behavior (including any characteristics that affect your view of this defendant's role in the offense):

   Traitorous acts; long term involvement; no remorse
            (See transcript attached)

2. Aggravating and/or mitigating factors concerning the offender's risk of recidivism:

            (See transcript attached)

3. Other aggravating and/or mitigating factors not adequately taken into account by the Guidelines (NOTE: If the defendant has cooperated with the government, please forward this information to the Bureau of Prisons community programs manager as a separate, confidential document):

            (See transcript attached)

B. If you disagree with the probation officer's estimate of the Parole Commission Guidelines, please give the reasons for your disagreement:

            Do not disagree

(Please see reverse side)

AO 235 (Rev. 8/85) Reverse

C. In assessing offense severity, the Parole Commission will consider unadjudicated offenses (alleged to be part of the total current transaction) that are supported by a preponderance of the evidence. Have any findings been made by the court as to this defendant's involvement in such unadjudicated offenses?

      (See transcript attached)

D. In multi-defendant cases, please give your assessment of this offender's relative culpability:

    This offender is much more culpable than the co-defendant, his son. However, the son, pursuant to the plea agreement, received only a 25 year sentence.

II. INFORMATION RELATIVE TO BUREAU OF PRISONS CLASSIFICATION   ☐ No Comment

A. What treatment or training should the Bureau of Prisons provide this offender?

☐ Drug Treatment-   ☐ Alcohol Treatment
☐ Mental Health Treatment   ☒ Medical Treatment - Diabetes
☐ Vocational Training   ☐ Education
☐ Other: _____

B. Recommended Institution (by institutional classification or name): Maximum security
Please indicate why this institution is recommended:

    Previous attempted escape; unprincipled and unremorseful

☐ No preference

III. OTHER COMMENTS:

☒ Inmate may have access
☐ Inmate may not have access
☐ Summary Attached

    I strenuously recommend that John Anthony Walker, Jr. not be released on parole at any time during the rest of his life. My reasons for making this recommendation are contained in the transcript of my sentencing remarks, delivered in open Court on November 6, 1986. I am attaching hereto a copy of this transcript. I urge that my remarks be brought to the attention o

IV. NOTIFICATION: each of the members of the Parole Commission.

  x   I wish to be notified of the date and place set for this prisoner's parole hearing.

  x   I wish to be notified of the Commission's decision in this case.

November 19, 1986   Alexander Harvey   ☒ Judge / ☐ Defense Counsel
Date   Name
            Chief United States District Judge

This form will be disclosed to the prisoner under the conditions and exceptions that apply to the presentence report (See 18 U.S.C. 4208(b))

Appendix C.
Affidavit Submitted by
Adm. William O. Studeman

UNITED STATES DISTRICT COURT
DISTRICT OF MARYLAND

United States of America   )
        Plaintiff,   )
)
        v.   )   CRIMINAL NO. H-85-0309
)
John Anthony WALKER, Jr.   )
        Defendant.   )
_____)

AFFIDAVIT OF WILLIAM O. STUDEMAN
DIRECTOR OF NAVAL INTELLIGENCE

1. I am William O. Studeman, a naval officer presently holding the rank of Rear Admiral. I was commissioned an Ensign in the Navy in 1963, and have served virtually continuously on active duty as a special duty naval intelligence line officer since that time. My present position is that of Director of Naval Intelligence, which I have held since September 1985. As Director of Naval Intelligence, I am responsible for the collection, analysis and distribution of intelligence information within the Naval Service. I am also the Navy's sponsor for counterintelligence programs executed by the Naval Security and Investigative Command, under the policy auspices of the Office of the Secretary of Defense. I offer this affidavit to the Court for any present use it may deem appropriate and for future use by any court of competent jurisdiction or by any administrative tribunal which may have cause to consider the case of John Anthony Walker.

2. John Anthony Walker enlisted in the Navy in 1956 and was enrolled in the basic Radioman training curriculum in February of that year. Having successfully completed that course of instruction, he was designated a Radioman and was sent to his first command, the destroyer escort, USS Johnny

EXHIBIT A

Hutchins. I believe it is important to understand that the Navy occupation
(or "rate") of Radioman is one of the most important and responsible jobs in
the fleet. The individuals chosen for that occupation are among the best and
brightest, necessarily so because the tasks are demanding and the
responsibilities are significantly greater than most young men are required
to assume. The Radiomen of the U.S. Navy, and their counterparts in the
other services, hold the keys to the nation's secrets. They transmit and
receive the communications containing those secrets, and they care for and
protect the cryptographic equipment, logic and enciphering systems that
prevent the exposure of transmitted messages to hostile powers. It was into
this select group that John Walker was placed, and he proved himself to be
adept in his rate and increasingly capable of assuming significant
responsibility. Within six years John Walker had advance to First Class
Petty Officer. Three years later he was promoted to Chief Petty Officer and
three years after that to Senior Chief Petty Officer. In 1967, only 11 years
after enlisting in the Navy, he was advanced to Warrant Officer One. The
following year he was given a permanent commission as a Warrant Officer Two,
and in 1978 was promoted to Warrant Officer Three. John Anthony Walker,
served the United States Navy for 20 years, always assuming an increasingly
greater range of responsibilities until his retirement from the Navy in 1976.
It was nearly ten years after his retirement before the United States would
learn that its confidence in John Walker was sadly misplaced.

3. In my professional opinion, the harm caused to the national security by
John Anthony Walker is of the gravest nature, and my opinion is buttressed by
information gained from debriefings of Vitaly Yurchenko who defected to the

2

United States from the Soviet Union in July of 1985 and provided a wealth of
valid intellignce information. Vitaly Yurchenko was a 25-year veteran of the
Soviet intelligence service, the K.G.B., with responsibilities for internal
security matters, including suspected espionage of K.G.B. officers. His
exposure to the Walker ring came as a result of Walker's arrest which was, at
first, believed by the Soviets to have been the result of K.G.B. compromise.
Because of his expertise in internal security matters, Yurchenko was briefed
on the Walker spy ring. From his briefings, Yurchenko learned the following:

a. The K.G.B. considered the Walker/Whitworth operation to be the most
important operation in the K.G.B.'s history.

b. The information obtained by Walker enabled the K.G.B. to decipher
over one million messages. Averaged over John Walker's career, this equates
to Soviet decryption of over 150 messages per day. This certainly ranks this
Soviet intelligence operation as one of the greatest espionage successes in
intelligence history.

c. The Walker case was handled by Department Sixteen of the K.G.B.
which handles only the most sensitive and important clandestine K.G.B.
operations around the world.

d. The K.G.B. officers who handled the Walker operation received
promotions and decorations for their successes.

e. So important was the Walker ring to the Soviets that K.G.B.
officers were assigned to the Soviet Embassy in Washington solely to receive
the information passed on by Walker.

3

f. Yurchenko related that a high K.G.B. official informed him that the information obtained from Walker would have been "devastating" to the United States in time of war.

4. In order to understand how such grave damage could be caused by one man, it is necessary to understand the function of a Radioman and the responsibilities entrusted to senior petty officers and commissioned officers. The primary function of a Radioman is to operate the communications systems of the Department of the Navy in order to allow the exchange of secure teletype, voice, facsimile data and other forms of communication between Navy senior and subordinate commands. Electrical distribution of naval messages is an essential activity designed to reach all levels of command in the Navy. Virtually all the information required to plan, operate, command, and maintain the military forces of the Department of Defense, all the services and our allies is exchanged electrically via communication systems, most of which are considered secure by virtue of their cryptographic cover. This naval communications system is operated by some of our brightest people who are given the tools, training and trust to protect the vital high technology systems and access to sensitive secrets which are placed in their hands. It is also important to understand the vulnerabilities inherent in naval communications.

5. Cryptographic systems are designed to encipher information so that only the holders of the system will be able to decipher that same information. Contemporary crypto-equipments accomplish enciphering and deciphering on the basis of complex mathematical components called "logic;" this cryptologic

4

works together with changeable cryptographic variables called "key." To decipher an intercepted message, an adversary must know both the cryptologic and the cryptokey. Since it is effectively impossible to ensure that the logic of a cryptosystem, which is part of the equipment, will not be compromised during the years it remains in effect, the security of our machine cryptosystems depends on ensuring the integrity of the associated key and the personnel who are responsible for the maintenance of the cryptologic and the security of cryptokeying material. Possession of "key" material will unlock the secrets of a nation which must be entrusted to encrypted communications.

6. The ultimate vulnerability of cryptosystems and all procedures designed to protect sensitive information lies at the human level. For this reason, personnel chosen for communications-related duties are carefully screened and indoctrinated in the especially sensitive nature of their positions and the fiduciary trust placed in them. No system ever designed can be invulnerable to the corrupt, cleared individual who has access to sensitive information.

7. The trust reposed in commissioned officers is similar to that described above, but is even more significant because officers are called upon to exercise both personal and organizational responsibilities, often for highly sensitive information. Thus,the radioman is personally responsible for himself, but his superior officer is responsible for both the crew under him and for the success or failure of the mission entrusted to him. With the enhanced responsibility comes significantly enhanced trust and, frequently, greater access to sensitive information. In the case of Chief Warrant

5

Officer John Walker, his commissioning led him into a variety of responsible positions, including both the training and supervision of enlisted Radiomen, control of communications security (COMSEC) material, including "key," and security of classified information at more than one duty station.

8. The importance of the individual spy cannot be overestimated in clandestine intelligence acquisition. Not even the formidable cryptosystems of the United States are safe when an adversary can employ a trusted agent to covertly obtain the protective logic and key which protect national security information. The information contained in encrypted messages may potentially include any or all national defense information of the United States. At a minimum, encrypted naval messages could be expected to contain future plans, ship locations and transit routes, military operation, intelligence activities and information, weapons and sensor data, naval tactics, terrorist threats, surface, subsurface and airborne doctrine and tactics, and similar information which could prove of incalculable value to hostile powers.

9. John Walker not only provided the Soviets with details related to cryptologic and key, he also provided classified documents which included information on communications architecture, future communications systems, and other military topics described in paragraph 8, above. These documents permitted the Soviets to develop a greater understanding of naval tactics and operations. In the interest of brevity, I will describe generically the types of information which have likely been traded to the Soviet Union through the years of this espionage enterprise. Paragraphs 10-12 deal primarily with data compromised through disclosure of COMSEC secrets.

6

Paragraphs 13-15 deal with other than COMSEC data. My conclusions concerning these compromises are based on my twenty-four years experience as a naval officer, as both a user and producer of intelligence information, and on my current responsibilities as Director of Naval Intelligence and the Senior Intelligence Officer for the Department of the Navy.

10. SHIP LOCATION AND TRANSIT INFORMATION. This is perhaps the most common type of information transmitted over naval communications circuits. Normally, this type of data is held confidential until the information is no longer valid, to minimize the potential vulnerability of naval units to detection and attack by hostile forces, to avoid disclosing naval tactics, and by reciprocal agreement with our allies with whom we regularly conduct naval operations. Today, with the constant threat of terrorist activity against U.S. vessels, this information is especially sensitive.

11. U.S. NAVAL OPERATIONS INFORMATION. Communications will invariably reveal classified technical information, intelligence data, intelligence surveillance activities or information critical to the United States in making decisions concerning the security of the nation and its foreign policy. If a hostile power were to obtain our decrypted communications, it would be able to adopt countermeasures, frustrate foreign policy and insert misleading data into the information collection process. An indirect benefit of obtaining this information would be the ability to analyze it for intelligence value, and to inferentially extrapolate the location and concentration of resources dedicated by the United States to obtaining similar information worldwide. Thus, disclosure of specific data can lead to

7

harmful results, both for the specific collection activity involved, and also for similar activities conducted worldwide by U.S. forces and other agencies of the government.

12. SPECIAL CATEGORY (SPECAT) INFORMATION. Frequently it is necessary to transmit information which is of such a degree of sensitivity that its disclosure must be limited to only those individuals with an absolute need to acquire this Special Category (SPECAT) data. The Walker espionage ring was, on several occasions, in a position to have access to SPECAT communications.

Some examples of operations that are planned and executed through SPECAT channels are:

a. COVERT MILITARY OPERATIONS: Disclosure of communications concerning covert operations jeopardized the United States' ability to conduct missions vital to the national defense and to world peace. The risks involve not only potential damage to the foreign relations policies of our government, but also danger to the lives of the personnel involved.

b. COUNTERINTELLIGENCE OPERATIONS: Only through the aggressive pursuit of counterintelligence initiatives such as double-agent operations and technical surveillance can the United States protect itself from the threat of espionage conducted against our defense establishment. Disclosure of SPECAT communications concerning such operations allows hostile intelligence services to develop countermeasures and techniques to render these operations ineffective.

8

c. HUMAN INTELLIGENCE (HUMINT) OPERATIONS: Humint is unquestionably the most fragile of intelligence sources, due to the difficulties in recruiting human agents, the ease with which they are lost, the personal danger often involved and because the quality of information is entirely dependent on the abilities of the individual recruited. Disclosure of any information relating to HUMINT operations, even the intelligence reports derived from HUMINT, can lead to loss of the source, personal harm to the agent and the insertion of false and misleading information through the agent once the target organization becomes aware.

d. EMERGENCY ACTION MESSAGES (EAMs) AND PROCEDURES: Emergency Action Messages are part of the procedural mechanism by which we ensure that nuclear strike capabilities will never be exercised by error. They contain the procedures and safeguards by which the military officer exercising responsibility for nuclear strike can be assured of his duties. Conversely, those same procedures and safeguards in the hands of a hostile power can reveal sufficient data to allow a first strike with the assurance that their opposite numbers have not yet been authorized to execute nuclear war.

13. ACCESS TO SUBMARINE COMMUNICATIONS AND RESERVE KEY MATERIAL. In addition to the naval communications which came to him by virtue of his rate, John Walker's commission led to dramatically greater exposure to other types of national defense information. For example, as a communications watch officer at the Submarine Forces, Atlantic Command (SUBLANT) during the 1967- 1969 time frame, he had access not only to the communications received and transmitted during his watch, but also to a great variety of classified

9

information. At SUBLANT the responsibilities with which he was entrusted enabled him to reveal emergency procedures for nuclear war planning, thus permitting him to significantly affect the nuclear deterrence value of U.S.submarine forces. John Walker gained similar responsibility and exposure to national defense information on the USS Niagara Falls where he was the communications officer. In this capacity, he was responsible for the entire radioman crew and its mission. He was also the custodian for all "key," which gave him unlimited access to reserve crypto materials. Having access to reserve cryptokey permits the spy to provide his principals with keying material long before it will be used. This, in turn, can allow a hostile force to prepare in advance to receive the encrypted transmissions and to develop the assets and procedures to read those transmissions as they are being transmitted. An enemy with this advantage can anticipate reactions and be prepared to counter them upon receipt of transmissions describing present intentions. As a collateral duty on the USS Niagara Falls, he was the TOP SECRET control officer with responsibility for all TOP SECRET material and was the officer in charge of ensuring that all communications and cryptographic materials were secure from unauthorized disclosure. The trust and responsibility reposed in him were of the highest order.

14. IMPACT ON U.S. STRATEGY, PLANS AND POLICIES. We have long known that the highest priority of Soviet espionage activity is the acquisition of cypher or cryptographic material. The advantages accruing to a nation which can read an adversary's communications are limitless, and impact on all aspects of national security. In addition to the ability to intercept and decrypt all types of naval communications, John Walker also gave the Soviets

10

232 • Appendix C

actual copies of defense plans, logistics information, weapons characteristics and tactical publications. The cumulative effect of these broadly based disclosures was to give the Soviets in-depth knowledge of U.S. national defense plans, policies, logistics data, force levels and tactics. This gave the Soviets an immense advantage in developing their own national defense plans. More important, it gave the Soviets an ability to make almost real-time tactical decisions because they knew the true strength of our forces, their plans for combat, the details of our logistic support and the tactical doctrine under which our forces operated. As acknowledged by Vitaly Yurchenko, this knowledge can mean the difference between victory and defeat in war. John Walker's espionage activity over almost two decades provided the Soviets insight into the very heart of this country's political/military objectives.

15. All national security depends for its support on personal integrity. The United States relied on John Walker's integrity throughout his naval career, giving him responsibility and access commensurate with that presumed integrity. His career-long exposure to cryptographic key which protects all the nation's secrets was significant, but grew geometrically once he became a commissioned officer. In addition, as a commissioned officer, John Walker taught the art of communications to other radiomen, was frequently the custodian of cryptographic materials, was responsible for overall security of communications and communications-related information for at least two duty stations and for physical security at one other.

16. After his retirement from the U.S. Navy, John Walker continued his espionage activities through agents who included his son, brother, and best friend, Jerry Whitworth. Through the information provided by Whitworth, the Soviets obtained detailed plans for primary, secondary and emergency communications circuits which are used by the National Command Authority to maintain contact with operational units. Whitworth and Walker provided the Soviets with sufficient data to permit them to gauge the true capabilities and vulnerabilities of the U.S. Navy. Beyond any doubt, they supplied the Soviets with an appreciation of our technological superiority and the motivation to dramatically and positively improve their military posture with respect to U.S. capabilities. The insights permitted by this espionage gave the Soviets the ability to exploit vulnerabilities of U.S. weapons and systems. We have seen clear signals of dramatic Soviet gains in all naval warfare areas, which must now be interpreted in light of the Walker/Whitworth conspiracy conducted over approximately two decades.

17. The damage done to national security from this conspiracy reaches beyond John Walker's personal access to classified information. From his associates, we know that John Walker also conducted assessing or spotting activities designed to provide the K.G.B. with names of other individuals who could be potentially recruited for espionage. The potential scope and impact of this activity, while uncertain, is enormous. The possibility exists that other naval personnel, identified by Walker as vulnerable to recruitment, could still be working for the Soviets.

18. We have little confidence that we understand the full extent and scope of the Walker conspiracy and the damage they have done. By any standard, however, John Walker clearly provided the Soviet Union with an extraordinarily successful espionage operation. The U.S. Navy and the nation have been seriously harmed by the operation. John Walker was once a trusted officer of the United States with responsibilities and benefits which reflected that high trust. His breach of faith and honor demonstrate how fragile the fiduciary relationships of such persons are when personal integrity is overcome by personal greed. In the case of John Walker, his abuse of that trust has jeopardized the backbone of this country's national defense and countless lives of military personnel. It is my judgment that recovery from his traitorous activity will take years and many millions of taxpayer dollars.

   On behalf of the Department of the Navy, I state that no sentence that this court can impose under the law could atone for the unprecedented damage and treachery perpetrated on this country by John Walker.

v/r

William O. Studeman
Rear Admiral
United States Navy

Subscribed and sworn to before me this 4th day of November, 1986.

Patrick A. Genzler
Lieutenant Commander
Judge Advocate General's Corps
United States Navy

Notary service provided in accordance with 10 U.S.C. sec. 936.

13

UNITED STATES DISTRICT COURT
DISTRICT OF MARYLAND

United States of America   )
      Plaintiff,   )
)
      v.   )   ``CRIMINAL NO. H-85-0309
)
Michael Lance Walker   )
      Defendant   )

AFFIDAVIT OF WILLIAM O. STUDEMAN
DIRECTOR OF NAVAL INTELLIGENCE

1. I am William O. Studeman, a naval officer presently holding the rank of

Rear Admiral. I was commissioned an Ensign in the Navy in 1963, and have

served virtually continuously on active duty as a special duty naval

intelligence line officer since that time. My present position is that of

Director of Naval Intelligence, which I have held since September 1985. As

Director of Naval Intelligence, I am responsible for the collection, analysis

and distribution of intelligence information within the Naval Service. I am

the Navy's sponsor for counterintelligence programs executed by the Naval

Security and Investigative Command, under the policy auspices of the Office

of the Secretary of Defense. My staff has been charged by the Department of

Defense with assessing the damage to our national security caused by the

espionage activities of John Walker and his coconspirator, including the

defendant in this case, Michael Lance Walker. I offer this affidavit to the

Court for any present use it may deem appropriate and for future use by any

court of competent jurisdiction or by any administrative tribunal which may

have cause to consider the case of Michael Lance Walker.

2. <u>The defendant's duties in the naval service.</u>

     a. Michael Lance Walker enlisted in the United States Naval Reserve on

EXHIBIT B

2 September 1982, and transferred to the Regular Navy on 13 December 1982.
After initial recruit training at Recruit Training Center, Great Lakes,
Illinois, the defendant reported for duty to Fighter Squadron 102 (VF-102) on
16 April 1983. VF-102 is a front-line combat unit, flying the most advanced
fighter aircraft in the Navy inventory, the F-14.

   b.   The defendant was routinely assigned several menial tasks, as are
most new recruits, but was ultimately selected to work in the squadron
administrative office as a Yeoman striker. The naval rating of Yeoman refers
to sailors who are specially trained to perform clerical, administrative, and
management-support tasks. In particular, as are most Yeoman, Michael Walker
was assigned to duties bringing him in frequent contact with classified
national defense information. Because of their direct contact with senior
officers and their concomitant access to sensitive information, Yeomen are
expected to exhibit discretion, reliability and trust. Michael Walker's
specific duties at VF-102 included receipting for and safeguarding all
classified information arriving at the squadron through registered mail.

   c.   On 31 January 1984, the defendant was transferred to the USS NIMITZ
(CVN-68), a nuclear-powered aircraft carrier. Again, he was rotated through
several short-term assignments on the NIMITZ, but ultimately ended in the
ship's Operations Administration office, as a Yeoman. In this office, Walker
had access to information concerning all aspects of the ship's operations.
In addition to being entrusted with access to safes containing classified
information, he also was trained to operate the ship's Message Processing and
Delivery System (MPDS), which is a computer system through which

2

communications traffic is distributed throughout the NIMITZ. He was also frequently assigned to work details that were to destroy superseded classified information accumulated onboard the NIMITZ. These materials, predominantly copies of naval messages but also including publications and manuals, were stored temporarily in a compartment on the ship and then periodically burned or transferred ashore for burning.

d. Throughout his naval career, Michael Walker impressed his superiors as an outstanding sailor, who was competent and reliable. This partially accounts for his selection for assignments in which reliability and trust were prerequisites. In fact, Michael Walker betrayed this trust by stealing over 1,500 classified documents with the intent of giving them to his father, John Walker, for transmission to the Soviet Union. He accomplished his thefts of classified information in several ways.

(1) While at VF-102, the defendant would either take copies of classified information he received for the squadron, if one of several copies could be taken without discovery, or photocopy them if only one copy was received. Through the use of codewords, Michael would sometimes inform his father that he had documents for delivery. For documents stolen from VF-102, he was paid $1,000.00 by the Soviets, through his father.

(2) On the NIMITZ, Walker sometimes stole documents from safes, cabinets or from desks in the Operations Administration office in which he worked. At other times, he printed extra copies of classified communications from the MPDS and stole them. Finally, he would use his access to the storage room for classified "burn bags" to open the bags and remove documents. Again, an elaborate scheme involving codewords was devised for

3

Michael to report to his father his success in obtaining classified
information.

e. Michael Walker and his father had discussed future assignments that
Michael could pursue so that his access-to classified information would
continue, and possibly progress to higher and more sensitive levels. The
totality of their conspiracy reveals a cunning, carefully constructed and
executed plan for systematically obtaining classified US national defense
information over a long term for the benefit of the Soviet Union. The
foundation of this plan was Michael Walker's ability to gain the confidence
and trust of his superiors in the Navy in order to maintain his access to
that information.

3. Classified Information Delivered to the Soviet Union. Although spanning
only a brief period, twenty-one months, compared to the long-term espionage
activities of his father, Michael Walker's treachery produced exceptionally
valuable information for the Soviet Union and represents a serious threat to
the war-fighting capability of the United States Navy. The information he
provided was varied and cut across a wide spectrum of Navy technical and
operational topics. Some of these are summarized below.

a. US NAVY WEAPONS SYSTEM CHARACTERISTICS AND EMPLOYMENT. Many of the
documents taken by Michael Walker and given to the Soviets by the
conspirators concerned technical details of the Navy's most modern weapons
systems used aboard the NIMITZ. This included not only offensive weapons,
used in combat with other ships and aircraft, but details of defensive

4

systems with which the 5,000 men aboard the NIMITZ could detect enemy forces and defend themselves from attacks. In addition to the purely technical details available from the stolen documents, the Soviets were given valuable insights into US tactics and procedures for naval and air warfare. The benefits of this information to an adversary are two-fold: first, the ability to exploit technical vulnerabilities in US weapons and thereby render them ineffective; and second, the ability to anticipate US actions in combat and contingency situations with resulting tactical advantages.

b. NUCLEAR WEAPONS CONTROL PROCEDURES. The use of nuclear weapons clearly carries the potential for escalating local tactical conflicts up to the level of global or strategic significance. Therefore, the procedures for every step in the decision-making, control and employment process for nuclear weapons are sensitive, explicitly documented, and strictly followed. It is of immense value to an adversary to know those procedures and to be able to accurately gauge the responsiveness and timing of our use of those procedures. Michael Walker transferred to the Soviets information on the procedures attendant to the use of nuclear weapons by naval forces.

c. CONTINGENCY TARGETING INFORMATION. Michael Walker passed to his father for the Soviets planning information identifying possible military targets in potentially hostile foreign countries. This information, if revealed to the target nations, would enable them to anticipate US attacks and dramatically increase expected casualties among US units.

d. US FORCES' ABILITY TO AVOID DETECTION AND ENGAGEMENT BY SOVIET

5

UNITS. Information obtained by Michael Walker and given to the Soviets described US capabilities to avoid or delay engagement by Soviet forces. Armed with this knowledge, the Soviets can upgrade their capabilities and thereby improve their ability to engage US vessels at a place and time of their choosing. The implications of this capability in potential combat situations are obvious.

e.   US NAVY ABILITY TO IDENTIFY HOSTILE FORCES. Similarly, other documents taken by Michael and provided to the Soviets by John Walker described US Navy capabilities to identify unknown vessels and determine hostile from friendly forces. This information can assist in development of countermeasures to our identification process and can enable the Soviets, client states, or terrorist groups to employ deception techniques to disguise the true identity or mission of their forces.

f.   COMMAND AND CONTROL PROCEDURES. Among the most damaging disclosures from Michael Walker's espionage is information relating to US command and control procedures. This information described standard US procedures for responding to contingencies. Knowledge of these procedures could allow the Soviets to achieve tactical surprise over US forces and gives them the ability to anticipate our military reactions to potential threats.

The most dangerous time in any tactical situation is the transition from peace-time to combat operations. This transition process can involve several thresholds during which the "Rules of Engagement," or procedures governing the military force our commanders may use, change in response to perceived

6

threats from hostile forces. As the perceived threat increases, higher
levels of authority are required to authorize more powerful responses. In
the aggregate, the information given to the Soviets by Michael Walker helps
them anticipate our actions and what force our commanders are allowed to use.
Thus forewarned, they can deceive our forces or gauge our posture to achieve
surprise. Of course, this same capability is available to any client states
or terrorist groups with whom the Soviets choose to share this information.

4. <u>Summary</u>. The damage to US national security, and particularly the
combat capability of the US Navy, done through Michael Walker's treachery can
be summarized as follows:

He revealed vulnerabilities of US weapons systems to the Soviets so that
they are now better able to employ their own forces in periods of increased
tension or hostility;

He revealed US knowledge and exploitation of Soviet vulnerabilities so
that they may correct those deficiencies and employ deception to confuse our
forces; and

He revealed US Navy tactics and control procedures, assisting the
Soviets in gaining surprise and tactical advantage in contingency and combat
situations.

7

We may never know the full extent of the damage done by Michael Walker's breach of the trust he bore as a member of the naval service. From what we do know, it is certain that he was willing to jeopardize the lives of his shipmates and the very ability of our country to defend itself.

v/a

W.O. Studeman

William O. Studeman
Rear Admiral
United States Navy

Subscribed and sworn to before me this <u>4th</u> day of <u>November</u>, 1986.

Patrick A. Genzler

Patrick A. Genzler
Lieutenant Commander
Judge Advocate General's Corps
United States Navy

Notary service provided in accordance with 10 U.S.C. sec. 936.

8

Index

Advice of Rights form, 65, 219
Air Force Office of Special Investigations, 119
Airtel, Boston's, 3–8, 9, 10
Algonquin House, Norfolk, Va., 5, 33, 119
American Society of Industrial Security, 82
Ames, Aldrich, 213
Andress, Beverly, 20–21; arrest of Arthur Walker, 110; Barbara Walker's visit to Norfolk and, 29–34; interview of Arthur Walker, 104, 107–8; surveillance of John Walker, 52; in Tom and Carol Manning case, 40–41; trial of Arthur Walker, 112, 115
Andress, Rod, 21
Andrews Air Force Base, 96
AO-235 forms, 198, 200–201, 220–21
Arlington, USS, Whitworth's service aboard, 139
Armed Forces Staff College, Norfolk Naval Base, 148, 158
Arnold, Bob, 64
Associated Agents (electronic equipment business), 36
Atlantic Submarine Force (SUBLANT), 4, 86
Ault, Richard L., 118–19, 120, 188

Baker, William, 69
Baltimore City Jail, Md., 162
Bamboo Snack Bar, Ladson, S.C., 4, 5, 31, 108, 178
Bank of Virginia branch, Norfolk,

Va., John Walker's safe-deposit box at, 186–87
Bazala (men's clothing store), Vienna, Austria, 88
Bennett, Fred Warren (John Walker's attorney), 68, 162, 163, 164, 171, 172, 177, 189, 193
Bennett, Thomas Francis, 139
Bernstein, Charles G., 67, 99–100, 171, 193
Bloch, Felix Stephen, 169, 217
Blue Ridge, USS, Arthur Walker and, 108
Blum, Howard, 190–91
Boley, Tom, 95, 152, 155–56
Bolin, Henry "Hank," 47, 48, 50
Bon Homme Richard, USS, Whitworth's service aboard, 139
books on Walker case, 68–69, 191, 210
Brahe, Bruce K., II, 58, 59, 114–15
Breezy Point Communications Center, Norfolk Naval Air Station, 157
Bryaer, Billy, 212
Buckley, H. William, 170; debriefing of John Walker, 121, 177; investigation and arrest of Michael Walker, 96, 99, 100; preparations for John Walker's trial, 165; preparations for Whitworth trial, 138; sentencing of John Walker, 193
Buckley, William F., 209
Buffalo, N.Y., Laura Walker Snyder's apartment in, 14–16
Bukashev, Yakov, 215
Bundeskriminalamt (BND), 166

Butner, N.C., Arthur Walker at federal penitentiary in, 210

Carrico, Jackie, 53
Carroll, Pamela Kay "P.K.," 18, 46, 150, 151, 153
Carter, Steve, 27, 91
Casablanca, John Walker's face-to-face meetings with Soviets in, 148–49, 186
Cecil County Jail, Md., 191
Christian Broadcasting Network (CBN), 100–101, 161–62
Christian Children's Fund, 111
Chrysler Museum, Norfolk, Va., 213
City of Virginia Beach Public School System, 151
Clarke, J. Calvitt, Jr.: Arthur Walker's trial and sentencing, 111, 114, 116, 121, 123, 124; recollections of Arthur's case, 127–28
code machines and settings, 85, 178, 216–17
Colvert, Barry D.: on Arthur Walker's involvement in espionage, 117, 120; on Arthur Walker's sentencing, 123; polygraph examinations, 10–11, 28, 42, 105–7, 114, 122, 149, 163, 164; visits Arthur Walker in prison, 124–26, 189, 210–12
Commander-in-Chief, Atlantic Fleet compound (CINCLANTFLT), 2, 209
Commander, Submarine Forces Atlantic (SUBLANT), 4, 86
Confidential Reports, Virginia Beach (detective agency), 4, 36, 150, 152, 157
Constellation, USS, Whitworth's service aboard, 141
Cosmopolitan magazine, 68
Culligan, Paul, 42, 43, 45; Laura Walker Synder interview, 11, 12, 14–15; and taped conversation of John and Laura Walker, 17–19

Daughter of Deceit (Laura Walker Snyder), 68–69
dead drops, 6, 8, 31, 54, 149, 185
Deane, Carroll Wayne, 104, 107
"Dear Friend" letter, 187; code letter

designations from, 84, 144; from drop package contents, 71–74, 75; from the early 1970s, 89–90
DeBrandt, Dennis, 43
debriefings of John Walker, 71, 74–75, 79, 82, 84, 121–22, 142–44, 145–46, 147–48, 177–89, 206–7
DeWitt, John, 192
Dion, John: arrest of John Walker, 61; plea agreements, 172; surveillance of John Walker, 45, 51, 54, 58, 60
Dole, Bob, 209
Donnelly, Brian, 113, 116, 121
drop package: contents of, 70–75, 99; discovery of John Walker's, 58–60, 114–15
drop sites, 54

Earley, Pete, 210
Eastern District of Virginia, 111, 112
Edward A. Garmatz Federal Building, Baltimore, Md., 174–75
Electronic Counterspy (business), 36
Enterprise, USS, Whitworth's service aboard, 142
espionage: as a capital offense, 113; death penalty for, 208–9; electronic espionage device given to John Walker by the Soviets, 85; espionage charges against Arthur Walker, 109, 113, 116; espionage charges against John Walker, 60, 63; espionage charges against Michael Walker, 96; laws, 172–73; proving, 10; U.S. Department of Justice in espionage cases, 51; Vienna as the espionage capital of the world, 88; weapons cautionary statement in espionage cases, 39
evidence against John Walker, 64, 76–80, 83–93, 153

Family of Spies: Inside the John Walker Spy Ring (Earley), 210
Farmer, William "Buck," 165, 166, 177, 183, 184
Federal Bureau of Investigation (FBI): Analytical Unit, 87, 138; Baltimore office, 66–67, 97, 100, 171, 181; Behavioral Science Unit, 119; Boston office, 2, 3, 7, 10; Buffalo office, 10, 11; file reviews,

14–15; Headquarters, 10, 13, 28, 35, 54, 87, 138; Latent Fingerprint Section, 90–91; Legal Division, 35; Special Photographic Unit, 54–55; Ten Most Wanted list, 40, 42; Washington FBI field office, 10; Whitworth investigation by San Francisco office, 134–38

Federal Bureau of Investigation (FBI), Norfolk, Va., office, 1, 20; arrest of John Walker, 60, 61–65; authorization for full field investigation of Walker case, 13, 28; code name for Walker case, 13; female agents, 20–21; Foreign Counterintelligence Squad (FCI), 2, 20–24; investigation and arrest of Arthur Walker, 103–10; preliminary investigation of Walker case, 13; search warrants against John Walker, 76, 81–93; surveillance of John Walker, 44, 45, 46, 47, 48–60; tracking beeper incident, 44, 54; Walker investigation conference at, 43–45; weapons cautionary statements, 39

federal grand jury: Arthur Walker's appearance before the, 109–10, 116, 161; John and Michael Walker before the, 160–61; John Walker's associates before the, 151–52

federal judicial system, 111
First Colonial High School, Virginia Beach, 47
First Directorate, The (Kalugin), 215
Foreign Counterintelligence Squad: Baltimore, Md., 100; Norfolk, Va., 2, 20–24
Foreign Intelligence Surveillance Court (FISC), Washington, D.C., 28, 35
Franklin, Joseph, 212
full field investigation (FFI), authorization for, 13, 28

Galvydis, Paul, 22
Germany, 165–69
Gorovoy, Vladimir, 203
Gotti, John, 212
Griego, Robert F., 138, 177
Grumman Tiger airplane, John

Walker's single-engine, 44–45, 81–82

Hale, Ed "Stump," 22–23, 39
Harvey, Alexander, II, 67, 174, 175, 194–201, 205
Heinz, Gary, 87, 92, 138
Helmich, Joseph, 86
Herford County Detention Center, Bel Air, Md., 99
Hibler, Neil, 119, 120
Hilltop Inn, Baltimore, Md., 171, 185
Hilton International, Vienna, Austria, 168, 169
History Channel, 69
Hitt, Keith, 95, 96, 155
Hodges, John, 20, 23, 38, 40; arrest of Arthur Walker, 110; interview of Arthur Walker, 107–8, 118; review of John Walker's flight logs, 81; surveillance of John Walker, 47, 48, 50, 52; trial of Arthur Walker, 112
Hollander, Ellen Lipton, 193
Holtz, Richard L. "Butch," 18, 21–22, 110
Horton, Brian Patrick, 2, 10, 96
Houlihan, Marty, 40–41
Howard, Edward Lee, 18
hypnotic interviews, 119–20

Internal Revenue Service, involvement in Walker case, 92, 93, 187
I Pledge Allegiance . . . : The True Story of the Walkers, an American Spy Family (Blum), 191

Jensen, Lowell, 113
Johnny Hutchins, USS, John Walker's service aboard, 25

Kalugin, Oleg, 215–18
Kempsville Professional Building, Virginia Beach, 82
Kenneally, Kevin, 21, 52, 152
KI-1A (cryptographic system), 140
Kimbrue, Pamela, 157–58
KL-47 code machine, 85, 178, 216–17
Klein, Daniel E., Jr., 68
Kolouch, James "Dr. K," 43, 85, 156,

Kolouch, James (*continued*)
170; arrest of John Walker, 62,
63–65, 66, 67, 69; arrest of
Michael Walker, 96, 99, 100;
debriefing of John Walker, 74–75,
121, 177, 183, 186, 189; the sentencing, 193; surveillance of John
Walker, 45, 51, 52, 54, 55; Whitworth investigation, 138
Komet Kitchen, Vienna, Austria, 88
Ku Klux Klan, 83–84

Ladson, S.C., Bamboo Snack Bar in,
4, 5, 31, 108, 178
Leavenworth, Whitworth's impris-
onment at, 184, 210
Lehman, John F., Jr., 157, 175, 176
Lewisburg, Pa.: John Walker at fed-
eral penitentiary in, 85, 210;
Michael Walker at federal peniten-
tiary in, 210
Linkov, Yuri, 203, 216
Los Angeles Times, 135, 137, 138
Lowe, Jackson, 43; arrest of John
Walker, 61, 62, 65, 67, 69; surveil-
lance of John Walker, 51, 53, 54,
55, 56
Lynnhaven Fish House, Virginia
Beach, 45

Majors, Dave, 100
manilla envelope, John Walker's, at
the time of his arrest, 64, 77–79, 80
Manning, Tom and Carol, 40–42
Manson, Charles, 176
Marion, Ill., John Walker at federal
correctional institution in, 34,
189, 210–12
Marsee, Mamie Patsy, 148–49, 151,
153, 158
Martin, John, 35, 45, 110, 172
Mason, Thomas B., 68, 163
McCall, Ron, 55
McDonald, Robert N., 67, 109, 162,
163; debriefing of John Walker,
177; in plea-bargaining process,
170, 171, 172, 174; the sentenc-
ing, 193
McDonalds, Tidewater Drive, Nor-
folk, Va., 49, 75
McKenzie, Francis, Jr., 55, 56, 165
McNally, Dan, 22, 156

media, Walker case and the, 68–69,
96–97, 116, 174, 175, 176, 199
Meekins, Samuel W., Jr., 113, 115,
116, 118, 121
Meese, Edwin, 113, 172, 209
messages, encoding, 85
Milburn, James, 87, 92, 138
Miller, Tommy E., 112, 116, 118,
120–21, 128–30
Minox cameras: camera factory in
Germany, 165, 166–67; used by
John Walker, 87, 164, 183
Molnar, Carol Ann, 158
Montgomery County Detention Cen-
ter, Md., 162
Morrison, Samuel L., 67
Muscovak, Jimi Elizabeth Thomas,
150–51

National Security Agency, 26–27, 91
Naval Investigative Service (NIS),
Walker investigation and, 2, 12,
38, 95, 152, 154–59, 209
Naval Training Communications Cen-
ter (NTCC), 141, 142
"Navy Warfare Publication Threat
Intelligence Summary Naval Air
Forces, The" (or NWP 12-8), 91
New York Times, 68
Niagara Falls, USS: John Walker's
service aboard, 6, 32, 90, 140, 143,
186, 188; Whitworth's service
aboard, 141
Nimitz, USS: classified documents
from, 58, 60, 71, 95, 96; Michael
Walker's service aboard, 4, 12, 74,
95, 96, 101, 155–56
no-parole recommendation filed by
Judge Harvey for John Walker, 198,
200–201, 220–21
Norfolk Naval Station: John Walker's
transfer to, 4; Norfolk Naval Air Station, 157; Nuclear Strike Planning
Branch at CINCLANTFLT, 2, 96
Norfolk Police Department, 18, 150;
police officers, 39
Norfolk, Va.: Barbara Walker's visit
to, 29–34; John Walker's residence, houseboat, vehicles, and
businesses in, 36, 44–45, 48, 76,
81–93; search warrants against
John Walker, 76, 81–93

North Korea, and USS *Pueblo* incident, 85, 216–17

Oceana Naval Air Station, Virginia Beach, Fighter Squadron VF-102 at, 32
Old Dominion University, Norfolk, Va., 95, 146, 150

Pentagon, 69
Petersburg, Va., Michael Walker at federal penitentiary in, 86, 210
Peterson, John, 138
plea agreements and plea-bargaining process, 162, 171–76
Pollard, Jonathan, 173, 212
polygraph examinations: of Arthur Walker, 104–7, 114; of Barbara Walker, 10–11, 28; of John Walker, 122, 164; of Laura Walker, 42; request for Barbara and Laura Walker, 10–11; U.S. Navy requirement for, 209
Portsmouth City Directory, 62
Portsmouth General Hospital, 38
Price, Walter, 12, 14, 29; Barbara Walker interview, 3–8, 11; "Dear Friend" letter to, 74
Prince, Phil, 149–50
Pueblo, USS, capture of the, 85, 86, 216–17
Puma, Roberta K., 146–47

Quantico, Va.: FBI Academy at, 2; hypnotic interview of Barbara Walker at, 119–20

Rafferty, Dick, 38–39
Ramada Inn, Rockville, Md., 60, 80, 146
Ranger, USS, Whitworth's service aboard, 139–40
Richards, Gerald B., 54–55; in Arthur Walker trial, 114; examination of contents of drop package, 58, 60, 66; examination of contents of manilla envelope, 77–79; on John Walker's low-technology operation, 70–71; trip to Germany and Austria, 165–69
Rivas, Daniel, Jr., 157, 158–59, 162
Robertson, Pat, 161

Robinson, June Laureen "Laurie," 19, 149–50, 151, 153, 158, 162
Rotor Readers, 85, 86
"RUS" letters, 134–38, 142, 184
Russoniello, Joseph, 165, 167–68

safe deposit box, John Walker's, 186–87
Saunders, John, 91
Schatzow, Michael: debriefing of John Walker, 177; in plea-bargaining process, 170, 171, 172, 174, 175–76; the sentencing, 193, 199; Walker investigation and, 67, 68, 109, 116, 138, 161, 162, 163, 165
Schoggen, Leida B., 177
Schrader, Francis "Ed," II, 22, 110
Scorpion, USS, disappearance of the, 86
Scranton, Pa., John Walker's home in, 4
search warrants against John Walker, 76–93
Seidel, Robert "Rob" J., Jr., 112, 115, 120–21, 130–32, 159
sentencing: of Arthur Walker, 123–26, 130; of John and Michael Walker, 193–201
700 Club, 161
7-Up cans used as signals, 55–56, 57, 79, 80
Sheafer, Edward D., Jr., 116
Simon Bolivar, USS, John Walker's service aboard, 4, 32
Sipe, Alan, 156
Sirhan Sirhan, 176
60 Minutes, 34
Smits, Bill, 138, 165, 166–67, 177
Snyder, Christopher, 43, 161–62
Snyder, Laura Walker (daughter), 3; apartment in Buffalo, N.Y., 14–16; attempted recruitment into espionage ring, 6, 7, 11, 42–43; book, 68–69; cooperates with investigation of her father, 11, 12, 13, 14–19; custody battle for son, 7, 161–62; polygraph examination, 10–11, 42; at the sentencing, 193; taped conversation with father, 17–19, 20
Snyder, Philip Mark, 43, 161
Social Service Bureau, Norfolk, Va., 42

Society of Old Crows, 82
Solomatin, Boris, 203, 215–16, 217
Souther, Glenn Michael, 18, 217–18
Soviets, the, 66–67, 144; defection of
    KGB officer to the U.S., 202–3; drop
    package contents to, 71–74, 75;
    electronic espionage device given
    to John Walker by, 85; espionage
    career of John Walker from the KGB
    perspective, 215–18; interest in
    Arthur Walker, 121, 123; John
    Walker's face-to-face meetings with,
    148–49, 165, 185–86; John Walker's
    visit to the Soviet embassy, 122,
    179–81, 215–16; KISS principle, 71;
    manilla envelope contents to,
    77–79; Soviet diplomat in Walker
    surveillance operation, 56–58, 59,
    114; Soviet success in Walker oper-
    ation, 70–71; travel restrictions, 37,
    59; "Walker class" Soviet sub-
    marines, 203
Springfield, Ill., John Walker in fed-
    eral prison hospital in, 212
Stauffer, Doug, 58, 59
strike packages, 2
Studeman, William O., 26, 203–6,
    222–42
Submarine Forces Atlantic (SUB-
    LANT), 4, 86
surveillance of John Walker, 44, 45,
    46, 47, 48–60
Swink, Gilbert R., 81
Szady, Dave, 13, 43; surveillance of
    John Walker, 45, 51, 53, 54, 56;
    telephone wiretaps, 35–36

Tamburello, Tony, 184
taped conversation of John and
    Laura Walker, 17–19, 20
television documentaries on Walker
    case, 68, 69
Terre Haute, Ind., Arthur Walker at
    federal penitentiary in, 124–26
Thurmond, Strom, 209
Tkachenko, Aleksey Gavrilovich,
    56–58, 59, 114

U.S. Attorney's Office: approval for
    wiretaps, 35; Arthur Walker's trial
    and, 112; trial preparation for
    John Walker at, 170

U.S. Court of Appeals for the Fourth
    Circuit, 123
U.S. Department of Justice: and
    Arthur Walker, 110, 113, 121; in
    espionage cases, 51; Internal Secu-
    rity Division, 35, 172; John and
    Michael Walker and, 157; National
    Security Section, 45
U.S. District Court, District of Mary-
    land, 26
U.S. Marshals Service, 162, 183
U.S. Navy: Arthur Walker's naval
    career, 103–4; Arthur Walker's pass-
    ing of unclassified technical manu-
    als and plans, 108–9, 112–13; back-
    ground investigation (BI) of Michael
    Walker, 99; classified documents
    from USS Nimitz, 58, 60, 71, 95, 96;
    COMSEC (communications secu-
    rity), 140, 141; confidential casualty
    report message list, 108–9, 112–13;
    damage control book, 108, 112; DEF-
    CON (defense condition) level, 121;
    found secret Navy documents from
    John Walker's house, 90–91; John
    Walker's sell of top secret crypto-
    graphic material, 178–81; John
    Walker's use of Navy personnel, 82,
    152; KL-47 code machine, 85, 178,
    216–17; military records of John and
    Arthur Walker, 12, 25–27; Navy
    radioman, 26; Rotor Reader, 85, 86;
    security clearances, 209; Special
    Category (SPECAT) information,
    178–79, 204–5; Studeman on dam-
    age caused by the Walker's espi-
    onage ring, 203–4, 205–6; Stude-
    man's affidavit, 222–42; testimony
    in Arthur Walker trial, 115–16;
    Whitworth's naval career, 139–42
U.S. State Department, 37

Vienna, Austria: John Walker's face-
    to-face meetings with Soviets,
    185–86; map of, 87, 92; trip to,
    168–69
"Vienna Procedure, The," 87–88, 92,
    165–69
Vietnam, 213, 216
Virginia Beach City Jail, Arthur
    Walker at, 118
VSE (Navy ship repair scheduling),

Arthur Walker and, 104, 106, 108, 112–13, 117, 121

Vukasin, John P., Jr., 184

Wagner, Charlie, 11

Wagner, Jack, 76

Waldrup, Randy, 2

Walker, Arthur James (brother), 4, 12, 14, 28, 30, 46, 164; alleged recruitment into espionage ring, 6, 11, 32–33; arrest of, 20, 21; case recollections, 127–33; in "Dear Friend" letter, 73, 74, 84; imprisonment, 124, 210; investigation and arrest of, 103–10; leniency for, 130, 131–32; military records of, 12, 25, 26; mystery of, 117–26; in Oakland City Jail, 183; parents, 103; polygraph examination, 104–7, 114; protective order for, 120–21; sentencing of, 123–26; telephone wiretap of, 28, 35–36; trial of, 111–16, 170; and Vienna map and instructions, 92; in Virginia Beach City Jail, 118

Walker, Barbara Joy Crowley (ex-wife), 12, 210; apartment in West Dennis, Mass., 3, 33; Arthur Walker and, 12, 14, 30, 32–33, 118; and "Dear Friend" letter, 74; discovery of ex-husband's spy activities, 3–8, 29–34; hypnotic interview of, 119–20; meeting with John, 33–34; polygraph examination, 10–11, 28; Price interview of, 3–8; at the sentencing, 193; visit to Norfolk, Va., 29–34

Walker, Cynthia (daughter), 3

Walker Enterprises (car radio shop), 108

Walker, Gary (half-brother), 74, 84, 145–46

Walker, John Anthony, Jr., 1, 28, 156; Advice-of-Rights form signed by, 65, 219; arrest of, 60, 61–69; Barbara Walker interview alleging spy activities of, 3–8; contents of drop package, 70–75; court hearings and appearances, 67–69; death of Aunt Amelia and, 46; debriefings of, 71, 74–75, 79, 82, 84, 121–22, 142–44, 145–46, 147–48, 177–89, 206–7; escape attempts, 162, 191–92; evidence against, 64, 76–80, 83–93, 153; FBI's discovery of drop package, 58–60, 114–15; Grumman airplane, 44–45, 81–82; home in Scranton, Pa., 4; imprisonment, 34, 85, 189, 210–12; interview about Arthur's involvement in espionage ring, 121–23; his manilla envelope at the time of his arrest, 64, 77–79, 80; meeting with Barbara, 33–34; meeting with Soviets in Casablanca, 148–49, 186; meeting with Soviets in Vienna, 185–86; military records of, 12, 25–27; no-parole recommendation filed by Judge Harvey, 198, 200–201, 220–21; in Oakland City Jail, 183; parents, 40; plea-bargaining and plea agreements, 162, 170, 171–73, 174–76; polygraph examinations, 122, 164, 191; proffer, 163–64; recruitment of Whitworth, 140, 142–44; residence, houseboat, vehicles, and businesses in Norfolk, Va., 36, 44–45, 48, 76, 81–93; safe deposit box, 186–87; search warrants against, 76–93; sentencing of, 193–201; spying activities, 29–33; surveillance of, 44, 45, 46, 47, 48–60; and taped conversation with daughter Laura, 17–19, 20; telephone wiretaps of, 28, 34, 35–47, 208; testimony in Whitworth's trial, 184; "The Vienna Procedure," 87–88, 92, 165–69

Walker, John Anthony, Sr. (father), 103

Walker, Laura. See Snyder, Laura Walker (daughter)

Walker, Margaret Ann (daughter), 3, 29, 151, 152, 162, 193

Walker, Margaret Loretta Scaramuzzo (mother), 46, 103, 164

Walker, Michael Lance (son), 4, 12, 28, 164; in "Dear Friend" letter, 72, 74, 84; debriefing of, 184–85; drop package contents from USS *Nimitz,* 58, 60, 71; Fighter Squadron VF-102, 32; imprisonment, 86, 210; investigation and arrest of, 94–102; NIS and, 155–56; in Oakland City Jail, 183; plea-bargaining and plea agree-

Walker, Michael Lance (*continued*)
  ments, 171, 173–76; polygraph
  examination, 191; recruitment into
  espionage ring, 74–75; sentencing
  of, 193–201; service aboard USS
  Nimitz, 4, 12, 74, 95, 96, 101
  155–56; summary of spying activi-
  ties by, 205–6
Walker, Rachel Allen (daughter-in-law),
  29, 32, 45–46, 95, 100–101, 102,
  151, 185, 193
Walker, Rita Claire Fritsch (sister-in-
  law), 103, 109, 110, 117, 123, 125
Wallace, Mike, 34
Wang, Bill, 62
Washington National Airport, 58
Washington Post, 69
Watkins, James D., 203
Weinberger, Caspar, 172, 176, 209
West Dennis, Mass., Barbara
  Walker's apartment in, 3, 33
Whittle, Richard H., 158
Whitworth, Brenda Reis, 138, 149
Whitworth, Jerry Alfred, 5, 6, 13, 26,
  149, 164; in "Dear Friend" letter,
  72–73, 74, 75, 84, 144; evidence

found implicating, 91, 92; imprisonment, 210; investigation and
  arrest of, 134–44; involvement in
  espionage, 75, 140–42, 187–88;
  recruitment into espionage ring,
  140, 142–44; "RUS" letters,
  134–38, 142, 184; trial of, 183–84
Wilkerson, Bill, 83
Williams, Kathy, 22
Wilson, Edwin, 212
wiretaps, telephone, 28, 34, 35–47, 208
Wolfinger, Joseph R. "Wolfie": arrest of
  John Walker, 62; arrest of Michael
  Walker, 100; debriefing of John
  Walker, 177; NIS and, 91, 158, 159;
  search warrants against John Walker,
  76; surveillance of John Walker, 46,
  49, 50, 51, 52–53, 54, 56; Walker
  investigation, 2, 8, 9, 12, 18, 20, 23,
  29, 34, 35, 37, 44
Wolling, Keith, 80

Yorktown battlefield, 208
Yurchenko, Vitaly, 144, 202–3

Zicarelli, Ray, 22

About the Authors

Robert W. Hunter was the case agent and lead investigator on the Walker espionage case. Born in 1936 in Johnstown, Pennsylvania, he received a bachelor's degree from Florida State University in 1962, served six years in the Air Force Reserves, and became a special agent with the FBI in 1966, fulfilling a boyhood dream. Hunter was assigned to New Orleans for one year and in June 1967 transferred to Norfolk, Virginia, where he stayed until his retirement in 1989.

During his last ten years with the Bureau, Hunter worked in the field of foreign counterintelligence. In that decade he was the case agent on the highest number of espionage convictions in the history of the FBI.

Since his retirement from the Bureau, Hunter has established a business as a private investigator. He is active in his church and enjoys fishing, music, reading, golfing, and walking.

Lynn Dean Hunter is a freelance writer, poet, and associate editor for the literary fiction journal *The Crescent Review*. A former college English teacher, she holds a bachelor's degree from Beloit College and a master's degree from Old Dominion University.

The Hunters live on an island in Virginia Beach, Virginia. They have five grown children, and they love hiking in the Blue Ridge Mountains, where they hope to retire one day.